THE DRONE MEMOS

Also by Jameel Jaffer

Administration of Torture: A Documentary Record from Washington to Abu Ghraib and Beyond (with Amrit Singh)

THE DRONE MEMOS

Targeted Killing, Secrecy, and the Law

Edited and introduced by Jameel Jaffer

THE NEW PRESS

NEW YORK
LONDON

Requests for permission to reproduce selections from this book should be mailed to:
Permissions Department, The New Press, 120 Wall Street, 31st floor, New York, NY
10005.

Published in the United States by The New Press, New York, 2016
Distributed by Perseus Distribution

LIBRARY OF CONGRESS CATALOGING-IN-PUBLICATION DATA

Names: Jaffer, Jameel, editor. | American Civil Liberties Union, sponsoring
  body.
Title: The drone memos : targeted killing, secrecy, and the law / edited and
  introduced by Jameel Jaffer.
Description: New York : The New Press, 2016.
Identifiers: LCCN 2016027796 (print) | LCCN 2016028118 (ebook) | ISBN
  9781620972595 (hardback) | ISBN 9781620972601 (e-book)
Subjects: LCSH: Targeted killing—United States. | War and emergency
  powers—United States. | Uninhabited combat aerial vehicles (International
  law) | Terrorism—Prevention—Law and legislation—United States. | BISAC:
  LAW / Constitutional. | POLITICAL SCIENCE / Political Freedom & Security /
  Terrorism. | POLITICAL SCIENCE / Political Freedom & Security /
  International Security.
Classification: LCC KF7225 .D76 2016 (print) | LCC KF7225 (ebook) | DDC
  344.7305/32517—dc23
LC record available at https://lccn.loc.gov/2016027796

The New Press publishes books that promote and enrich public discussion and
understanding of the issues vital to our democracy and to a more equitable world. These
books are made possible by the enthusiasm of our readers; the support of a committed
group of donors, large and small; the collaboration of our many partners in the
independent media and the not-for-profit sector; booksellers, who often hand-sell New
Press books; librarians; and above all by our authors.

www.thenewpress.com

Book design and composition by Bookbright Media
This book was set in Minion Pro and Alternate Gothic No. 2

Printed in the United States of America

10 9 8 7 6 5 4 3 2 1

I know not what answer to give you, but this, that Power always Sincerely, conscientiously, *de très bon Foi*, believes itself Right. Power always thinks it has a great Soul, and vast Views, beyond the Comprehension of the Weak; and that it is doing God Service, when it is violating all his Laws. . . . And I may be deceived as much as any of them, when I Say, that Power must never be trusted without a Check.

—John Adams to Thomas Jefferson, 1816

Remove everything that has no relevance to the story. If you say in the first chapter that there is a rifle hanging on the wall, in the second or third chapter it absolutely must go off. If it's not going to be fired, it shouldn't be hanging there.

—Anton Chekhov, 1887

It's basically a hit list. . . . The Predator [drone] is the weapon of choice, but it could also be someone putting a bullet in your head.

—John Rizzo, former acting general counsel, CIA, 2011

CONTENTS

THE DRONE MEMOS

INTRODUCTION

ONE
Chekhov's Drones

The sun had yet to rise when missiles launched by CIA drones struck a clutch of buildings and vehicles in the lower Kurram tribal agency of Pakistan, killing four or five people and injuring another. It was February 22, 2016, and the American drone campaign had entered its second decade. Over the next weeks, officials in Washington and Rome announced that the U.S. military would use the Sigonella air base in Sicily to launch strikes against targets in Libya. American strikes in Yemen killed four people driving on a road in the governorate of Shabwah and eight people in two small villages in the governorate of Abyan. A strike in Syria killed an Indian citizen believed to be a recruiter for the self-styled "Islamic State," and another strike killed a suspected Islamic State fighter in northern Iraq. A particularly bloody series of drone strikes and airstrikes in Somalia incinerated some 150 suspected militants at what American officials described as a training camp for terrorists. In southeastern Afghanistan, a series of drone strikes killed twelve men in a pickup truck, two men who attempted to retrieve the bodies, and another three men who approached the area when they became worried about the others.

Over just a short period in early 2016, in other words, the United States deployed remotely piloted aircraft to carry out deadly attacks in six countries across Central and South Asia, North Africa, and the Middle East, and it announced that it had expanded its capacity to carry out attacks in a seventh. And yet with the possible exception of the strike in Somalia, which garnered news coverage because of the extraordinary death toll, the drone attacks did not seem to spark controversy or reflection. As the 2016 presidential primaries were getting under way, sporadic and sketchy reports of strikes in remote regions of the world provided a kind of background noise—a drone in a different sense of the word—to which Americans had become inured. Questions about the morality, wisdom, and lawfulness of the drone program had receded, though they had not been answered.

This book is an effort to bring those crucial questions to the fore once again. The documents collected here supply much of what is known about the legal and policy framework for the U.S. government's practice of "targeted killing"—the killing of suspected terrorists and militants, typically using armed drones, often away from conventional battlefields—and collectively they set out the rules that govern drone strikes carried out by the United States today. The legal memos, white papers, and speeches presented here are also a record of official decisions that remain deeply unsettling to many people around the world, including to many Americans. A reflection of a deep transformation in American attitudes, the documents are a measure of the extent to which the perceived demands of counterterrorism are erasing rule-of-law strictures that were taken for granted only a generation ago.

Senior officials in the administration of President Barack Obama variously described drone strikes as "precise," "closely supervised," "effective," "indispensable," and even the "only game in town"—but what they emphasized most of all is that the drone strikes they authorized were lawful.

In this context, though, "lawful" had a specialized meaning. Except at the highest level of abstraction, the law of the drone campaign had not been enacted by Congress or published in the U.S. Code. No federal agency had issued regulations relating to drone strikes, and no federal court had adjudicated their legality. Obama administration officials insisted that drone strikes were lawful, but the "law" they invoked was their own. It was written by executive branch lawyers behind closed doors, withheld from the public and even from Congress, and shielded from judicial review.

Secret law is unsettling in any context, but it was especially so in this one. For decades the U.S. government had condemned targeted killings, characterizing them as assassinations or extrajudicial executions. On its face, the drone campaign signified a dramatic departure from that position—a departure that demanded explanation, at the very least. It was far from obvious what distinguished American drone strikes from the targeted killings the United States had historically rejected as unlawful. Nor was it clear how these targeted killings could be reconciled with international human rights law, with a decades-old executive order that bans assassinations, with the constitutional guarantee of due process, or, for that matter, with domestic laws that criminalize murder.

The scale of the drone campaign, and the human cost of it, made government secrecy even more disquieting. The United States was carrying out lethal strikes not only on actual battlefields, but in places far removed from them as well. The first strike President Obama authorized killed at least nine people in the tribal areas of Pakistan. An early strike in Yemen, albeit one carried out with cruise missiles rather than drones, killed two families, including as many as twenty-one children—and, according to the *New York Times*, "left behind a trail of cluster bombs that subsequently killed more innocents." By the end of President Obama's first term, American strikes had killed several thousand people in Pakistan, Yemen, and Somalia, including many hundreds of civilian bystanders. The deaths of innocents raised sharp moral questions, and the moral questions gave urgency to the legal ones.

Early in 2010, American media organizations began to report that Anwar al-Aulaqi, an American, had been added to "kill lists" maintained by the CIA and JSOC—the U.S. military's Joint Special Operations Command. Al-Aulaqi had once been a preacher at a mosque near Falls Church, Virginia. He had condemned the September 11 attacks, encouraged "interfaith dialogue," and been invited to dine at the Pentagon. In the weeks after the attacks, however, the FBI became suspicious of al-Aulaqi's earlier contact with several of the hijackers. FBI agents interviewed al-Aulaqi repeatedly and placed him under constant surveillance. In 2002, citing a "climate of fear [and] intimidation," al-Aulaqi left the United States for the United Kingdom. Two years later he returned to Yemen, where he had spent much of his childhood and where most of his family still lived.

But al-Aulaqi's past followed him to Yemen. Soon after he arrived there, the United States pressured the Yemeni government to detain him. He was imprisoned without trial. By the time he was freed eighteen months later—the FBI having been unable to provide the Yemeni government with evidence to justify his continued imprisonment—his views toward the United States had hardened. In online videos, and in an English-language magazine called *Inspire,* he became an unforgiving critic of U.S. policies and, in some instances, an apologist for attacks against Americans. In 2009, a Nigerian, Umar Farouk Abdulmutallab, tried to detonate plastic explosives on a Christmas Day flight from Amsterdam to Detroit; American intelligence officials came to suspect that he had been equipped by al-Qaeda in the Arabian Peninsula, a Yemen-based group, and that he had been instructed by al-Aulaqi. By early 2010, American intelligence officials were describing al-Aulaqi as the "bin Laden of the Internet" and "the most dangerous man in the world"—and they had marked him for death.

Intelligence officials' claims about al-Aulaqi were exceptionally grave ones, but the astonishing revelation that the government intended to carry out the deliberate and premeditated targeted killing of one of its own citizens—something the United States had not done since at least the Civil War—brought the debate about the government's drone campaign into American courtrooms. I traveled to Sana'a, Yemen's capital, in the spring of 2010 with Ben Wizner, one of my colleagues at the American Civil Liberties Union, to meet with Nasser al-Aulaqi, Anwar's father. At the offices of a Yemeni human rights organization, Dr. al-Aulaqi, an American-trained economist who had gone on to become a minister in Yemen's government and then the president of Yemen's largest university, asked us, disbelievingly, whether the U.S. Constitution could possibly permit what the government was proposing to do. When Ben and I returned to New York, we worked with Pardiss Kebriaei and Maria LaHood at the Center for Constitutional Rights to develop a challenge to the lawfulness of the government's kill lists.

It was a bizarre death-penalty case in which there was no indictment, the accused was in hiding overseas, and the prosecutors, who had already pronounced the sentence, were apoplectic at the suggestion that there should be anything resembling a trial. In the fall of 2010, John Bates, a federal district court judge, presided over a hearing in which Justice Department lawyers argued that the Constitution permits the government to kill suspected terrorists without judicial process, and we argued in response that if the Constitution meant anything at all, it surely meant that the government could not kill its own citizens without ever justifying its actions to a court. In his subsequent ruling, Bates wrote that the case was "unique and extraordinary," and he conceded that it raised profound questions about "the proper role of the courts in our constitutional structure," but he nonetheless dismissed the case on procedural and jurisdictional grounds. Nine months later, with the court having declined to intervene, a drone strike in Yemen's northern al-Jawf governorate killed al-Aulaqi and three others, including Samir Khan, the twenty-five-year-old American who published and edited *Inspire*.

Less expected—and more shocking—was the U.S. government's killing, two weeks later, of Anwar's American-born son, Abdulrahman. A gangly, bookish sixteen-year-old, Abdulrahman had set out from his grandparents' home in Sana'a determined to find his father. Not knowing where to look, he traveled by bus to the southern governorate of Shabwah, where his extended family lived. He learned there of the drone strike that had killed his father hundreds of miles to the north. While President Obama was at Fort Myer in Virginia describing the killing of Anwar al-Aulaqi as "a tribute to our intelligence community," sixteen-year-old Abdulrahman was in the remote province of Shabwah struggling to come to terms with his father's death. One evening he and his cousins stopped by the side of the road at the kind of informal, open-air restaurant that is common in Yemen. A group of men already gathered there were roasting lamb over an open fire. Abdulrahman and his companions set out a blanket on the ground. They would probably have heard the buzz of drones overhead; perhaps they would have seen a flash of light. Hours later, when other family members arrived at the site, they found only a crater, scattered body parts, and the remnants of American missiles.

We filed another suit, this time on behalf of the estates of Anwar and Abdulrahman al-Aulaqi and Samir Khan. Judge Bates had rejected our earlier effort, but we hoped another judge might be more receptive to a case that sought after-the-fact judicial review of the government's actions—especially because those actions had resulted in the death of a sixteen-year-old boy. Hina Shamsi, my colleague who argued the case, pressed the court to consider the implications of closing the courthouse door. But this second case was also dismissed, with the government contending again that the lawfulness of drone strikes was for the political branches to decide, and with Judge Rosemary M. Collyer ultimately holding that legal remedies that would have been available in other contexts were not available in this one.

The litigation relating to the strikes that killed the three Americans in Yemen prompted a degree of public reflection about the drone campaign and forced the government to clarify and defend some of its positions. It also compelled courts to confront (if not answer) important legal questions relating to the government's policies. But the debate generated by the litigation was a narrow one, focusing mainly on the scope of the U.S. government's authority to kill its own citizens, and even that debate was distorted by secrecy and selective disclosure. Government officials declared that Anwar al-Aulaqi had been an "operational terrorist," but they declined to disclose the evidence that supported this charge. They withheld memos in which the Justice Department concluded that the government could kill terrorism suspects without justifying its actions to a court. They intimated that the killing of sixteen-year-old Abdulrahman had been inadvertent, but they declined to supply an on-the-record account of the strike that resulted in his death, and they withheld the results of their post-strike investigations. They controlled most of the information and disclosed only what they chose to.

This book is possible because the secrecy surrounding American drone strikes has begun, at the margins, to erode. The documents collected here shed light on how a president committed to ending the abuses associated with the Bush administration's "war on terror" came to dramatically expand one of the practices most identified with that war, and they supply a partial view of the legal and policy framework that underlies that practice. But while many of the documents collected here were meant to be defenses of the drone campaign, ultimately they complicate, at the very least, the government's oft-repeated argument that the campaign is lawful. To be sure, even the existence of these documents is an indication of the extent to which the drone campaign is saturated with the language of law. Perhaps no administration before this one has tried so assiduously to justify its resort to the weapons of war. But the rules that purportedly limit the government's actions are imprecise and elastic; they are cherry picked from different legal regimes; the government regards some of them to be discretionary rather than binding; and even the rules the government concedes to be binding cannot, in the government's view, be enforced in any court. If this is law, it is law without limits—law without constraint.

There is something ironic, and even sad, in the fact that the expansion and normalization of the drone campaign was overseen by President Obama, a onetime professor of constitutional law who was elected after promising to end the lawless national security policies of the administration that preceded his. Perhaps it is also true, though, that only President Obama could have overseen it. When President George W. Bush left office, he was unpopular and distrusted. The evidence he had cited to justify the invasion of Iraq had been exposed as a fiction. His administration's torture policies were widely viewed as an embarrassment and an outrage. The Supreme Court had repeatedly rejected his policies relating to military detention and prosecution. It is doubtful that the courts or the public would have allowed him to expand the drone campaign.

But many Americans who were appalled when Bush ordered extrajudicial detention were untroubled when Obama ordered extrajudicial killing. If they appreciated the breadth of the power Obama had claimed, they assumed he would use the power wisely. Equally significant, some of the scholars and human rights lawyers who might otherwise have been expected to harshly criticize Obama's targeted-killing policies were part of Obama's administration and deeply involved in developing the policies.

Several months before the 2012 presidential election, when it appeared that Americans might not give President Obama a second term, administration officials began to worry privately that the powers they had claimed for themselves might soon be in the hands of another president. They began to consider ways of narrowing the powers they had asserted. By this point, though, the administration had already persuaded a federal judge that the courts had no role to play in determining whether (or when) an American citizen could be targeted by his own government. The administration was already on its way toward persuading another judge that the government should not have to present evidence even after a targeted killing had been carried out. The powers claimed by the Obama administration had become entrenched—so entrenched that they could not readily be surrendered. This was even more true in early 2016, when Obama administration officials turned once again to the question of what legacy they would leave to their successors.

Now the lethal bureaucracy whose growth Obama personally oversaw will be turned over to a new administration. The powers Obama claimed will be wielded by another president. Perhaps as significant is the jarring fact that the practice of targeted killing—*assassination*, as it would once have been called, without a second thought—no longer seems remarkable, and the fact that the United States now boasts a legal and bureaucratic infrastructure to sustain this practice. Eight years ago the targeted-killing campaign required a legal and bureaucratic infrastructure, but now that infrastructure will demand a targeted-killing campaign. The question the next president will ask is not whether the powers Obama claimed should be exploited, but where, and against whom.

TWO

"The Tight Leash"

President Obama inherited the "war on terror." On the day he took office, more than 35,000 Americans were deployed in Afghanistan and some 144,000 were deployed in Iraq. The National Security Agency had been engaged in warrantless domestic surveillance for seven years. The U.S. military was imprisoning 242 men at the Guantánamo Bay Naval Base in Cuba and more than 650 others at Bagram Air Base in Afghanistan. Two dozen men had been charged before military commissions. Federal courts were weighing whether the CIA could rely on the "state secrets" privilege to quash litigation over the torture of prisoners in the agency's secret prisons overseas, whether human rights groups could challenge the constitutionality of national security surveillance, and whether the government had authority to imprison American terrorism suspects without charge or trial.

Obama disavowed some of the Bush administration's most extreme national security policies, but he made the drone campaign emphatically his own. Campaigning for the White House, Obama pledged to end the wars in Afghanistan and Iraq and said he would not lightly commit American lives and resources to new conflicts. When he took office, he saw armed drones as a less costly and more surgical alternative to the kinds of large-scale wars in which the United States was mired. Even as he struggled to end the U.S. involvement in Afghanistan and Iraq, he authorized the CIA and the military to expand the use of missile-equipped MQ-1 Predator drones and MQ-9 Reaper drones in other theaters. Very quickly the armed drone—touted as distant, efficient, and precise—became identified with a president said to have the same qualities.

Bush had approved drone strikes, but relatively few took place on his watch—about fifty in Pakistan, and most in the last year of his second term. Within two years of Obama's January 2009 inauguration, the pace of drone strikes had increased roughly sixfold, and the number of drone deaths had quadrupled. Many of the strikes were in Afghanistan. (The Bureau of Investigative Journalism, a U.K.-based research group, would later declare Afghanistan to be "the most heavily drone-bombed country in the world.") But other strikes were not on conventional battlefields—they were in the tribal areas of Pakistan, where fighters sympathetic to the Afghan Taliban found refuge; in Yemen, where al-Qaeda in the Arabian Peninsula was thought to be gathering force; and in Somalia, where fighters loyal to al-Shabaab, a militant Islamist group, were consolidating their hold over large parts of the capital, Mogadishu.

In 2010 alone, the CIA carried out 128 strikes in the tribal areas of Pakistan, killing more than 700 people. In the same year, U.S. operations in Yemen killed some 37 people, and in the following year they killed more than 200. Between the spring of 2010 and the fall of 2011, the United States carried out more than one hundred drone strikes in Libya as part of an effort to enforce a no-fly zone and end the Libyan government's attacks against civilians. To be sure, there were pauses in the drone campaign's growth. Drone strikes in Yemen were suspended for almost a year after a May 2010 strike mistakenly killed a deputy provincial governor who was attempting to broker a truce. The CIA briefly suspended drone strikes in Pakistan in late 2011 after U.S. forces mistakenly killed twenty-four Pakistani soldiers. Still, President Obama's first term saw the drone program expand on every axis: more strikes, with more drones, in more countries.

The escalating drone campaign required an administrative infrastructure. To manage the expansion of the program, and to regulate it, the president oversaw the design of a new bureaucracy responsible for nominating suspected militants to government "kill lists." In regular meetings, more than a hundred government officials would assemble by videoconference to discuss whom the drone operators should kill next. The National Counterterrorism Center developed a "disposition matrix," a database that associated the names of suspected terrorists with the resources being used to "track them down." The president's counterterrorism adviser chaired a committee at the National Security Council to consider the center's nominations. The president himself approved the criteria used by the committee as well as the kill lists. As covert killings became a significant part of the CIA's mandate, the agency developed its own process for identifying targets. Eventually some 20 percent of the CIA's analysts would be "targeters" tasked with the job of identifying individuals for the agency to recruit, imprison, or kill.

In bureaucratizing the program, the president normalized it. Hundreds of civilian officials became accustomed to participating in decision-making about extrajudicial killing. In the *Washington Post*, Greg Miller observed that the president had "transform[ed] ad-hoc elements into a counterterrorism infrastructure capable of sustaining a seemingly permanent war."

The drone campaign's expansion and the rise of a bureaucratic infrastructure to oversee it was accompanied by a loosening of targeting standards. While the Bush administration had used drone strikes to target relatively senior leaders of al-Qaeda and associated forces, the new administration took a broader approach. A 2010 study by the New America Foundation concluded that only 8 percent of the Obama administration's drone targets in Pakistan were affiliated with al-Qaeda, compared to 25 percent under the Bush administration, and that relatively few of the Obama administration's strikes were aimed at leaders of militant groups, as opposed to foot soldiers. Many of the strikes in Pakistan were not aimed at specific, known individuals at all. Instead, they were "signature" strikes—strikes aimed at individuals or groups on the basis of conduct that was thought to suggest engagement in militant activity. Other strikes were carried out as a service to Pakistan, rather than because the targets were thought to present any direct threat to the United States. Richard Blee, one of the architects of the CIA's drone program, told *New York Times* journalist Mark Mazzetti, "In the early days, for our consciences we wanted to know who we were killing before anyone pulled the trigger. Now we're lighting these people up all over the place."

By the middle of 2010, the vast majority of those whom the CIA was killing in Pakistan were individuals whose identities the CIA did not know. Some of these strikes would have been of questionable legality even if they had taken place on a conventional battlefield. One 2013 study concluded that at least four of fourteen predicates then being used by the United States in "signature" strikes were not "legally adequate" under the laws of war because they failed to distinguish between those who were lawful targets and those who were not.

Signature strikes caused large numbers of civilian casualties. In March 2011, a CIA strike in Pakistan killed upwards of twenty-six people, the agency having apparently mistaken a meeting of tribal elders for something more sinister. There were other mistakes, many of them documented by independent research and human-rights groups. In places like Yemen and Waziristan, the mere fact that a person was carrying a gun did not mean that he was a militant in any meaningful sense of the word, let alone that he presented an immediate threat to American interests. Nor was it the case that only militants rode in flatbed trucks, or moved back and forth across the Afghanistan–Pakistan border, or assembled in groups—yet the CIA's signature strikes in Pakistan were reportedly based on such assumptions. CIA documents obtained by the *Washington Post* indicate that the agency sometimes selected its targets on the basis of "the extent of 'deference' they had been shown when arriving at a suspect site." State Department personnel "joke[d]" that the CIA would assume that any "three guys doing jumping jacks" were in fact a terrorist training cell.

"What is the definition of someone who can be targeted?" journalist Tara McKelvey asked Cameron Munter, who had served as U.S. ambassador to Pakistan between October 2010 and July 2012. "The definition is a male between the ages of 20 and 40," Munter responded. "My feeling is one man's combatant is another man's—well, a chump who went to a meeting."

In some instances the U.S. government seems to have assumed that those who came to the aid of individuals injured in drone strikes were themselves lawful targets—the theory apparently being that first responders were likely to be associates of those initially targeted. Even human rights researchers accustomed to documenting the worst abuses found it hard to accept that such a cruel and obviously unlawful practice could possibly have been authorized by the Obama administration. After a point, however, the accounts of witnesses became too numerous and detailed to dismiss. On the basis of a three-month study that included interviews with eyewitnesses, family members of victims, and local journalists, the London-based Bureau of Investigative Journalism identified fifteen "double-tap" strikes in which the CIA had targeted people who had gone to the aid of those injured in drone strikes or who had tried to extract bodies from the rubble.

The Bureau also identified cases in which the CIA had targeted militants' funerals in the expectation that mourners would include other militants. After a CIA strike killed Khwaz Wali Mehsud, a mid-ranking Taliban commander, the agency fired missiles into the crowd of mourners at his funeral, reportedly on the theory that other Taliban commanders, including Baitullah Mehsud, then the leader of the Pakistani Taliban, would be in attendance. Baitullah Mehsud escaped unharmed, but the June 2009 strike killed eighty-three people, including forty-five civilians, some of whom were children. It was not an isolated case. The Bureau identified eighteen other instances in which the CIA had targeted funerals. Human rights clinics at the law schools of Stanford University and New York University identified others.

Because signature strikes in Pakistan had caused large numbers of civilian casualties, President Obama balked at permitting the CIA and the JSOC to carry out such attacks in Yemen. In the spring of 2012, though, President Obama signed off on a modified version of the authority, giving the two forces license to carry out what were labeled "terrorist attack disruption strikes." A senior administration official insisted that the CIA would not engage in the kinds of signature strikes that had caused significant civilian casualties in Pakistan, but he conceded that the new policy was meant to "broaden the aperture slightly." The several months that followed the policy shift were by far the bloodiest of the Yemen campaign, with some two dozen strikes resulting in more than two hundred deaths.

Much of this was invisible to Americans—or visible only through a fog. The U.S. government rarely even acknowledged drone strikes outside conventional battlefields, let alone explained them. Only a handful of Western journalists managed to visit the sites that American missiles destroyed, and only a particularly dauntless few managed to interview survivors. In the Western press, at least, it was uncommon to find eyewitness accounts. Reports about individual strikes relied heavily, and often exclusively, on the statements of anonymous military and intelligence officials.

Senior officials did make rare on-the-record statements about bystander casualties. In the summer of 2011, John Brennan, who was then President Obama's top counterterrorism adviser, declared that there had not been "a single collateral death" for more than a year "because of the exceptional proficiency" and "precision" of the government's weapons. Later, Senator Dianne Feinstein, the chair of the Senate committee tasked with overseeing the CIA, stated that the number of civilian casualties associated with the drone program had "typically been in the single digits" each year. In early 2012, Obama answered a question about the drone program during a live Web interview. The United States was "careful," he said, and drone strikes had not caused large numbers of civilian casualties. "It is important for everybody to understand that this thing is kept on a very tight leash."

The administration finally published official casualty statistics in the summer of 2016, announcing that, over the seven-year period ending on December 31, 2015, "counterterrorism strikes outside the areas of active hostilities" had killed between 64 and 116 noncombatants (294). But though this statement was heralded as a transparency milestone, it was only marginally more credible than the statements that had been offered earlier by Brennan and Feinstein. Independent research groups that had carefully tracked public information about drone strikes—the Bureau of Investigative Journalism, the Long War Journal, and the New America Foundation—had used varying methodologies, but all of them had arrived at numbers far higher than the government's, estimating that total bystander casualties ranged from several hundred to more than a thousand. The adminstration insisted that the independent analyses were incorrect, but it rejected demands that it publish the more granular information that would have allowed for a meaningful comparison of the independent analyses with the government's own. Human rights groups, including the ACLU, pressed the government to release information about individual strikes—the dates of the strikes, the locations, the number of casualties, and the combatant or civilian status of the people killed—but the government declined to do so, citing national security considerations.

One reason for the chasm between official and unofficial accounts of bystander casualties almost certainly had to do with the assumptions the government was making about the legal status of those killed. The *New York Times* reported in 2012 that the government was counting "all military males in strike zones as combatants" except where it had "explicit intelligence" that "posthumously proved them innocent." Defense Department documents later obtained by *The Intercept* were consistent with this report, indicating that analysts labeled those killed in drone strikes "EKIAs"—enemies killed in action—except where there was evidence showing that they were innocent bystanders. The administration denied that it had adopted a presumption of combatant status, but official documents—including the Defense Department's Law of War Manual—strongly suggested that the military, at least, had adopted exactly that.

This presumption mattered. In Yemen, Somalia, and Waziristan, the U.S. government had few sources on the ground who could reliably identify targets. It was heavily reliant on partner intelligence services whose motives were uncertain and whose information was often unreliable. The United States' signals-intelligence capability—its ability to intercept telephone calls, emails, and other electronic communications—was also limited. A 2013 Defense Department report complained that signals intelligence was "poor," but it also stated that signals intelligence often accounted for "more than half" of the intelligence used to justify strikes.

Even with the most powerful technology, only so much could be gleaned through visual surveillance conducted from fifteen thousand feet overhead. Tellingly, the U.S. government did not learn until the summer of 2015 that the leader of the Waziristan-based "Haqqani network," which had been responsible for attacks against U.S. troops in Afghanistan, had died a year earlier. Likewise, it did not learn until the summer of 2015 that the leader of the Taliban, Mullah Muhammad Omar, had died two years earlier in a Pakistani hospital. With all of its human and technical resources, the United States had remarkably little visibility into the groups it was endeavoring to eradicate, or into the communities with which it believed those groups were entangled.

The October 2011 strike that killed sixteen-year-old Abdulrahman al-Aulaqi was, if one accepts the explanations of anonymous American officials, the result of these limitations—or, more precisely, the result of the willingness of American officials to authorize lethal force notwithstanding these limitations. American officials who declined to be named on the record told reporters that the strike had been aimed at Ibrahim al-Banna, an operative of al-Qaeda in the Arabian Peninsula who turned out not to be at the site. The man whom the government thought was al-Banna was someone else. The deaths of Abdulrahman and six others—including Abdulrahman's seventeen-year-old cousin—were of course regrettable, the unnamed officials said, but the strike was lawful and justified and fully consistent with the U.S. government's policies.

Many Americans were willing to overlook bystander casualties because government officials insisted that drone strikes were effective—indeed, that drone strikes abroad were the only means of averting terrorist attacks at home. If the drone campaign was "effective," though, it was effective only in the narrow sense that drone strikes sometimes killed their targets. By other measures, the campaign was a failure. Most militants who were killed were not sophisticated terrorists intent on attacking the United States, but rather low-level foot soldiers focused principally on local or regional conflicts. The perception that the United States was indifferent to the lives of Muslims alienated local populations and drove new recruits to the very terrorist and insurgent groups the

United States was trying to eliminate. New leaders quickly replaced the ones the United States killed. Between 2009 and 2013, al-Qaeda in the Arabian Peninsula grew from 200 or 300 fighters to more than 1,000, and it shifted its focus from local concerns to international ones. In the spring of 2016, there were reportedly 1,000 AQAP fighters in one southern Yemeni city alone. While the United States succeeded in weakening some groups, other groups arose in their place, and the new groups were sometimes more ruthless than the ones the United States had weakened.

Farea al-Muslimi, a Yemeni human rights activist, testified to the U.S. Congress in the spring of 2013 about the way the drone campaign had affected his community and country. Al-Muslimi had previously lived in the United States as an exchange student, and he told the committee about that experience—what he described as "one of the best years" of his life. "I am who I am today because the U.S. State Department supported my education," he said. In the United States, he had learned about American culture, managed his school's basketball team, and gone trick or treating at Halloween. His "most exceptional experience," he said, had been getting to know his host family, and particularly the U.S. Air Force pilot who had become "like a father" to him, taking him to church and accompanying him to the mosque. "I went to the U.S. as an ambassador for Yemen," al-Muslimi explained, but "I came back to Yemen as an ambassador of the U.S."

Al-Muslimi told the committee that a drone strike had hit his village only six days before, and he questioned why the strike had been necessary. The reported target, Hameed al-Radmi, was well known in the area and could easily have been arrested by local authorities, he said. And while the strike had killed al-Radmi, it had also killed three others and terrorized the entire village. Previously, al-Muslimi said, what the villagers knew of the United States was based on the stories he had told them about his experiences in the United States—"the friendships and values" he had described to them "helped them understand the America that I know and love." Now, though, the villagers would associate the United States with lethal drones. There was "intense anger" against the United States, he said. "What violent militants had previously failed to achieve, one drone strike accomplished in an instant."

Al-Muslimi was talking about Yemen, but the drone campaign fueled anti-Americanism in Pakistan, too. While the Pakistani intelligence community had tacitly consented to drone strikes, among ordinary Pakistanis the drone campaign was overwhelmingly unpopular. Some Pakistanis who thought of the Pakistani Taliban as an existential threat to the nation believed the drone campaign was driving young men into the group's arms. A Pew Research Center poll completed in June 2012 found that only 17 percent of Pakistanis supported U.S. drone strikes in Pakistan, even if those strikes were carried out "in conjunction with the Pakistani government" and aimed at "leaders of extremist organizations." Ninety-four percent of Pakistanis believed that drone strikes were killing "too many" innocent people.

To most Americans, the drones were an abstraction associated with security, but to many Pakistanis and Yemenis the drones were an ever-present and fearsome threat. David Rohde, a *New York Times* journalist who was held captive by the Taliban in the tribal areas of Pakistan for seven months, wrote afterward about his experience: "From the ground, drones are terrifying weapons that can be heard circling overhead for hours at a time. They are a potent, unnerving symbol of unchecked American power." Law students at Stanford and NYU who conducted interviews in Pakistan to assess the effects of the drone campaign there reached similar conclusions.

> Drones hover twenty-four hours a day over communities in northwest Pakistan, striking homes, vehicles, and public spaces without warning. Their presence terrorizes men, women, and children, giving rise to anxiety and psychological trauma among civilian communities. Those living under drones have to face the constant worry that a deadly strike may be fired at any moment, and the knowledge that they are powerless to protect themselves.

One of the people whom the Stanford and NYU students spoke to had lost both legs in a drone strike. He told them, "[E]veryone is scared all the time. When we're sitting together to have a meeting, we're scared there might be a strike. When you can hear the drone circling in the sky, you think it might strike you. We're always scared. We always have this fear in our head."

In part because they believed drone strikes were fueling

anti-American sentiment, some officials who had once been closely associated with the drone campaign began to express doubts that the campaign was working. They "felt the urgency of counterterrorism strikes was crowding out consideration of a broader strategy against radicalization." Cameron Munter, the former U.S. ambassador to Pakistan, said after he retired in the fall of 2012 that some strikes had saved lives but that the United States was not using armed drones judiciously. "Do we want to win some battles and lose the war?" he asked. In March 2011, he had tried unsuccessfully to veto a CIA strike that reportedly killed four militants but also as many as thirty-nine civilians. (Anne Patterson, Munter's predecessor, had also tried unsuccessfully to veto some strikes, believing that the strikes would be counterproductive.) The March 2011 strike led other officials, including Tom Donilon, the president's national security adviser, to question whether drone strikes were backfiring. In early 2013, retired general Stanley McChrystal, who had commanded U.S. forces in Afghanistan, warned that the drone campaign might be compromising the United States' longer-term strategic interests. "What scares me about drone strikes is how they are perceived around the world," the general told Reuters. "The resentment created by American use of unmanned strikes . . . is much greater than the average American appreciates. They are hated on a visceral level, even by people who've never seen one or seen the effects of one."

Many others harbored doubts. The director of the International Crisis Group's Horn of Africa project told the *New York Times*: "What we've seen time and time again is that there's a whole swath of middle-ranking commanders who are well trained, experienced and eager to step into the shoes of their departed colleagues." Admiral Dennis Blair, who served as President Obama's first director of national intelligence, voiced related misgivings, acknowledging that the drone program "play[ed] well domestically" but warning that any damage done to the national interest "only shows up over the long term." In an op-ed in the *New York Times*, Blair complained, "American officials dealing with Pakistan now spend most of their time haggling over our military and intelligence activities, when they should instead be pursuing the kind of comprehensive social, diplomatic, and economic reforms that Pakistan desperately needs and that would advance America's long-term interests."

The drone campaign was problematic as a counterterrorism strategy for another reason, too: every successful drone strike extinguished a potential source of intelligence. The administration knew this, of course, but it was reluctant to risk American lives in capture missions, and for good reasons it was unwilling to add new numbers to the tainted prison at Guantánamo, which it had said it would close. Administration officials may also have been wary of the judicial and public oversight that would have been associated with detention and prosecution. Saxby Chambliss, who was then the most senior Republican on the Senate Intelligence Committee, accused the administration of killing people who should instead have been detained and interrogated. "Their policy is to take out high-value targets, versus capturing high-value targets," the legislator told the *New York Times*. "They are not going to advertise that, but that's what they are doing." John Bellinger, who had helped develop the targeted-killing policy during the Bush administration, levied the same charge. The Obama administration "has decided that instead of detaining members of al-Qaida [at Guantánamo] they are going to kill them," he said at a conference in the spring of 2013.

Chambliss and Bellinger might have had partisan motives for their statements, but others reached similar conclusions. In April 2015, Micah Zenko, a widely respected analyst at the Council on Foreign Relations, noted that despite the Obama administration's "unqualified preference" for capturing rather than killing suspected terrorists, capture operations appeared to be remarkably rare—Zenko thought there had been fewer than a dozen since the fall of 2011. "Terrorists are being killed continuously at a safe distance with little apparent regard for or interest in retrieving the intelligence that they possess," Zenko wrote. Perhaps this meant that the United States was killing people who might otherwise have been sources of important information about terrorist organizations and their plans. Or perhaps, Zenko speculated, the United States was unwilling to undertake risky capture operations because the vast majority of its targets were low-level fighters who were unlikely to have intelligence. In that case, though, did they present a significant enough threat to justify the use of lethal force?

The United States did very deliberately forgo killing in favor of capture in at least one instance. In 2013, the CIA and JSOC proposed targeting Mohamad Mahmoudal al-Farekh, an American whom some in the CIA and the Pentagon believed had taken on a significant role in al-Qaeda, but apparently al-Farekh was never targeted. Attorney General Eric Holder doubted that al-Farekh was a significant enough figure to justify the use of lethal force and believed that he could be captured and prosecuted. At a closed hearing in July 2013, members of the House Intelligence Committee pressed military and intelligence officials to explain why al-Farekh had not yet been killed. After the CIA informed Pakistan of his whereabouts, Pakistan detained al-Farekh late in 2014 and turned him over to the United States. He was arraigned in New York in April 2015.

And yet killing was the norm, and capture the rare exception. "You see the puff of smoke, and he's gone," Paul Pillar, a former deputy director of the CIA's counterterrorism center, told the *Washington Post*. "When you rely on a particular tactic, it starts to become the core of your strategy." At the end of 2015, Phil Klay, a U.S. Marine Corps veteran, wrote in the *New York Times*, "What was once a tactic within the broader military and civilian efforts that characterized counterinsurgency has now become the whole thing, never mind that it seems to be alienating wide segments of the globe."

At this point even those who insist that drone strikes are the only effective means of averting terrorist attacks cannot deny that the United States is caught in a seemingly inescapable loop: the threat of terrorism supposedly necessitates drone strikes, but drone strikes inarguably fuel the terrorist threat. If drone strikes are a cure, they are also part of the disease. Many officials insist that the drone campaign is necessary, but none can plausibly say that it is working. "How do you get beyond this attrition warfare?" one former military commander asked David Rohde. "I don't think we've answered that question yet."

———

Controversy over drone strikes compelled the Obama administration to discuss the campaign publicly in more detail. In a speech to the American Society of International Law in the spring of 2010, State Department legal adviser Harold Koh briefly addressed criticisms of the drone campaign and offered emphatic assurances that the campaign was fully consistent with international law (119–125). The following year, John Brennan, then the president's chief counterterrorism adviser, explained why, in the government's view, the United States' authority to use military force against suspected terrorists was not "restricted solely to 'hot battlefields' like Afghanistan" (161–166). In the spring of 2012, Holder delivered an address at Northwestern University Law School in which he explained and defended the government's claimed authority to carry out the targeted killing of American terrorism suspects in particular (191–198). There were other addresses as well, each one building incrementally on the one that preceded it.

The first crest of this effort came in May 2013, when President Obama delivered a major address at the National Defense University (259–270). The speech, sober and reflective, seemed intended to signal a turning point in the nation's struggle against terrorism. The country had been at war for more than a decade, the president noted, and the country still faced the threat of terrorism, though the nature of that threat had changed. But "no nation could preserve its freedom in the midst of continual warfare," he observed. "This war, like all wars, must end."

Obama defended the effectiveness of the drone campaign, asserting that drone strikes had taken "dozens of highly skilled al Qaeda commanders, trainers, bomb makers and operatives" off the battlefield. He also defended its legality, insisting that the United States was "at war" with al-Qaeda and associated forces and that the drone program was part of "a war waged proportionally, in last resort, and in self-defense." The president also made clear that he expected armed drones to continue to be used "beyond the Afghan theater."

He conceded, however, that drone strikes had resulted in civilian casualties and adversely impacted public opinion overseas, and that the use of lethal force gave rise to moral questions distinct from the legal ones. "The same human progress that gives us the technology to strike half a world away," the president said, "also demands the discipline to constrain that power."

The previous day, the president disclosed, he had signed classified Presidential Policy Guidance—what became known as the drone "playbook"—to govern the use of lethal force against suspected terrorists (225–252). Under the new playbook, the United States would use lethal force only against individuals who posed a "continuing, imminent threat to U.S. persons," and only if there was "near certainty" that the target was present at the site and "near certainty" that non-combatants would not be injured or killed. Moreover, it would use lethal force only if the government assessed that capture was "not feasible," that the country in whose territory the strike would take place was unable or unwilling to address the threat itself, and that there were "no other-reasonable alternatives." After the president's speech, administration officials offered an additional commitment: responsibility for drone strikes would gradually be shifted from the CIA to the military. Placing more authority with the Defense Department, administration officials suggested, would permit the government to disclose more information about individual strikes.

The new playbook seemed to promise a fundamental transforma-tion of the drone program—including, perhaps, an end to signature strikes—but there was reason to be skeptical. For one thing, the play-book applied only "outside areas of active hostilities." The administra-tion did not explain what it meant by this phrase, but after the president's speech, officials indicated to reporters that the playbook would not immediately be applied to the CIA's drone campaign in Pakistan.

In addition, some of the playbook's operative terms were vague, elastic, and even contradictory. In what kinds of circumstances would capture be deemed "infeasible"? Did infeasibility entail only an opera-tional judgment, or did it entail a political one as well? And any cap-ture operation always involves *some* risk; how much risk would be too much, and what kinds of risks would be considered? Likewise, in what kinds of circumstances would another nation be deemed "unable" or "unwilling" to take action? The administration did not say. The target-ing standard the administration described was most perplexing of all. What kind of threat could be both "imminent" and "continuing"?

At least some of the skepticism about the new playbook turned out to be justified. Despite presidential assurance that strikes would be pur-sued only if there was "near certainty" that non-combatants would not be injured or killed, the CIA and JSOC continued to carry out strikes that killed innocent bystanders, including children. In its April 2015 report, the Open Society Justice Initiative, an international human rights group, identified four such strikes. The Bureau of Investigative Journalism documented many others, including a December 2013 strike on a wedding procession that killed twelve people, at least eight of whom were civilians. Human Rights Watch investigated the latter strike and questioned whether the strike complied with the laws of war. Even the CIA apparently questioned the wisdom of the strike, which was carried out by JSOC.

The government also continued to conduct signature strikes. In January 2015, a signature strike on a compound in Pakistan killed two aid workers—Italian Giovanni Lo Porto and American Warren Weinstein—whom al-Qaeda had taken hostage several years earlier. A series of apparent signature strikes in Yemen in the first half of 2015 killed several dozen people.

And though the administration had suggested that the CIA's involvement in targeted killing would be phased out, the phase-out was incomplete. The congressional committees tasked with overseeing the CIA pushed back against the proposed move, insisting, plausibly or not, that the agency was simply more adept than the military at carrying out targeted strikes. Senator Dianne Feinstein, the chair of the Senate Intelligence Committee, contended that she had seen the CIA "exercise patience and discretion specifically to prevent collateral damage" and that she was not yet persuaded that the military could do the same. On at least two occasions, members of Congress inserted language in spending bills to undermine efforts to shift control of the program to the Pentagon. When in early 2015 the administration revived its plan to shift control of the drone program to the military, the Senate Intelligence Committee resisted, sending a classified letter that reportedly warned against any narrowing of the CIA's role. The administration did finally manage to scale down the CIA's role in lethal strikes in the first half of 2016, after a key CIA official was replaced, but even then the agency remained deeply involved in identifying targets for elimination.

In the end, the May 2013 decision to impose stricter limitations on drone strikes seems to have had an effect only at the margins. President Obama was surely right to say, at the National Defense University, that the ill-defined and borderless war begun by his predecessor "must end," and he was surely right to subject drone strikes to more stringent controls. But he did not end the war, and the introduction of the playbook seems hardly to have slowed the drone campaign's expansion. To the contrary, with each passing month, the drone campaign seems to cross some new geographic border, or some new legal line.

THREE

Secrecy, and the Fiction of It

At a press briefing in 2011, Jake Tapper, the White House correspondent for ABC News, questioned Jay Carney, the White House press secretary, about why the government had killed Anwar al-Aulaqi:

TAPPER: You said that [al-Aulaqi] was demonstrably and provably involved in operations. Do you plan on demonstrating—

CARNEY: I should step back. He is clearly—I mean "provably" may be a legal term. I think it has been well established, and it has certainly been the position of this administration and the previous administration that he is a leader in—was a leader in [al-Qaeda in the Arabian Peninsula]; that AQAP was a definite threat, was operational, planned and carried out terrorist attacks that, fortunately, did not succeed, but were extremely serious—including the ones specifically that I mentioned, in terms of the would-be Christmas Day bombing in 2009 and the attempt to bomb numerous cargo planes headed for the United States. And he was obviously also an active recruiter of al Qaeda terrorists. So I don't think anybody in the field would dispute any of those assertions.

TAPPER: You don't think anybody else in the government would dispute that?

CARNEY: Well, I wouldn't know of any credible terrorist expert who would dispute the fact that he was a leader in al Qaeda in the Arabian Peninsula, and that he was operationally involved in terrorist attacks against American interests and citizens.

TAPPER: Do you plan on bringing before the public any proof of these charges?

CARNEY: Again, the question makes us—has embedded within it assumptions about the circumstances of his death that I'm just not going to address.

TAPPER: How on earth does it have—I really don't understand. How does—he's dead. You are asserting that he had operational control of the cargo plot and the Abdulmutallab plot. He's now dead. Can you tell us, or the American people—or has a judge been shown . . .

CARNEY: Well, again, Jake, I'm not going to go any further than what I've said about the circumstances of his death and—

TAPPER: I don't even understand how they're tied.

CARNEY:—the case against him, which, again, you're linking. And I think that . . .

TAPPER: You said that he was responsible for these things.

CARNEY: Yes, but again—

TAPPER: Is there going to be any evidence presented?

CARNEY: I don't have anything for you on that.

TAPPER: Do you not see at all—does the administration not see at all how a President asserting that he has the right to kill an American citizen without due process, and that he's not going to even explain why he thinks he has that right, is troublesome to some people?

CARNEY: I wasn't aware of any of those things that you said actually happening. And again, I'm not going to address the circumstances of [al-Aulaqi's] death. I think, again, it is an important fact that this terrorist, who was actively plotting—had plotted in the past, and was actively plotting to attack Americans and American interests, is dead. But I'm not going to—from any angle—discuss the circumstances of his death.

Carney's uncharacteristic descent into near gibberish when discussing the government's summary killing of an American citizen reflected a broader policy of obfuscation. Top Obama administration officials demanded that virtually every aspect of the drone campaign be kept from the public. Statistics on civilian casualties were treated as top secret. So were the identities of those targeted for elimination, and, more fundamentally, the standards and procedures by which individuals were added to kill lists. Withheld, too, was much of the legal reasoning developed to undergird the program, and the evidence that purportedly justified individual strikes, including the strikes that killed Americans.

The stonewalling went beyond the public and press. Basic information was kept secret even from the courts and Congress. Citing national security concerns, the Justice Department refused to tender its drone memos to the congressional intelligence committees, agreeing to surrender one of the memos—and just one—only after Senator Ron Wyden threatened to filibuster a vote on John Brennan's confirmation as CIA director. The administration withheld that memo from other legislators for another fifteen months.

Responding to lawsuits filed in the federal courts, the CIA argued that national security considerations precluded it even from confirming or denying that the drone campaign existed, let alone that the agency had any role in it. When courts rejected that argument, the agency grudgingly acknowledged that it had relevant records but still insisted that national security considerations precluded it from describing the records or even saying how many there were. When it was forced to retreat from *that* position, the agency described the records in only the most generic terms and contended that none could safely be released.

Official secrecy infected every discussion of the program. Congressional testimony was heard in closed session. Judicial hearings were likewise closed to the public, judicial filings sealed, and judges' opinions redacted. One secret justified another—a secret fact required a secret brief, and a secret brief called for a secret hearing, and a secret hearing led to a secret judicial opinion. At a closed hearing in the summer of 2015, one appellate judge wondered aloud whether there was something "counterintuitive" about it all. The more secrets there were, the more there needed to be.

But notwithstanding the government's courtroom machinations, the official secrecy surrounding the program was also, in significant part, a fiction. Nearly everything about the program was classified top secret, but high government officials frequently disclosed selected information about the program's scope, legal basis, and targets through anonymous leaks to the media. To marshal public support, officials used the media to paint a self-serving picture. The program was "narrow" and "closely supervised," they said. Bystander casualties were said to be the rare exception, if they occurred at all. (Again, it was not until 2016 that the administration published official casualty statistics.) The targets were "plotting attacks."

In 2012, the ACLU and ProPublica, a nonprofit journalism group, identified more than two hundred instances in which individuals identified only as "government officials," "intelligence officials," or "White House officials" supplied reporters with statements relating to, among other things, the identity of the government's targets, the process by which individuals were added to kill lists, the success of individual strikes, and the purported infrequency of bystander casualties. Jack Goldsmith, who briefly led the Office of Legal Counsel under President George W. Bush, wrote that "the global picture [was] one of a concerted and indeed official effort by the [U.S. government] to talk publicly about and explain the CIA drone program—almost always in a light favorable to the administration, or at least to the person or interest[s] of the person who [was] speaking to the reporter."

The fiction of secrecy is a phenomenon with a long pedigree in the sphere of national security, but here it took on absurd dimensions. Senior government officials filed declarations asserting that certain information about the drone program could not be disclosed without compromising national security, and then the very same information would be leaked to the media. The chair of the Senate Intelligence Committee had publicly acknowledged the CIA's role in the drone campaign, but the government insisted in court that the CIA's role was still a classified fact. Statements by members of Congress "are not official government disclosure[s]," the government wrote in its legal briefs. In the summer of 2014, the U.S. Court of Appeals for the Second Circuit published one of the Justice Department's legal memos relating to targeted killings. No matter. In a bizarre footnote buried toward the end of a subsequently filed legal brief, the government declared that it still considered the memo's contents to be secret.

As the Jake Tapper–Jay Carney exchange highlights, both secrecy and the fiction of it extended to the strike that killed Anwar al-Aulaqi. In the summer of 2010, after the ACLU and the Center for Constitutional Rights filed suit on behalf of Anwar's father, CIA director Leon Panetta submitted a "state secrets" declaration asserting that the case could not be litigated "without risking or requiring the disclosure of classified and privileged intelligence information that must not be disclosed." (Adding yet another layer of secrecy, this declaration itself remained hidden from public view until the CIA was compelled to release a redacted version in a separate case.) The CIA made a similar argument two years later when the ACLU and the Center for Constitutional Rights returned to court to challenge the lawfulness of the strikes that had killed al-Aulaqi, Samir Khan, and sixteen-year-old Abdulrahman. The court lacked the information it would need to decide the case, the CIA told the judge, adding that even if the agency were to provide the relevant information, the court would "hardly [be] competent to evaluate it."

At some level it was unsurprising that the Obama administration wanted to avoid difficult questions about al-Aulaqi's targeting. Al-Aulaqi, after all, was an American citizen, and the contours of the president's unilateral authority to target people for death, especially off the battlefield, remains controversial even today. It is also the case that the instinct toward excessive secrecy in the national security sphere transcends political party and administrations. The George W. Bush administration was equally secretive about its counterterrorism policies, and one can feel confident that future administrations—whatever their rhetorical commitment to openness—will have more or less the same propensities.

More notable than the Obama administration's efforts to control information, and certainly more consequential, was that their efforts encountered so little resistance in the courts. It was not simply that the courts upheld the administration's invocation of the state-secrets privilege in litigation involving al-Aulaqi. Federal judges also deferred to the administration's narrow construction of the Freedom of Information Act. In a September 2011 opinion, Judge Rosemary Collyer of the United States District Court in Washington, D.C., held that the Freedom of Information Act did not require the CIA to disclose anything at all about the program—not even the fact of its involvement in it. "Confirming the existence or nonexistence of pertinent agency records on drone strikes," Judge Collyer wrote, could "reasonably be expected" to compromise national security.

In New York, Judge Colleen McMahon reached a similar conclusion, albeit more reluctantly, in consolidated Freedom of Information Act cases filed by the ACLU and the *New York Times*. The case, she wrote in January 2013, "implicate[d] serious issues about the limits on the power of the Executive Branch under the Constitution and laws of the United States, and about whether we are indeed a nation of laws, not of men." More disclosure, she wrote, would help the public better understand the "war on terror"—that "ill-defined yet vast and seemingly ever-growing exercise in which we have been engaged for well over a decade." Noting that senior administration officials had "mount[ed] an extensive public relations campaign" about targeted killings, Judge McMahon expressed skepticism about the government's motives for withholding the memos. If senior officials could claim publicly that targeted killings were legal, what legitimate security justification could there be for their refusal to say why? Judge McMahon also admitted deep misgivings about the legality of the government's policies. "The Founders contemplated that traitors would be dealt with by the courts of law, not by unilateral action of the Executive," she wrote.

But despite her stated belief that disclosure would serve the public interest, her doubts about the government's motives for secrecy, and her concerns about the lawfulness of the conduct that the government was concealing, Judge McMahon declined to second-guess the government's classification decisions. She was "constrained" to rule for the government, she explained. Indeed, in her view, she lacked authority to do otherwise. "The Alice-in-Wonderland nature of this pronouncement is not lost on me," she wrote, but "I can find no way around the thicket of laws and precedents that effectively allow the [government] to proclaim as perfectly lawful certain actions that seem on their face incompatible with our Constitution and laws, while keeping the reasons for its conclusion a secret."

———

Because the executive branch exercised such tight control over information relating to the drone campaign, government officials could easily deflect inconvenient questions. The public simply did not have the information it needed to evaluate the government's decisions. Overbroad secrecy impoverished public debate and corrupted the democratic process.

A less-appreciated upshot of the secrecy was that public debate focused to an unusual degree on policy makers rather than policy. One of the most important stories about the drone program appeared on the front page of the *New York Times* in May 2012. In more than six thousand words, Scott Shane and Jo Becker explored the tensions between the Obama administration's stated declared principles and its actual policies. The story supplied a slew of important new details about the drone program, but to judge by their quotes, administration officials were less interested in addressing the program than in testifying to the strength of character of the officials who were devising and implementing it. Aides described President Obama as "a student of writings on war by Augustine and Thomas Aquinas" who believed he needed to "take moral responsibility for such actions." Colleagues of John Brennan, the president's counterterrorism adviser, described Brennan in similar terms. Brennan was "a priest whose blessing ha[d] become indispensable to Mr. Obama, echoing the president's attempt to apply the 'just war' theories of Christian philosophers to a brutal modern conflict." Harold Koh, who was then the State Department's legal adviser, extended the conceit. "If John Brennan is the last guy in the room with the president, I'm comfortable, because Brennan is a person of genuine moral rectitude," Koh said. "It's as though you had a priest with extremely strong moral values who was suddenly charged with leading a war."

Koh's prominent role in defending the targeted-killing campaign was itself evidence that the administration was trading on the perceived trustworthiness of its officials. One would not ordinarily have expected the State Department's legal adviser to be one of the most visible defenders of a program involving the summary killing of suspected terrorists. Moreover, before assuming the post of legal adviser, Koh had been a prominent and widely respected advocate for international law and human rights. From his prestigious perch at Yale Law School, he had been an early and outspoken critic of the Bush administration's torture policies. He was a hero to a generation of progressive lawyers, including to me and many of my ACLU colleagues. And within the Obama administration, he was a critic of some aspects of the drone program, advocating greater transparency and reportedly questioning the notion that the laws of war authorized the United States to carry out strikes beyond conventional battlefields. But all of this made Koh's public support for the program exceptionally valuable to the administration. Koh's speech at the meeting of the American Society of International Law in March 2010 (119–125) was crucial to the administration's communications effort precisely because it was Koh who delivered it. In his book about the Obama administration's national security policies, journalist Daniel Klaidman writes that some drone operators even contemplated printing T-shirts that said, "Drones: If they're good enough for Harold Koh, they're good enough for me."

Of course, the media focused on the integrity and personal qualities of the officials overseeing the targeted-killing program for multiple reasons. Even if the administration had been entirely transparent about its use of military and paramilitary force abroad, it would have been surprising if some news articles did not delve into the backgrounds and personalities of the officials who were directing that force. It was surely legitimate for reporters to ask whether the officials whose fingers were on the trigger, so to speak, were women and men of sound judgment and character.

But a major reason the question of personality became so central was that the government's policies were secret. Secrecy made it difficult to debate the standards governing the kill lists, or the accuracy of the government's drones, or the persuasiveness of its legal theories. The American public supported the program, but their support, by and large, was not based on any intimate knowledge of the program's parameters and consequences. Americans did not—could not—know the program's full scope, or the legal basis for it, or its effectiveness at averting terrorist attacks, or the extent to which it had resulted in the deaths of innocents. Americans were supporting the program, as journalist Tom Junod wrote in *Esquire*, because President Obama had "asked for their trust as a good and honorable man surrounded by good and honorable men and women" and because he had "dispatched men of proven integrity to put their integrity on the line in defense of the Lethal Presidency."

Michael Hayden, who had approved, defended, and overseen controversial (and illegal) national security programs as head of the CIA and National Security Agency, said something similar to the *New York Times*. The drone program "rests on the personal legitimacy of the president," Hayden observed. He wondered whether this was sustainable. "I have lived the life of someone taking action on the basis of secret [Justice Department] memos, and it ain't a good life. Democracies do not make war on the basis of legal memos locked in a D.O.J. safe." Hayden, no doubt, had complicated motives for offering that observation, but his critique was entirely fair.

———

Over time, the gap between what the government said was secret and what was actually secret became increasingly difficult for the government to manage and increasingly difficult for the courts to ignore. The

CIA and military were carrying out almost daily strikes in multiple countries. The campaign required an enormous investment of resources as well as the sustained attention of the president and many other senior officials. "The effort and infrastructure of the drone campaign," journalist David Sanger observed, had "become so sprawling that the official refusal to discuss the subject [had] become ludicrous."

One important inflection point came in the spring of 2013. The ACLU had filed a Freedom of Information Act request three years earlier for records relating to civilian casualties. The CIA had responded, reflexively, that "[t]he existence or nonexistence of CIA records responsive to this request . . . is a currently and properly classified fact, the disclosure of which reasonably could be expected to cause damage to national security." At a hearing in the fall of 2012, however, a three-judge panel of the D.C. Circuit questioned whether the CIA could legitimately reject the ACLU's request for records when intelligence officials had acknowledged the drone program and publicly defended it. Judge Thomas Griffith, a conservative jurist with a libertarian bent, seemed particularly offended by the chasm between what the government said was secret and what was truly so. He interrogated the CIA's attorney about the government's long record of unofficial disclosures: "Are you aware of *any* case in which we have been confronted with allegations of such widespread . . . and strategic leaking at such a high level? Are you aware of *any* case that's like this?"

In March 2013, the panel ordered the CIA to respond to the ACLU's records request, ruling that the government had acknowledged an "intelligence interest" in the drone program even if it had not acknowledged its precise role in it. It "strains credulity," Judge Merrick Garland wrote for the court, to suggest that the CIA possessed no records relating to the program. Garland, whom President Obama would nominate to the U.S. Supreme Court after Justice Antonin Scalia's death in February 2016, cited multiple instances in which senior officials had discussed the drone program in interviews and public speeches. The government's assertions about the need for secrecy were entitled to a degree of deference, Judge Garland wrote, but here the CIA was "ask[ing] the courts . . . to give their imprimatur to a fiction of deniability that no reasonable person would regard as plausible." Quoting a World War II–era opinion by Justice Felix Frankfurter, Garland wrote: "There comes a point where . . . [c]ourt[s] should not be ignorant as judges of what [they] know as men and women." He continued: "We are at that point with respect to the question of whether the CIA has any documents regarding the subject of drone strikes."

The court's ruling was narrow—it did not require the CIA to disclose records, only to list and describe them, and it left open the important question of how granular the CIA's descriptions would have to be. Still, the ruling had a larger significance. It made clear that there was a limit to the deference the court would accord to the government's insistence that secrecy was necessary. It strengthened the hand of those within the administration who favored more transparency about the program. The ruling was esoteric—it explored the difference between a "Glomar" response, in which an agency refuses to confirm or deny that it possesses relevant records, and a "no-number no-list" response, in which an agency acknowledges that it has records but refuses to list or describe them—but its message was unmistakable: the government, as a matter of law, owed the public a fuller account of its policies.

If the D.C. Circuit's opinion was one indication that the tide might be turning, a subsequent ruling from the Second Circuit was another. A few months after President Obama delivered his major address at the National Defense University, the Second Circuit heard the appeal by the ACLU and *New York Times* of Judge McMahon's "Alice in Wonderland" ruling. The appeal focused principally on whether the Justice Department could withhold a July 2010 memo written by the Office of Legal Counsel, or OLC, authorizing the killing of Anwar al-Aulaqi. At a hearing in the fall of 2013, the three-judge panel picked up where the D.C. Circuit had left off, peppering the government's attorney with questions about why the July 2010 memo had not been publicly released. "We want to take a few things out of the bottle," Judge Jon O. Newman told the government's attorney, who had spent the previous hour contending that nothing could be disclosed without compromising national security.

A few months later, the Second Circuit held that the Justice Department's categorical withholding of the July 2010 OLC memo was unlawful. Writing for the court, Judge Newman noted that the OLC's analysis overlapped with the contents of a white paper that had been leaked to and published by *Newsweek* and then authenticated by the government.

He noted that senior officials had invoked the OLC's analysis in an effort to reassure legislators and the public that the killing of al-Aulaqi was lawful, and that John Brennan—by then the CIA director—had told Congress that the OLC analysis "establishe[d] the legal boundaries" within which the government could operate. Against this background, Judge Newman wrote, the government could "no longer validly claim that the legal analysis in the Memorandum is a secret."

The Second Circuit decision was tightly reasoned, but many assumed the Obama administration would petition the Supreme Court to review it, if only to buy time. As it happened, though, the Second Circuit issued its decision just as the Senate was considering President Obama's nomination of David Barron, the author of the July 2010 OLC memo, to another federal appellate court. Some progressive and libertarian senators were reluctant to confirm Barron—or even to allow a vote on his confirmation—without first seeing the memos he had written and evaluating what they might portend for his performance on the bench. To secure votes, the administration made the July 2010 OLC memo available to all members of Congress and quietly signaled that it would forgo the opportunity to ask the Supreme Court to review the appellate court's ruling. As a result, two things happened: the Second Circuit published the memo in the summer of 2014, and Barron took his seat on the federal bench.

From a certain perspective, the Second Circuit's publication of the July 2010 OLC memo represented an important and in some respects unprecedented victory for transparency. The D.C. Circuit's earlier decision had required the CIA to respond to a Freedom of Information Act request, but did not require the agency to release any document. The Second Circuit's ruling, by contrast, required the disclosure of a nominally "top secret" document that the government had argued, however implausibly, could not be disclosed without causing "exceptionally grave harm" to national security.

But the victory for transparency was limited. The appeals court published one memo but declined to order the disclosure of others. In the memo it published, many crucial passages—including an eleven-page section discussing the factual basis for the al-Aulaqi strike—were redacted.

And though transparency advocates hoped the Second Circuit's ruling would have a domino effect, it did not. In the months after the ruling, both Judge McMahon in New York and Judge Collyer in Washington, D.C., issued sweeping rulings permitting the government to withhold other documents relating to the drone campaign, including other OLC memos. In an October 2015 decision, moreover, the Second Circuit affirmed Judge McMahon's opinion, holding that nine OLC memos could be withheld in their entirety. The court reasoned that some of the memos related to a particularly sensitive document whose existence the government had not acknowledged. (The court was almost certainly referring, in error, to a document that the government *had* in fact acknowledged—a September 2001 "Memorandum of Notification" in which President George W. Bush approved the CIA's overseas black sites as well as its targeted-killing campaign.) The ACLU had argued that the OLC memos were effectively the law of the targeted-killing campaign, and that as such they could not permissibly be withheld from the public. The court reasoned, however, that the memos could not be considered "law" because they had not been formally adopted by the Defense Department or CIA.

In President Obama's last year in office, Judge McMahon did pressure the administration to release another handful of crucial documents about the drone campaign, including the PPG—the Presidential Policy Guidance—that President Obama had signed in May 2013 (225–252). In connection with yet another Freedom of Information Act lawsuit filed by the ACLU, Judge McMahon expressed skepticism at the administration's argument that the PPG could be withheld in its entirety and demanded that the document be turned over to her for review. In response to her order, and to avoid an adverse ruling, the administration reconsidered its position and agreed to make a redacted version of the PPG public. It published the PPG, together with several related documents, in the summer of 2016.

On the whole, though, judicial rulings in the FOIA cases had only a marginal effect on the secrecy surrounding the drone campaign. For the most part, the government itself decided what to disclose and what to keep secret. In most of the instances in which courts compelled the government to disclose information, they did so only after concluding that the government had already "officially acknowledged" the information it sought to withhold—i.e., only after concluding that the information had already been disclosed. Despite the substantial resources invested by the ACLU, the *New York Times,* and others in litigation, disclosures about the drone campaign were almost always a matter of executive discretion. Some Obama administration officials were uncomfortable with this state of affairs, and in the summer of 2016, when the administration released official casualty statistics, President Obama issued an executive order committing the government to providing regular updates (299–304). It was a laudable effort to establish a new baseline for transparency about the drone campaign, but of course the next president may decide to amend the executive order, or even to rescind it. She may be unwilling to adopt the transparency protocols that President Obama resisted for seven years and adopted only in the last year of his second term. Better to have the executive order than not to have it, but whatever else the executive order may be, the order is a reminder that transparency about the drone campaign remains a matter of executive grace.

FOUR
Law Without Limits

FBI agents arrested Jose Padilla at O'Hare Airport in Chicago on May 8, 2002. A thirty-two-year-old American who had spent the previous months in Afghanistan and Pakistan, Padilla was initially held on a material-witness warrant, with the government asserting that his testimony was needed in connection with the investigation into the 9/11 attacks. Over the next few weeks, though, the government did not seek Padilla's testimony or charge him with any crime. Instead, in what would become a defining event in the nascent war on terror, President Bush issued an order directing that Padilla be held by the military as an "enemy combatant." Attorney General John Ashcroft, who happened to be visiting Russia at the time, explained in a dramatic televised address from Moscow—a "fear-inducing video hookup," *Time* magazine called it—that Padilla had been plotting to build and detonate a "dirty bomb" that would have released radioactive material over Washington, potentially killing thousands. The FBI transferred Padilla to the custody of the Defense Department, and for the next three years Padilla was held in a military brig in Charleston, South Carolina. He was held in solitary confinement, subjected to a soul-crushing regime of complete sensory deprivation, and denied access to counsel.

The Padilla case was controversial for many reasons, but chief among them was that the government was imprisoning without charge or trial an American who had been apprehended not on a foreign battlefield, but within the United States. Embedded in the Bush administration's handling of the Padilla case was the claim that the battlefield of the "war on terror" knew no geographic limits. The claim was an audacious one, and in fact it was so broad, and so unsupported by existing precedent, that the Bush administration ultimately decided that it did not want the Supreme Court to consider the validity of it. In the fall of 2005, in an effort to keep the case out of the high court, President Bush ordered that Padilla be transferred back to the custody of the Justice Department, and federal prosecutors in Florida filed an indictment charging Padilla with having attended a training camp in Afghanistan. Remarkably, the indictment made no mention of al-Qaeda or the dirty-bomb plot that had ostensibly justified Padilla's designation as an enemy combatant. The allegations that Ashcroft had described so vividly from Moscow had turned out to be the fabrications of another prisoner whom the CIA had brutally tortured. Ultimately, Padilla was convicted and sentenced to twenty-one years in federal prison, with the government abandoning a request for a longer sentence in exchange for Padilla's agreement not to introduce evidence of the abuse he had suffered while in military detention—an extortive tit for tat.

When President Obama took office, his administration eschewed the rhetoric of "global war," calling it distracting and counterproductive. The administration also filed an indictment against Ali al-Marri, the one remaining "enemy combatant" still being held inside the United States, which many observers took to mean that the administration would abandon the Bush administration's legal claim about the geographic scope of the battlefield. John Brennan, who was then the president's counterterrorism adviser, said in the summer of 2009 that the mindset of "global war" had served to "validate al-Qaida's twisted worldview." Four years later, in his remarks at the National Defense University, Obama insisted that the country should define its struggle against terrorism "not as a boundless 'Global War on Terror,' but rather as a series of persistent targeted efforts to dismantle specific networks of violent extremists that threaten America" (264).

But President Obama did not abandon the Bush administration's core legal claim, even if he declined to embrace it enthusiastically. When Obama's senior advisers defended the drone campaign publicly, they resurrected essentially the same arguments they were purported to have disavowed. "The United States does not view our authority to use military force against al-Qaida as being restricted solely to 'hot' battlefields like Afghanistan," John Brennan said in the fall of 2011 (164). The Justice Department said the same thing in a November 2011 white paper. *Any* U.S. operation against al-Qaeda or its affiliates, the Justice Department declared, would be part of an armed conflict, "even if it were to take place away from the zone of active hostilities" (171). At a speech before the American Society of International Law in April 2016, Harold Koh's successor as State Department legal adviser, Brian Egan, emphasized that the United States did not claim authority to carry out targeted killings wherever it pleased. Rather, Egan said, the administration would use lethal force in other nations only if those nations consented or proved "unable or unwilling" to address the threats themselves. At the same time, though, Egan reaffirmed the administration's view that *every* action against al-Qaeda or the Islamic state, *wherever carried out*, should be viewed as an action taken in connection with armed conflict (276–278).

And in fact the claim that the United States was engaged in a borderless war against terrorist groups was foundational to the Obama administration's defense of the drone campaign. It was this claim that permitted the Obama administration to contend that drone strikes— even those carried out "away from the zone of actual hostilities"—were governed *not* by human rights law, which bars the use of lethal force except in very limited circumstances, but by the laws of war, which are more permissive of state violence and less protective of individual rights. If the administration had conceded that human rights law governed, the United States would have been legally empowered to use lethal force only as a last resort, and only in response to concrete and specific threats that were truly imminent. Where human rights law controlled, the entire apparatus of the drone campaign—the "nomination" process, the "kill lists," signature strikes—would have been obviously and inarguably unlawful.

By characterizing the struggle against terrorism as a borderless war, the United States performed a remarkable feat of legal alchemy, transforming what would otherwise have been the illegal and extrajudicial killing of civilians into the ostensibly legitimate exercise of military force. Unlawful assassination became supposedly lawful targeting. Many of the U.S. government's targets were nowhere near Afghanistan or Iraq or any other actual battlefield, but the theory, in its boldest form, was that the battlefield is everywhere because terrorists can be found anywhere. It was this theory that the Bush administration had pioneered to justify the military detention of Jose Padilla, and it was this same theory—a modified version of it, to be sure, but still quite recognizably a version of it—that the Obama administration relied upon to kill suspected terrorists and insurgents in places like Somalia and Yemen.

The theory rested on dubious foundations. As a matter of domestic law, the administration relied principally on the Authorization for Use of Military Force that Congress passed in the fall of 2001. "The AUMF itself does not set forth an express geographic limitation on the use of force it authorizes," the Justice Department observed (93, 172). It is doubtful, though, that many of the legislators who authorized military force in the weeks after the September 2001 attacks believed they were approving a global war, let alone one to be waged against groups that did not even exist at the time. "None of us, not one who voted for it, could have envisioned we were voting for the longest war in American history, [o]r that we were about to give future presidents the authority to fight terrorism as far-flung as Yemen and Somalia," Senator Dick Durbin told *Politico*.

Nor had the Supreme Court adopted the administration's premise. In 2006, the U.S. Supreme Court held in *Hamdan v. Rumsfeld* that the United States was engaged in an armed conflict with al-Qaeda, but that case involved the detention of an individual apprehended in Afghanistan in 2002—that is, at a time and place in which the United States was indisputably at war. And while an appeals court subsequently upheld the detention at Guantánamo of a handful of men who had been detained outside Afghanistan, the Supreme Court had not reviewed those rulings, and in any event most of the men whose detention was at issue in those cases allegedly had some link to the hostilities in Afghanistan, even if they had not been detained there.

The position the Obama administration staked out was also difficult to reconcile with international law. The United States was not involved in hostilities in Yemen, Somalia, or Pakistan that rose to a level that would trigger the application of the laws of war. Even if one accepted that the United States was at war *in* these countries, which groups was it at war *with*? Some of the groups the United States was fighting—for example, al-Shabaab in Somalia—appeared to have only loose connections with "core" al-Qaeda, the organization behind the September 2001 terrorist attacks. The Obama administration took the position that some of the groups were "associated" with al-Qaeda in a way that rendered them targetable, but international law does not support a conception of association as broad as the one the administration articulated.

Outside Washington, the administration's borderless-battlefield theory was rejected almost universally. "Right now, there isn't a government on the planet that agrees with our legal rationale for these operations, except for Afghanistan and maybe Israel," former CIA director Michael Hayden acknowledged in 2012. The International Committee for the Red Cross, the foremost authority on the laws of war, categorically rejected the claim that the United States was engaged in a borderless conflict: "The ICRC does not share the view that a conflict of global dimensions is or has been taking place." The ICRC's legal adviser, Jelena Pejic, noted that "the great majority of states" had not accepted the United States' position, and she wondered what would happen if they did. "It is disturbing, as a practical matter," she wrote, "to envisage the potential ramifications" if other nations "were to likewise rely on the concept of a 'global battlefield.'"

The Presidential Policy Guidance that President Obama signed in May 2013 and described the following day at the National Defense University was in part a concession to those who rejected the paradigm of borderless war. The administration did not abandon the claim that the law of war governed strikes conducted outside actual battlefields, but it said that it would apply a new, more stringent set of rules to those strikes. The new rules gestured toward human rights principles but did not fully reflect them. A mishmash of ideas borrowed from different legal paradigms, the new rules relied on what Stanford Law School professor

Shirin Sinnar has called "rule of law 'tropes'"—concepts meant to preserve executive discretion while conjuring an aura of legal constraint. Indeed, the new rules were discretionary on their face. The administration made clear that it would make a policy decision as to where the new rules would be applied, and that even where the new rules applied, the president would retain the authority to waive the rules in particular instances.

One important respect in which the new framework was at odds with human rights law had to do with targeting standards. Taken together, human rights conventions, treaties, and supporting case law permit a state to use lethal force in response to threats that are "imminent," but the use of lethal force in response to non-imminent threats constitutes a violation of a *jus cogens* norm—that is, a norm so fundamental and well settled that no departure from it is permitted. Where human rights law governs, states must exhaust other options before resorting to lethal force, and the imminence requirement helps enforce that principle. Perhaps the person believed to be a threat may turn out not to pose a threat at all, or perhaps he will abandon the threatening conduct, or perhaps the threat can be addressed with some measure short of lethal force. The imminence requirement is meant to ensure that the state uses lethal force only when there is no other option.

The imminence requirement is also closely connected to procedural considerations. The U.S. Constitution prohibits the government from depriving a person of his or her life without "due process of law," and this prohibition crystallizes a foundational principle of human rights law. As one American court has observed, "every instrument or agreement that has attempted to define the scope of international human rights has 'recognized a right to life coupled with a right to due process to protect that right.'"

In his 2012 speech at Northwestern University Law School, Attorney General Eric Holder argued that "'due process' and 'judicial process' are not one and the same" (197)—and Holder was right about this. There are contexts in which domestic and international law permit the government to deprive individuals of their rights, and even their lives, without first presenting evidence to a judge. Many believe that police officers use force too readily, for example, but no one proposes that police officers should submit applications to judges before responding, even with lethal force, to threats they reasonably believe to be imminent. Beyond battlefields, though, a government's authority to use lethal force without prior judicial review is strictly limited, and it is limited in part by the imminence requirement. Except on actual battlefields, "imminence" marks the line between situations in which lethal force can be used without prior judicial approval and situations in which it cannot be.

In his May 2013 speech, Obama invoked the imminence requirement but softened it, stating that lethal force would be used only against individuals who present a "*continuing*, imminent threat." Attorney General Holder explained some of the thinking behind this shift in his earlier speech at Northwestern. Whether a particular target presents a sufficiently immediate threat, he said, "incorporates considerations of the relevant window of opportunity to act, the possible harm that missing the window would cause to civilians, and the likelihood of heading off future disastrous attacks against the United States." Holder continued: "[t]he Constitution does not require the President to delay action until some theoretical end-stage of planning—when the precise time, place, and manner of an attack become clear. Such a requirement would create an unacceptably high risk that our efforts would fail, and that Americans would be killed" (196).

The argument has superficial appeal, but it does not withstand scrutiny, because it takes into account only one side of the balance. It gives weight to the potential harm associated with delaying the use of lethal force, but it overlooks the risks of using lethal force prematurely. These latter risks—that lethal force might be used against the wrong target, that it might be used against someone who does not in fact present a threat, that it might be used against someone who does not present a *serious* threat, that it might be used against someone whose capture is feasible, that it might result in bystanders being injured or killed unnecessarily—these risks are not part of the calculus Holder describes. And while Holder rightly observed that the government may have to act without knowing "the precise time, place, and manner" in which the feared attack would be carried out, he overlooked all of the other ways in which the government's knowledge might be incomplete. In Holder's imagined scenario, the government is dealing with *known* terrorists who are *known* to be planning attacks continuously—but this assumes a degree of certainty the government will rarely, if ever, have.

Moreover, neither Holder in his Northwestern University speech, nor President Obama, in his speech at the National Defense University, grappled with the *procedural* implications of abandoning or relaxing the imminence requirement. Again, when human rights law relieves the government from the usual requirement of prior judicial review, it does so because of the threat's imminence. However, if the requirement of imminence is abandoned, or if the concept is distended so radically as to allow for nominating processes and standing "kill lists," the rationale for releasing the government from the requirement of prior judicial review dissolves. Holder observed that "military and civilian officials must often make *real-time decisions* that balance the need to act, the existence of alternative options, the possibility of collateral damage, and other judgments—all of which depend on expertise and immediate access to information that only the Executive Branch may possess *in real time*." This argument has force, though, only if the government is in fact responding in real time to imminent threats, rather than responding—as it often is—with bureaucratic deliberation over weeks or months to threats that reveal themselves only gradually and that may come to fruition, if at all, only months or years after first identified.

As it became clear that few drone strikes were directed at individuals thought to present truly imminent threats, and that many strikes were preceded by bureaucratic deliberation, some began to question why federal courts should not be involved in assessing, in advance of lethal strikes, whether the government's proposed targets were legitimate ones. "Having the executive being the prosecutor, the judge, the jury and the executioner all in one is very contrary to the traditions and the laws of this country," Senator Angus King of Maine observed. Senator Dianne Feinstein, the Senate Intelligence Committee chair, indicated in February 2013 that she would hold hearings to consider the establishment of some kind of drone court. John Brennan, then the CIA director, revealed that the administration had discussed the possibility of a judicial oversight mechanism and he allowed that the idea was "worth considering."

In the end, though, no specific proposal emerged from Congress or the administration. Some supporters of the government's drone campaign concluded that the establishment of a drone court would constitute an intolerable encroachment on the president's war powers. Many critics of the campaign—including those of us at the ACLU—believed that creating a court to sign off on drone strikes would further normalize the broad use of lethal force in areas far removed from actual battlefields. The apparent lawlessness of the expanding drone campaign was alarming, but involving federal judges in targeting decisions did not seem like the right answer.

————

The question of what role the judiciary should play in relation to the drone campaign was presented most sharply in the litigation involving Anwar al-Aulaqi. From a certain perspective, al-Aulaqi's case presented the strongest possible argument for the involvement of the American judiciary, because al-Aulaqi was an American citizen whose right to invoke the protection of the U.S. Constitution was indisputable, and because U.S. officials had acknowledged publicly that al-Aulaqi had been added to government kill lists. Still, when I and my colleagues filed suit on behalf of Anwar's father in the summer of 2010, we did not ask the court to review the government's targeting decisions. Instead, we asked the court to review the legal framework within which those targeting decisions would be made. The brief we filed on Dr. al-Aulaqi's behalf stressed that distinction:

> Outside of armed conflict, both the Constitution and international law prohibit targeted killing except as a last resort to protect against concrete, specific, and imminent threats of death or serious physical injury. The summary use of force is lawful in these narrow circumstances only because the imminence of the threat makes judicial process infeasible. A targeted killing policy under which individuals are added to kill lists after a bureaucratic process and remain on these lists for months at a time plainly goes beyond the use of lethal force as a last resort to address imminent threats, and accordingly goes beyond what the Constitution and international law permit.

Foreshadowing Holder's remarks at Northwestern University, the Obama administration vehemently rejected the notion that the judiciary should oversee what the government characterized as wartime targeting decisions. Affording Dr. al-Aulaqi the relief he sought, the government argued in legal papers, "would constitute an ex ante command to military and intelligence officials that could interfere with lawful commands issued by the President, who is constitutionally designated as Commander-in-Chief of the armed forces and constitutionally responsible for national security." The government further warned: "Courts have neither the authority nor expertise to assume these tasks."

But as administration officials surely knew, Dr. al-Aulaqi was not asking the court to interfere with real-time targeting decisions. That is, he was not asking the court, as the government misdescribed it at oral argument, to "stand at the shoulder of the President as he was trying to decide whether there was 'an imminent threat to the security of U.S. nationals.'" He was asking the court to do something quite different: *to say what the law was.* Even if real-time targeting decisions would be based on information available only to intelligence and military personnel, a court tasked with protecting constitutional rights should not defer to the government's view of the relevant legal framework, Dr. al-Aulaqi argued. How could it possibly make sense, he asked, to allow the executive branch to decide for itself the scope of its authority to use lethal force against its own citizens?

At oral argument, Judge Bates seemed troubled by the government's contention that the judiciary had no role to play. The judge pressed Douglas Letter, the senior Justice Department lawyer representing the government in court:

> How is it that judicial scrutiny is required when the United States decides to target a U.S. citizen overseas for electronic surveillance, and judicial scrutiny is permitted when the United States takes the property of U.S. citizens overseas, but judicial scrutiny is prohibited, in your view, on the political question doctrine, when the United States decides to target a U.S. citizen overseas for death? How does that all make sense?

That seeming skepticism aside, Judge Bates ultimately accepted the government's argument, finding that Dr. al-Aulaqi lacked "standing" to
assert his son's constitutional rights and that, in any event, at least in
the circumstances presented, "the Executive's unilateral decision to kill
a U.S. citizen overseas [was] constitutionally committed to the political branches and judicially unreviewable." In the judge's view, the core
question presented by the case—that is, under what circumstances the
government could lawfully carry out the killing of a U.S. citizen alleged
to be an enemy of the state—was a "political question," meaning a question assigned to Congress and the executive branch, not to the courts.

Judge Bates's ruling would have been consequential enough if it had
stopped there but, at the administration's urging, he went further. At
oral argument the judge had raised the possibility that, if he dismissed
the lawsuit, Dr. al-Aulaqi—or someone else—would bring another suit
after Anwar al-Aulaqi's killing had been carried out. If such a suit were
filed, Judge Bates asked at oral argument, would the government argue
that the political question doctrine barred *that* suit as well? "I believe
we would, your honor," Letter conceded. Returning to that question in
his opinion, Judge Bates adopted the administration's view, holding that
the political question doctrine would bar *any* suit relating to al-Aulaqi's
killing. "Any after-the-fact judicial review of the Executive's decision to
employ military force abroad," he wrote, "would reveal a lack of respect
due coordinate branches of government and create the potentiality of
embarrassment of multifarious pronouncements by various departments on one question."

The U.S. government killed Anwar al-Aulaqi, Samir Khan, and
Abdulrahman al-Aulaqi less than a year after Judge Bates issued his
opinion. When, as the judge had forecast, the ACLU and the Center for
Constitutional Rights filed a second suit seeking a measure of accountability for the deaths, the Obama administration stuck to its script. In
legal papers and in court, the administration argued that the new suit
was barred by the political question doctrine, and that the Constitution
supplied no right of redress in any event. At oral argument, Hina Shamsi, my ACLU colleague, contended that the government's interpretation
of the Constitution was indefensible, and Judge Rosemary Collyer, who
presided over the case, seemed astonished at the breadth of the government's theory. She told the government's lawyer:

> The argument you're making isn't tied to these facts. It's
> tied to an assertion of authority that says that the Court has
> no role in this. None, none, none. . . . [Y]ou see, the scope
> of your argument is what concerns me. It just would gobble
> up all of the air in the room.

But although she ultimately rejected the administration's politi-cal question argument, Judge Collyer dismissed the suit. She was not persuaded that the killing of Samir Khan and Abdulrahman al-Aulaqi implicated the Constitution at all, because there was no publicly avail-able evidence that either of them had been specifically targeted. She rec-ognized that Anwar al-Aulaqi had been targeted, but she concluded that U.S. law afforded no remedy even if his constitutional rights had been violated. "In this delicate area of warmaking, national security, and foreign relations, the judiciary has an exceedingly limited role," Judge Collyer wrote. The questions the plaintiffs had raised, she continued, echoing the Obama administration's argument, were for the political branches to answer. National security officials "must be trusted."

The Obama administration's arguments in court were based in part on memos written by the Office of Legal Counsel, the component of the Justice Department whose central function is to provide controlling legal advice to executive branch agencies. Practically speaking, the OLC's opinions are often the last word on the legality of whatever action the agencies are contemplating, because many of the issues the OLC considers are never adjudicated by the courts. This is especially true in the national security realm, where the government's policies and activi-ties are often immunized from judicial review by secrecy and jurisdic-tional doctrines.

The OLC has sometimes been called the "conscience" of the execu-tive branch, but the office's reputation was gravely damaged during the presidency of George W. Bush. In the years following 9/11, the office signed off on the NSA's warrantless wiretapping program in opinions that failed to contend with, or even cite, controlling Supreme Court precedent. OLC lawyers also drew other dubious conclusions aggran-dizing executive power, concluding, for example, that the military could operate inside the United States without complying with the

Fourth Amendment. Prisoners thought to be associated with al-Qaeda were not entitled to the protections of the Geneva Conventions, OLC opinions said, nor were prisoners entitled to file habeas corpus petitions challenging the lawfulness of their detention. In the early years of the Bush administration, the OLC served more as consigliere than conscience.

Most significantly, the OLC's lawyers concluded in a series of now notorious memos that the president could lawfully permit interrogators to use torture. Those memos, still a shocking read, reasoned that the brutal interrogation techniques proposed by the CIA—confining prisoners in small boxes, slamming them against walls, waterboarding them—were not so severe that they constituted torture under federal law. Even if the techniques amounted to torture, the OLC wrote, the president could lawfully authorize interrogators to employ them in defense of the nation. The OLC's memos were intended to be a golden shield, penned to give the administration legal cover and to ensure that officials would never be prosecuted for authorizing the methods the CIA had proposed.

Intent on restoring the OLC's credibility, President Obama staffed the office with lawyers with impeccable legal credentials. Among them were David Barron and Marty Lederman. Barron had taught for a decade at Harvard Law School following a stint with the Clinton administration's OLC. Early in his career he had served as a law clerk to Judge Stephen Reinhardt on the U.S. Court of Appeals for the Ninth Circuit, and to Justice John Paul Stevens on the U.S. Supreme Court—two highly respected jurists. Lederman had also worked in the Clinton administration's OLC, going on to represent labor unions in private practice before joining the faculty of Georgetown Law School. In 2009, Barron and Lederman collaborated on an article several hundred pages long about the president's constitutional authority as commander in chief. Published in the *Harvard Law Review*, the article, rejecting views associated with the Bush administration's OLC, concluded that Congress has broad authority to regulate presidential power during wartime.

It was Barron and Lederman to whom senior administration officials turned when they wanted to know whether they could order the killing of Anwar al-Aulaqi. The two lawyers gave oral approval for the killing early in 2010, following up with a seven-page written memo

addressed to Attorney General Holder (61–72). Alerted by a law professor's blog post to questions they had overlooked, Barron and Lederman penned another, much longer memo that was finalized in July 2010
(73–117), just days before Anwar al-Aulaqi's father filed the first of his
lawsuits against the government. It was this July 2010 memo that the
U.S. Court of Appeals for the Second Circuit published, with redactions, four years later as the Senate was considering President Obama's
nomination of Barron to the federal bench.

In the days following the July 2010 memo's publication in 2014,
some commentators compared the document favorably to those that
had been written a decade earlier by the Bush administration's OLC,
observing that the memo written by Barron and Lederman identified key precedents, offered plausible readings of them, and addressed
anticipated counterarguments. These observations had the effect, if not
always the intent, of short-circuiting any sustained reflection on the
arguments the Obama administration's OLC had endorsed. Evaluated
on its own terms, however, the July 2010 memo was deeply flawed.

While Barron and Lederman found it unnecessary to endorse the
strongest version of the borderless-battlefield theory, they reasoned that
the 2001 Authorization for Use of Military Force invested the president with power to use military force thousands of miles away from
the battlefield in Afghanistan, and against a group that did not exist
when the 9/11 attacks were carried out and whose connections to core
al-Qaeda were at best murky (92–97). They reasoned that the proposed
killing would be an exercise of "lawful public authority," and that
consequently domestic criminal laws—including the laws that crimi-
nalized murder—would not apply (78–88). The two lawyers also concluded that the Fourth and Fifth Amendments did not entitle al-Aulaqi
to judicial process in advance of the contemplated strike (113–117). To
the extent the Constitution protected al-Aulaqi, they wrote, its requirements would be fully satisfied by secret deliberations within the executive branch (116).

These arguments were not dictated by precedent. Nor were they the
best reading of the law. To reach their conclusions, Barron and Lederman construed very broadly the cases in which the courts had affirmed
the president's war powers, and they construed very narrowly the cases
in which the courts had recognized individual rights.

And there were deeper problems with their analysis. To begin with, Barron and Lederman oversimplified the test the Supreme Court has used to determine what procedural safeguards the government must afford before depriving an individual of his property, liberty, or life. In a forty-year-old case called *Mathews v. Eldridge*, the court wrote that identifying the demands of "due process" requires consideration of "three distinct factors": first, the significance of the private interest at stake; second, "the risk of an erroneous deprivation of such interest through the procedures used, and the probable value, if any, of additional or substitute procedural safeguards"; and, third, the government's interest, including the "burdens that the additional or substitute procedural requirement would entail." Barron and Lederman acknowledged the relevance of *Mathews* but then failed to apply its framework, instead emphasizing, in an analysis of less than three pages, the deference often extended to the executive branch in times of war (113–115).

Relatedly, Barron and Lederman failed to contend with the procedural implications of the fact that al-Aulaqi was believed to present a "continuing and imminent" threat rather than a truly imminent one. One of their unstated assumptions seems to have been that the threat was so immediate that the government did not have time to present evidence to a court before acting, but by the time Barron and Lederman finished their memo, six months had passed since the CIA and JSOC had added al-Aulaqi to their respective kill lists. In this light, it is at least questionable why the perceived threat was thought to be so immediate as to preclude deliberation or judicial review. The very fact that Barron and Lederman were writing a legal memo was evidence that there was time for deliberation.

Although portions of the July 2010 OLC memo remain redacted, Barron and Lederman also appear not to have addressed the question of whether the Constitution would require some form of judicial process *after* the contemplated killing of al-Aulaqi. Presumably the two OLC lawyers were asked to address only the question of what process was required *before* the strike—but can that question really be answered in isolation? Barron and Lederman rightly observed that the Supreme Court had not always required the government to obtain a judge's approval before depriving a person of his property, liberty, or life, but all of the cases they cited are ones in which some form of judicial review would have been available after the deprivation. The Supreme Court has never held that the government can lawfully deny an individual *any* judicial forum in which to vindicate a constitutional claim. To the contrary, it has taken care to avoid this result. And yet this was the result that the Obama administration was actually proposing. It was not proposing that judicial review should be deferred. As would become clear in the al-Aulaqi litigation, the administration was proposing that judicial review should be denied altogether.

The memo's argument that CIA personnel involved in the killing of al-Aulaqi would be exercising "public authority" was also flawed. Under the laws of war, members of regular armed forces are entitled to a "privilege of belligerency"—meaning that so long as their conduct is consistent with the laws of war, they are immunized from prosecution under the domestic laws of the countries in which they operate. Barron and Lederman acknowledged that CIA personnel would not be entitled to any similar privilege or immunity. To Barron and Lederman, though, this fact was not determinative, because in their view the CIA's contemplated conduct, even if not *privileged* by the laws of war, would not *contravene* the laws of war, either. This was a defensible position, but oddly the two lawyers did not acknowledge—at least in the passages that are available to us—that the U.S. government had taken precisely the opposite position for almost a decade. At Guantánamo Bay, the Defense Department had charged prisoners with war crimes for having participated in hostilities without the privilege of belligerence—that is, for having done, albeit with more primitive weapons, exactly what the CIA was proposing to do. It had filed war crimes charges against Omar Khadr, a Canadian prisoner who had been captured at age fifteen, for allegedly having thrown a grenade that killed a U.S. medic in Afghanistan. It had filed similar charges against Mohamed Jawad, an Afghan prisoner whose family said he was twelve when he was captured, for allegedly having thrown a grenade at a passing American convoy. In both cases, the alleged war crime was the mere fact of unprivileged belligerency.

Again, parts of the July 2010 memo have been blacked out by the government, but it appears that Barron and Lederman failed to contend with these cases. And while the two lawyers observed that the Defense Department's "then-current" manual for military commissions did not "endorse the view that the commission of an unprivileged belligerent act, without more, constitutes a violation of the international law of war," they neglected to mention that the then-current manual had been issued only weeks before, and that the passage they quoted had been inserted precisely because of the concern that the earlier version of the manual would have made the CIA's drone strikes war crimes. They also failed to note that, while the Obama administration was no longer using the phrase "war crime" to describe Omar Khadr's conduct, it had not abandoned Khadr's prosecution. To the contrary, it was continuing to prosecute Khadr in a tribunal whose jurisdiction had historically been understood to extend only to war crimes.

———

Dr. al-Aulaqi, Anwar's father, did not appeal Judge Collyer's decision dismissing his suit. The government's statements had prepared him, at some level, for his son's death—though of course he thought the summary killing to be unjustified. But Dr. al-Aulaqi could not fathom the death of his sixteen-year-old grandson, and still less could he understand the government's refusal to explain its actions. "A country that believes it does not even need to answer for killing its own is not the America I once knew," Dr. al-Aulaqi wrote in the *New York Times*. After Judge Collyer's ruling, he lost faith that the American legal system would offer his family anything resembling justice, and he instructed us to abandon the case.

We cannot know how a higher court would have ruled, but surely the American government owed Dr. al-Aulaqi an explanation, at the very least. And whatever one thinks of the argument that it should not be required to present evidence to judges *before* carrying out targeted killings, the idea that courts would exceed their proper role by engaging in an after-the-fact review is decidedly weak. American courts are already accustomed to engaging in after-the-fact review of the government's use of force. Police officers make split-second decisions on the basis of information that is available only to them, but courts review their decisions later. After-the-fact review cannot reverse the use of lethal force, but it can nonetheless provide a kind of accountability. Over time, it can also generate a body of law that clarifies when the government can permissibly use lethal force and when the Constitution prohibits it from doing so.

The fact that targeted killings are carried out for "national security" reasons does not make this kind of after-the-fact review less appropriate or less necessary. Indeed, the Supreme Court has already recognized as much. In the 2004 case of *Hamdi v. Rumsfeld*, the nation's highest court reviewed the detention of Yasser Hamdi, an American citizen who had been captured by the Northern Alliance in Afghanistan in 2001 and turned over to the U.S. military. The U.S. military transferred him to Guantánamo Bay and then, when it determined that he was an American citizen, to a naval brig in Norfolk, Virginia. When Hamdi challenged his detention, the Bush administration argued that whatever process Hamdi was owed because of his citizenship had already been supplied to him by the executive branch, and that any judicial review of Hamdi's detention would be "constitutionally intolerable."

Writing for a plurality of the court, Justice Sandra Day O'Connor disagreed. The government had a weighty interest in ensuring "that those who have in fact fought with the enemy during a war do not return to battle against the United States," Justice O'Connor wrote. But this did not mean that an American detained by the military should be denied a meaningful opportunity to challenge his detention. "It is during our most challenging and uncertain moments that our Nation's commitment to due process is most severely tested; and it is in those times that we must preserve our commitment at home to the principles for which we fight abroad," Justice O'Connor continued. In her view, Hamdi was entitled to both "notice of the factual basis" for his designation as an "enemy combatant" and a "meaningful opportunity to rebut the government's allegations before a neutral decisionmaker." Four members of the court would have gone further and prohibited Hamdi's detention in the absence of a criminal proceeding and conviction.

The Supreme Court also held in two celebrated cases—*Rasul v. Bush* in 2004 and *Boumediene v. Bush* in 2008—that federal courts had jurisdiction to review the detention of foreign citizens imprisoned as enemy combatants at Guantánamo. The Bush administration strongly opposed the prisoners' right to file habeas corpus petitions, arguing the prisoners possessed no constitutional right of judicial review, and that it would be improper as a constitutional matter for the courts to "second-guess" the military's decisions. In a proud moment, the Supreme Court rejected these arguments, and now, eight years after *Boumediene*, district court judges in Washington, D.C., have heard dozens of prisoners' petitions. In these cases, judges opine on the scope of the government's authority and assess the sufficiency of the government's evidence—in other words, they perform essentially the same tasks they would perform in the context of suits challenging the lawfulness of targeted killings.

The U.S. government has never supplied compelling reasons for denying court review of the lawfulness of drone strikes. After-the-fact judicial review would not intrude on the authority of the commander in chief any more than it did in cases like *Hamdi*, *Rasul*, and *Boumediene*. In the post-strike litigation before Judge Rosemary Collyer, the government argued that after-the-fact review would be unworkable because it would require disclosure of classified facts. Even the mere possibility that sensitive facts might be disclosed, the government argued, would have a chilling effect on intelligence sources. Yet the same concerns were raised in the Supreme Court's detention cases and rejected. Additionally, many of the classified facts the government was seeking to protect in the case before Judge Collyer would have had to be disclosed if the government had prosecuted Anwar al-Aulaqi rather than killed him. In a criminal trial, the government would have had to specify the charges against al-Aulaqi and substantiate those charges with evidence. Why should less be demanded of the government when it imposes a death sentence unilaterally? It makes little sense to require the government to present a persuasive justification to a judge when it locks up a terrorism suspect but not when it kills the suspect summarily. As Georgetown Law professor David Cole has observed, "Leaked accounts to the *New York Times* are no substitute for legal or democratic process."

This is not to say that it follows inevitably from the court's detention cases that the Constitution requires after-the-fact judicial review of targeted killings, or even that the Constitution permits such review. But in important respects, the argument that after-the-fact judicial review should be available in a case like al-Aulaqi's is far stronger than it was in the detention cases. Hamdi was on an actual battlefield, but al-Aulaqi was far away from one. The prisoners at Guantánamo were foreign citizens, but al-Aulaqi was an American whose entitlement to protection under the Fourth and Fifth Amendments could not be seriously disputed. And while wrongful detention is in some sense reversible, wrongful killing is not. As Yale Law School professor Owen Fiss has written, "More procedure, not less, should be required when the taking of life hangs in the balance." The irreversibility of a targeted killing only heightens the need for clear limits on the government's authority and for some mechanism by which those limits can be enforced.

———

The drone campaign presents critical questions about the scope of executive authority to use lethal force, and about the way that authority is exercised and overseen. With a new administration in the offing, these questions take on new urgency. A dangerous legacy of the Obama presidency is a legal regime in which executive branch actors are judge, jury, and executioner—one in which executive actors decide for themselves both the breadth of their authority to use lethal force and, even outside actual battlefields, the permissibility of using lethal force in any particular instance. It is a framework in which the government can carry out deliberate and premeditated killings on the basis of evidence that is never disclosed, and on the basis of legal rules that are neither fully articulated to the public nor reviewed by any court. And it is a framework in which the government can kill a sixteen-year-old boy—one of its own citizens—without explaining why.

President Obama himself seemed to recognize the unsustainability of this framework in his remarks at the National Defense University in 2013. "The same human progress that gives us the technology to strike half a world away," the president said, "also demands the discipline to constrain that power." But, as the documents collected here underscore, President Obama's administration did not meaningfully constrain the power. Nor did Congress or the courts. It is a distressing and ominous fact, and a testament to the failure of all three branches of government, that the drone campaign is not subject to any meaningful constraint that could not be lifted by a stroke of the next president's pen.

EDITOR'S NOTE

Collected in the following pages are sixteen documents that together supply much of what we know of the law and policy underlying the U.S. government's practice of "targeted killing"—the killing of suspected terrorists and militants, typically using armed drones, often away from conventional battlefields. Some of the documents were disclosed in response to litigation under the Freedom of Information Act; others the government disclosed of its own accord; and others are transcripts of public speeches delivered by government officials.

I have transcribed and reset the documents to make them more readable. For documents other than public speeches, original pagination is indicated in the margin. I have omitted the government's classification markings, as well as markings relating to processing under the Freedom of Information Act. I have abridged some of the speeches to exclude passages that address issues other than targeted killing; omitted text is marked with three asterisks. In some instances, I have preserved formatting (e.g., distinctive letterhead, signature blocks) to give the reader a sense of the original document.

The government's redactions to documents released under the Freedom of Information Act are indicated with black bars. Readers especially interested in the extent to which the government has redacted the documents should be aware that, because the documents presented here have been transcribed and reset, the length of the redactions in them corresponds only roughly to the length of the redactions in the originals.

THE DRONE MEMOS

1

Office of Legal Counsel Memorandum

February 19, 2010

"Lethal Operation Against Shaykh Anwar Aulaqi ███████████"

In late 2009 or early 2010, the Justice Department's Office of Legal Counsel orally approved the targeting of Anwar al-Aulaqi, an American citizen. The OLC produced this written memo a few weeks later. The memo addresses the implications of an executive order that bans "assassinations," as well as "applicable constitutional limitations due to Aulaqi's United States citizenship." This version of the memo, which was provided to the journalist Jason Leopold and the ACLU in connection with FOIA litigation, is heavily redacted. Many of the redactions appear to relate to the OLC's analysis of the assassination ban.

The document from which this text was transcribed is posted at: www.ACLU.org/TDM/OLCMemo1.

Feb. 19, 2010

MEMORANDUM FOR THE ATTORNEY GENERAL

Re: Lethal Operation Against Shaykh Anwar Aulaqi ███████████

███████████████████████████████ has asked for your views on the legality of the Central Intelligence Agency's ("CIA") proposed use of lethal force in Yemen against Shaykh Anwar Aulaqi, a U.S. citizen who the CIA assesses is a senior leader of Al-Qa'ida in the Arabian Peninsula. ██ Under the conditions and factual predicates as represented by the CIA and in the materials provided to us from the Intelligence Community, we believe that a decisionmaker, on the basis of such information, could reasonably conclude that the use of lethal force against Aulaqi would not violate the assassination ban in Executive Order 12333 or any applicable constitutional limitations due to Aulaqi's United States citizenship. This memorandum confirms oral advice setting forth this conclusion. ██████████████

I.

██

2

3

4

consistent with the assassination ban in Executive Order 12333[2]
killings in self-defense are not
assassinations

5

---

[2] Section 2.11 of Executive Order 12333 provides that "[n]o person employed by or acting on behalf of the United States Government shall engage in, or conspire to engage in, assassination." 46 Fed. Reg. 59941 (Dec. 4, 1981).

The question that remains is whether Aulaqi's status as a U.S. citizen imposes any constitutional limitations that would preclude the proposed lethal action

being a U.S person

does not give a member of al-Qa'ida a constitutional immunity from attack.

This conclusion finds support in Supreme Court case law addressing whether a U.S. citizen who acts as an enemy combatant may be subject to the use of certain types of military force. *See Hamdi v. Rumsfeld*, 542 U.S. 507, 521–24 (2004) (plurality opinion); *cf. also Ex parte Quirin*, 317 U.S. 1, 37–38 (1942) ("[c]itizens who associate them-

6 selves with the military arm of the enemy government, and with its aid, guidance and direction enter [the United States] bent on hostile acts," may be treated as "enemy belligerents" under the law of war).

Because Aulaqi is a U.S. citizen, the Fifth Amendment's Due Process Clause, as well as the Fourth Amendment, likely applies in some respects, even while he is abroad (in this case, in Yemen). *See Reid v. Covert*, 354 U.S. 1, 5–6 (1957) (plurality opinion); *United States v. Verdugo-Urquidez*, 494 U.S. 259, 269–70 (1990); *see also In re Terrorist Bombings of U.S. Embassies in East Africa*, 552 F.3d 157,167–68 (2d Cir. 2008). In *Hamdi*, a plurality of the Supreme Court used the *Mathews v. Eldridge* balancing test to outline the due process rights of a U.S. citizen captured on the battlefield in Afghanistan and detained in the United States, explaining that "the process due in any given instance is determined by weighing 'the private interest that will be affected by the official action,' against the Government's asserted interest, 'including the function involved' and the burdens the Government would face in providing greater process." *Hamdi*, 542 U.S. at 529 (plurality opinion) (quoting *Mathews v. Eldridge*, 424 U.S. 319, 335 (1976)).

the plurality in *Hamdi* stated that "[t]he parties agree that initial captures on the battlefield need not receive the process we discuss here; that process is due only when the determination is made to *continue* to hold those who have been seized," and the plurality thus found it "unlikely that this basic process will have the dire impact on the central functions of warmaking that the Government forecasts." 542 U.S. at 534 (plurality opinion). ███ ███ on the battlefield, the Government's interests and burdens preclude offering a process to judge whether a detainee is truly an enemy combatant ████████████████

███ In the case of a member, associate, or affiliate of al-Qa'ida operating abroad in circumstances where capture is infeasible, and it is known that the individual ████████████████ continued and imminent threat ██ given the weight of the government's interest in using an authorized means of force to respond to an imminent threat posed by the activities of a person operating as a member, associate, or affiliate of an enemy force. ██ to the extent Fourth Amendment principles are relevant in the context of operations against a U.S. person who is a member of al-Qa'ida and whose activities pose a continued and imminent threat, the proposed lethal operation would not violate the Fourth Amendment, ████████ *Verdugo-Urquidez*, 494 U.S. at 273–74 ("Application of the Fourth Amendment to these circumstances [i.e., foreign policy operations] could significantly disrupt the ability of the political branches to respond to foreign situations involving our national interest.") ████████████████████████████████ This conclusion draws further support from the fact that, even in domestic law enforcement operations, the Supreme Court has noted that "if the suspect threatens the officer with a weapon or there is probable cause to believe that he has committed a crime involving the infliction or threatened infliction of serious physical harm, deadly force may be used if necessary to prevent escape and if, where feasible, some warning has been given." *Tennessee v. Garner*, 471 U.S. 1, 11–12 (1985). ████████████████ where ████████████ a capture operation is infeasible and ████ the targeted person is part of a

7

dangerous enemy force and poses a continued and imminent threat to U.S. persons or interests, the use of lethal force would not violate the Fourth Amendment.

        For these reasons, and on these understandings, we do not believe the Constitution prohibits the proposed lethal action,

        does not violate the assassination ban in Executive Order 12333.

        Please let us know if we can be of further assistance.

David J. Barron
Acting Assistant Attorney General

Office of Legal Counsel Memorandum

July 16, 2010

"Applicability of Federal Criminal Laws and the Constitution to Contemplated Lethal Operations Against Shaykh Anwar al-Aulaqi"

David Barron and Marty Lederman, the two lawyers who wrote the Office of Legal Counsel's February 19, 2010, memo authorizing the proposed killing of Anwar al-Aulaqi, realized during the spring of 2010 that their analysis was incomplete. To address issues their earlier memo had overlooked, Barron and Lederman drafted another memo. This memo, a redacted version of which was released to the ACLU and the *New York Times* in June 2014 after the U.S. Court of Appeals for the Second Circuit ruled that the government had waived its right to withhold it, addresses, among other things, the application of domestic criminal laws, the relevance of al-Aulaqi's citizenship, the geographic scope of the armed conflict against al-Qaeda, and the application of the Fourth and Fifth Amendments.

The document from which this text was transcribed is posted at: www. ACLU.org/TDM/OLCMemo2.

Office of the Assistant Attorney General   *Washington, D.C. 20530*

July 16, 2010

MEMORANDUM FOR THE ATTORNEY GENERAL

Re: Applicability of Federal Criminal Laws and the Constitution to Contemplated Lethal Operations Against Shaykh Anwar al-Aulaqi

* * *

II.[*]

We begin our legal analysis with a consideration of section 1119 of title 18, entitled "Foreign murder of United States nationals." Subsection 1119(b) provides that "[a] person who, being a national of the United States, kills or attempts to kill a national of the United States while such national is outside the United States but within the jurisdiction of another country shall be punished as provided under sections 1111, 1112, and 1113." 18 U.S.C. § 1119(b).[6] In light of the nature of the contemplated operations described above, and the fact that their target would be a "national of the United States" who is outside the United States, we must examine whether section 1119(b) would prohibit those operations. We first explain, in this part, the scope of section 1119 and why it must be construed to incorporate the public authority justification, which can render lethal action carried out by a governmental official lawful in some circumstances. We next explain in part III-A

---

[*] [Ed.: When the U.S. Court of Appeals for the Second Circuit ordered the disclosure of this memo, it permitted the government to withhold the entirety of the memo's first section, which, the court stated, relates to "intelligence gathering activities."]

[6] *See also* 18 U.S.C. § 1119(a) (providing that "national of the United States" has the meaning stated in section 1011(a)(22) of the Immigration and Nationality Act, 8 U.S.C. § 1101(a)(22)).

why that public authority justification would apply to the contemplated DoD operation. Finally, we explain in part III-B why that justification would apply to the contemplated CIA operation. As to each agency, we focus on the particular circumstances in which it would carry out the operation.

A.

Although section 1119(b) refers only to the "punish[ments]" provided under sections 1111, 1112, and 1113, courts have construed section 1119(b) to incorporate the substantive elements of those cross-referenced provisions of title 18. *See, e.g., United States v. Wharton*, 320 F.3d 526, 533 (5th Cir. 2003); *United States v. White*, 51 F. Supp. 2d 1008, 1013–14 (E.D. Ca. 1997). Section 1111 of title 18 sets forth criminal penalties for "murder," and provides that "[m]urder is the unlawful killing of a human being with malice aforethought." *Id.* § 1111(a). Section 1112 similarly provides criminal sanctions for "manslaughter," and states that "[m]anslaughter is the unlawful killing of a human being without malice." *Id.* § 1112. Section 1113 provides criminal penalties for "attempts to commit murder or manslaughter." *Id.* § 1113. It is therefore clear that section 1119(b) bars only "unlawful killings."[7]

This limitation on section 1119(b)'s scope is significant, as the legislative history to the underlying offenses that the section incorporates makes clear. The provisions section 1119(b) incorporates derive from sections 273 and 274 of the Act of March 4, 1909, ch. 321, 35 Stat. 1088, 1143. The 1909 Act codified and amended the penal laws of the United States. Section 273 of the enactment defined murder as "the unlawful killing of a human being with malice aforethought," and section 274 defined manslaughter as "the unlawful killing of a human being without

---

[7] Section 1119 itself also expressly imposes various procedural limitations on prosecution. Subsection 1119(c)(1) requires that any prosecution be authorized in writing by the Attorney General, the Deputy Attorney General, or an Assistant Attorney General, and precludes the approval of such an action "if prosecution has been previously undertaken by a foreign country for the same conduct." In addition, subsection 1119(c)(2) provides that "[n]o prosecution shall be approved under this section unless the Attorney General, in consultation with the Secretary of State, determines that the conduct took place in a country in which the person is no longer present, and the country lacks the ability to lawfully secure the person's return"—a determination that "is not subject to judicial review," *id.*

malice." 35 Stat. 1143.[8] In 1948, Congress codified the federal murder
and manslaughter provisions at sections 1111 and 1112 of title 18 and
retained the definitions of murder and manslaughter in nearly identical
form, *see* Act of June 25, 1948, ch. 645, 62 Stat. 683, 756, including the
references to "unlawful killing" that remain in the statutes
today—references that track similar formulations in some state murder
statutes.[9]

---

[8] A 1908 joint congressional committee report on the Act explained that
"[u]nder existing law [i.e., prior to the 1909 Act], there [had been] no statutory definition of the crimes of murder or manslaughter." Report by the Special Joint Comm. on
the Revision of the Laws, Revision and Codification of the Laws, Etc., H.R. Rep. No. 2,
60th Cong. 1st Sess., at 12 (Jan. 6, 1908) ("Joint Committee Report"). We note, however, that the 1878 edition of the Revised Statutes did contain a definition for manslaughter (but not murder): "Every person who, within any of the places or upon any
of the waters [within the exclusive jurisdiction of the United States] unlawfully and
willfully, but without malice, strikes, stabs, wounds, or shoots at, otherwise injures
another, of which striking, stabbing, wounding, shooting, or other injury such other
person dies, either on land or sea, within or without the United States, is guilty of the
crime of manslaughter." Revised Statutes § 5341 (1878 ed.) (quoted in *United States
v. Alexander*, 471 F.2d 923, 944–45 n.54 (D.C. Cir. 1972)). With respect to murder,
the 1908 report noted that the legislation "enlarges the common-law definition, and
is similar in terms to the statutes defining murder in a large majority of the States."
Joint Committee Report at 24; *see also Revision of the Penal Laws: Hearings on S.
2982 Before the Senate as a Whole*, 60th Cong., 1st Sess. 1184, 1185 (1908) (statement
of Senator Heyburn) (same). With respect to manslaughter, the report stated that
"[w]hat is said with respect to [the murder provision] is true as to this section, manslaughter being defined and classified in language similar to that to be found in the
statutes of a large majority of the States." Joint Committee Report at 24.

[9] *See, e.g.*, Cal. Penal Code § 187(a) (West 2009) ("Murder is the unlawful killing of a human being, or a fetus, with malice aforethought."); Fla. Stat. § 782.04(1)(a)
(West 2009) (including "unlawful killing of a human being" as an element of murder);
Idaho Code Ann. § 18-4001 (West 2009) ("Murder is the unlawful killing of a human
being"); Nev. Rev. Stat. Ann. § 200.010 (West 2008) (including "unlawful killing of a
human being" as an element of murder); R. I. Gen. Laws § 11-23-1 (West 2008) ("The
unlawful killing of a human being with malice aforethought is murder."); Tenn. Code
Ann. § 39-13-201 (West 2009) ("Criminal homicide is the unlawful killing of another
person"). Such statutes, in turn, reflect the view often expressed in the common law
of murder that the crime requires an "unlawful" killing. *See, e.g.*, Edward Coke, *The
Third Part of the Institutes of Laws of England* 47 (London, W. Clarke & Sons 1809)
("Murder is when a man of sound memory, and of the age of discretion, unlawfully
killeth within any county of the realm any reasonable creature *in rerum natura* under
the king's peace, with malice fore-thought, either expressed by the party, or implied
by law, so as the party wounded, or hurt, &c. die of the wound, or hurt, &c. within
a year and a day after the same."); 4 William Blackstone, *Commentaries on the Laws
of England* 195 (Oxford 1769) (same); *see also A Digest of Opinions of the Judge Advo-*

As this legislative history indicates, guidance as to the meaning of [14] what constitutes an "unlawful killing" in sections 1111 and 1112—and thus for purposes of section 1119(b)—can be found in the historical understandings of murder and manslaughter. That history shows that states have long recognized justifications and excuses to statutes criminalizing "unlawful" killings.[10] One state court, for example, in construing that state's murder statute explained that "the word 'unlawful' is a term of art" that "connotes a homicide with the absence of factors of excuse or justification," *People v. Fiye*, 10 Cal. Rptr. 2d 217, 221 (Cal. App. 1992). That court further explained that the factors of excuse or justification in question include those that have traditionally been recognized, *id.* at 221 n.2. Other authorities support the same conclusion. *See, e.g., Mullaney v. Wilbur*, 421 U.S. 684, 685 (1975) (requirement of "unlawful" killing in Maine murder statute meant that killing was "neither justifiable nor excusable"); *cf. also* Rollin M. Perkins & Ronald N. Boyce, *Criminal Law* 56 (3d ed. 1982) ("Innocent homicide is of two kinds, (1) justifiable and (2) excusable.").[11] Accordingly, section 1119

---

cates General of the Army 1074 n.3 (1912) ("Murder, at common law, is the unlawful killing by a person of sound memory and discretion, of any reasonable creature in being and under the peace of the State, which malice aforethought either express or implied.") (internal quotation marks omitted).

[10] The same is true with respect to other statutes, including federal laws, that modify a prohibited act other than murder or manslaughter with the term "unlawfully." *See, e.g., Territory v. Gonzales*, 89 P. 250, 252 (N.M. Terr. 1907) (construing the term "unlawful" in statute criminalizing assault with a deadly weapon as "clearly equivalent" to "without excuse or justification"). For example, 18 U.S.C. § 2339C makes it unlawful, *inter alia*, to "unlawfully and willfully provide[] or collect[] funds" with the intention that they be used (or knowledge they are to be used) to carry out an act that is an offense within certain specified treaties, or to engage in certain other terrorist acts. The legislative history of section 2339C makes clear that "[t]he term 'unlawfully' is intended to embody common law defenses." H.R. Rep. No. 107–307, at 12 (2001). Similarly, the Uniform Code of Military Justice makes it unlawful for members of the armed forces to, "without justification or excuse, unlawfully kill[] a human being" under certain specified circumstances. 10 U.S.C. § 918. Notwithstanding that the statute already expressly requires lack of justification or excuse, it is the longstanding view of the armed forces that "Killing a human being is *unlawful*" for purposes of this provision "when done without justification or excuse." Manual for Courts-Martial United States (2008 ed.), at IV–63, art. 118, comment (c) (1) (emphasis added).

11

does not proscribe killings covered by a justification traditionally recognized, such as under the common law or state and federal murder statutes. *See White*, 51 F. Supp. 2d at 1013 ("Congress did not intend [section 1119] to criminalize justifiable or excusable killings.").

B.

Here, we focus on the potential application of one such recognized justification—the justification of "public authority"—to the contemplated DoD and CIA operations. Before examining whether, on these facts, the public authority justification would apply to those operations, we first explain why section 1119(b) incorporates that particular justification.

The public authority justification, generally understood, is well-accepted, and it is clear it may be available even in cases where the particular criminal statute at issue does not expressly refer to a public authority justification.[12] Prosecutions where such a "public authority" justification is invoked are understandably rare, *see* American Law Institute, Model Penal Code and Commentaries § 3.03 Comment 1, at 24 (1985); *cf. VISA Fraud Investigation*, 8 Op. O.L.C. 284, 285 n.2, 286 (1984), and thus there is little case law in which courts have analyzed the scope of the justification with respect to the conduct of government

---

[12] Where a federal criminal statute incorporates the public authority justification, and the government conduct at issue is within the scope of that justification, there is no need to examine whether the criminal prohibition has been repealed, impliedly or otherwise, by some other statute that might potentially authorize the governmental conduct, including by the authorizing statute that might supply the predicate for the assertion of the public authority justification itself. Rather, in such cases, the criminal prohibition simply does not apply to the particular governmental conduct at issue in the first instance because Congress intended that prohibition to be qualified by the public authority justification that it incorporates. Conversely, where another statute expressly authorizes the government to engage in the *specific* conduct in question, then there would be no need to invoke the more general public authority justification doctrine, because in such a case the legislature itself has, in effect, carved out a specific exception permitting the executive to do what the legislature has otherwise generally forbidden. We do not address such a circumstance in this opinion.

officials.[13] Nonetheless, discussions in the leading treatises and in the Model Penal Code demonstrate its legitimacy. *See* 2 Wayne R. LaFave, *Substantive Criminal Law* § 10.2(b), at 135 (2d ed. 2003); Perkins & Boyce, *Criminal Law* at 1093 ("Deeds which otherwise would be criminal, such as taking or destroying property, taking hold of a person by force and against his will, placing him in confinement, or even taking his life, are not crimes if done with proper public authority."); *see also* Model Penal Code § 3.03(1)(a), (d), (e), at 22–23 (proposing codification of justification where conduct is "required or authorized by," inter alia, "the law defining the duties or functions of a public officer. . ."; "the law governing the armed services or the lawful conduct of war"; or "any other provision of law imposing a public duty"); National Comm'n on Reform of Federal Criminal Laws, A Proposed New Federal Criminal Code § 602(1) ("Conduct engaged in by a public servant in the course of his official duties is justified when it is required or authorized by law."). And this Office has invoked analogous rationales in several instances in which it has analyzed whether Congress intended a particular criminal statute to prohibit specific conduct that otherwise falls within a government agency's authorities.[14]

---

[13] The question of a "public authority" justification is much more frequently litigated in cases where a private party charged with a crime interposes the defense that he relied upon authority that a public official allegedly conferred upon him to engage in the challenged conduct. *See generally* United States Attorneys' Manual tit. 9, Criminal Resource Manual § 2055 (describing and discussing three different such defenses of "governmental authority"); National Comm'n on Reform of Federal Criminal Laws, A Proposed New Federal Criminal Code § 602(2); Model Penal Code § 3.03(3)(b); *see also United States v. Fulcher*, 250 F.3d 244, 253 (4th Cir. 2001); *United States v. Rosenthal*, 193 F.2d 1214, 1235–36 (11th Cir. 1986); *United States v. Duggan*, 743 F.2d 59, 83–84 (2d Cir. 1984); Fed. R. Crim. P. 12.3 (requiring defendant to notify government if he intends to invoke such a public authority defense.) We do not address such cases in this memorandum, in which our discussion of the "public authority" justification is limited to the question of whether a particular criminal law applies to specific conduct undertaken by *government agencies* pursuant to their authorities.

[14] *See, e.g.,* Memorandum for ▮▮ *see also Visa Fraud Investigation*, 8 Op. O.L.C. at 287–88 (concluding that civil statute prohibiting issuance of visa to an alien known to be ineligible did not prohibit State Department from issuing such a visa where "necessary" to facilitate important

16   The public authority justification does not excuse all conduct of
public officials from all criminal prohibitions. The legislature may
design some criminal prohibitions to place bounds on the kinds of governmental conduct that can be authorized by the Executive. Or, the legislature may enact a criminal prohibition in order to delimit the scope
of the conduct that the legislature has otherwise authorized the Executive to undertake pursuant to another statute.[15] But the recognition that
a federal criminal statute may incorporate the public authority justification reflects the fact that it would not make sense to attribute to Congress the intent with respect to each of its criminal statutes to prohibit
all covered activities undertaken by public officials in the legitimate
exercise of their otherwise lawful authorities, even if Congress has
clearly intended to make those same actions a crime when committed
by persons who are not acting pursuant to such public authority. In
some instances, therefore, the better view of a criminal prohibition may
well be that Congress meant to distinguish those persons who are acting pursuant to public authority, at least in some circumstances, from
those who are not, even if the statute by terms does not make that distinction express. *Cf. Nardone v. United States*, 302 U.S. 379, 384 (1937)
(federal criminal statutes should be construed to exclude authorized
conduct of public officers where such a reading "would work obvious
absurdity as, for example, the application of a speed law to a policeman
pursuing a criminal or the driver of a fire engine responding to an
alarm").[16]

Here, we consider a federal murder statute, but there is no general
bar to applying the public authority justification to such a criminal pro-

---

Immigration and Naturalization Service undercover operation carried out in a
"reasonable" fashion).

[15] See, *e.g., Nardone v. United States*, 302 U.S. 379, 384 (1937) (government
wiretapping was proscribed by federal statute); ███████████████████
███████████████

[16] In accord with our prior precedents, each potentially applicable statute must
be carefully and separately examined to discern Congress's intent in this respect—
such as whether it imposes a less qualified limitation than section 1119 imposes. *See
generally, e.g.,* ████████████████ *United States Assistance to Countries that
Shoot Down Civil Aircraft Involved in Drug Trafficking*, 18 Op. O.L.C. 148 (1994); *Application of Neutrality Act to Official Government Activities*, 8 Op. O.L.C. 58 (1984).

hibition. For example, with respect to prohibitions on the unlawful use of deadly force, the Model Penal Code recommended that legislatures should make the public authority (or "public duty") justification available, though only where the use of such force is covered by a more particular justification (such as defense of others or the use of deadly force by law enforcement), where the use of such force "is otherwise expressly authorized by law," or where such force "occurs in the lawful conduct of war." Model Penal Code § 3.03(2)(b), at 22; *see also id.* Comment 3, at 26. Some states proceeded to adopt the Model Penal Code recommendation.[17] Other states, although not adopting that precise formulation, have enacted specific statutes dealing with the question of when public officials are justified in using deadly force, which often prescribe that an officer acting in the performance of his official duties must reasonably have believed that such force was "necessary."[18] Other states have more broadly provided that the public authority defense is available where the government officer engages in a "reasonable exercise" of his official functions.[19] There is, however, no federal statute that is analogous, and neither section 1119 nor any of the incorporated title 18 provisions setting forth the substantive elements of the section 1119(b) offense, provide any express guidance as to the existence or scope of this justification.

Against this background, we believe the touchstone for the analysis of whether section 1119 incorporates not only justifications generally, but also the public authority justification in particular, is the legislative intent underlying this criminal statute. We conclude that the statute should be read to exclude from its prohibitory scope killings that are encompassed by traditional justifications, which include

---

[17] *See, e.g.,* Neb. Rev. Stat. § 28-1408(2)(b); Pa. C.S.A. § 504(b)(2); Tex. Penal Code tit. 2, § 9.21(c).

[18] *See, e.g.,* Ariz. Rev. Stat. § 13-410.C; Maine Rev. Stat. Ann. tit. 17, § 102.2.

[19] *See, e.g.,* Ala. Stat. § 13A-3-22; N.Y. Penal Law § 35.05(1); LaFave, *Substantive Criminal Law* § 10.2(b), at 135 n. 15; *see also* Robinson, *Criminal Law Defenses* § 149(a), at 215 (proposing that the defense should be available only if the actor engages in the authorized conduct "when and to the extent necessary to protect or further the interest protected or furthered by the grant of authority" and where it "is reasonable in relation to the gravity of the harms or evils threatened and the importance of the interests to be furthered by such exercise of authority"); *id.* § 149(c), at 218–20.

the public authority justification. There are no indications that Congress had a contrary intention. Nothing in the text or legislative history of sections 1111–1113 of title 18 suggests that Congress intended to exclude the established public authority justification from those that Congress otherwise must be understood to have imported through the use of the modifier "unlawful" in those statutes (which, as we explain above, establish the substantive scope of section 1119(b)).[20] Nor is there anything in the text or legislative history of section 1119 itself to suggest that Congress intended to abrogate or otherwise affect the availability under that statute of this traditional justification for killings. On the contrary, the relevant legislative materials indicate that in enacting section 1119 Congress was merely closing a gap in a field dealing with entirely different kinds of conduct than that at issue here.

The origin of section 1119 was a bill entitled the "Murder of United States Nationals Act of 1991," which Senator Thurmond introduced during the 102d Congress in response to the murder of an American in South Korea who had been teaching at a private school there. *See* 137 Cong. Rec. 8675–77 (1991) (statement of Sen. Thurmond). Shortly after the murder, another American teacher at the school accused a former colleague (who was also a U.S. citizen) of having committed the murder, and also confessed to helping the former colleague cover up the crime. The teacher who confessed was convicted in a South Korean court of destroying evidence and aiding the escape of a criminal suspect, but the individual she accused of murder had returned to the United States before the confession. *Id.* at 8675. The United States did not have an extradition treaty with South Korea that would have facilitated prosecution of the alleged murderer and therefore, under then-existing law, "the Federal Government ha[d] no jurisdiction to prosecute a person residing in the United States who ha[d] murdered an American abroad except in limited circumstances, such as a terrorist murder or the murder of a Federal official." *Id.*

---

[20] In concluding that the use of the term "unlawful" supports the conclusion that section 1119 incorporates the public authority justification, we do not mean to suggest that the absence of such a term would require a contrary conclusion regarding the intended application of a criminal statute to otherwise authorized government conduct in other cases. Each statute must be considered on its own terms to determine the relevant congressional intent. *See supra* note 16.

To close the "loophole under Federal law which permits persons who murder Americans in certain foreign countries to go punished," *id.*, the Thurmond bill would have added a new section to title 18 providing that "[w]hoever kills or attempts to kill a national of the United States while such national is outside the United States but within the jurisdiction of another country shall be punished as provided under sections 1111, 1112, and 1113 of this title." S. 861, 102d Cong. (1991) (incorporated in S. 1241, 102d Cong. §§ 3201–03 (1991)). The proposal also contained a separate provision amending the procedures for extradition "to provide the executive branch with the necessary authority, in the absence of an extradition treaty, to surrender to foreign governments those who commit violent crimes against U.S. nationals." 137 Cong. Rec. 8676 (1991) (statement of Sen. Thurmond) (discussing S. 861, 102d Cong., § 3).[21] The Thurmond proposal was incorporated into an omnibus crime bill that both the House and Senate passed, but that bill did not become law.

In the 103d Congress, a revised version of the Thurmond bill was included as part of the Violent Crime Control and Law Enforcement Act of 1994. H.R. 3355 § 60009, 103d Cong. (1994). The new legislation differed from the previous bill in two key respects. First, it prescribed criminal jurisdiction only where both the perpetrator and the victim were U.S. nationals, whereas the original Thurmond bill would have extended jurisdiction to all instances in which the victim was a U.S. national (based on so-called "passive personality" jurisdiction[22]). Second, the revised legislation did not include the separate provision from the earlier Thurmond legislation that would have amended the procedures for extradition. Congress enacted the revised legislation in 1994

---

[21] The Thurmond proposal also contained procedural limitations on prosecution virtually identical to those that Congress ultimately enacted and codified at 18 U.S.C. § 1119(c). *See* S. 861, 102d Cong. § 2.

[22] *See* Geoffrey R. Watson, *The Passive Personality Principle*, 28 Tex. Int'l L.J. 1, 13 (1993); 137 Cong. Rec. 8677 (1991) (letter for Senator Ernest F. Hollings, from Janet G. Mullins, Assistant Secretary, Legislative Affairs, U.S. State Department (Dec. 26, 1989), submitted for the record during floor debate on the Thurmond bill) (S4752 ("The United States has generally taken the position that the exercise of extraterritorial criminal jurisdiction based solely on the nationality of the victim interferes unduly with the application of local law by local authorities.").

as part of Public Law No. 103-322, and it was codified as section 1119 of title 18. *See* Pub. L. No. 103-322, § 60009, 108 Stat. 1796, 1972 (1994).

Thus, section 1119 was designed to close a jurisdictional loophole—exposed by a murder that had been committed abroad by a private individual—to ensure the possibility of prosecuting U.S. nationals who murdered other U.S. nationals in certain foreign countries that lacked the ability to lawfully secure the perpetrator's appearance at trial. This loophole had nothing to do with the conduct of an authorized military operation by U.S. armed forces or the sort of ██████████████ CIA counterterrorism operation contemplated here. Indeed, prior to the enactment of section 1119, the only federal statute expressly making it a crime to kill U.S. nationals abroad, at least outside the special and maritime jurisdiction of the United States, reflected what appears to have been a particular concern with protection of Americans from terrorist attacks. *See* 18 U.S.C. § 2332(a), (d) (criminalizing unlawful killings of U.S. nationals abroad where the Attorney General or his subordinate certifies that the "offense was intended to coerce, intimidate, or retaliate against a government or a civilian population").[23] It therefore would be anomalous to now read section 1119's closing of a limited jurisdictional gap as having been intended to jettison important applications of the established public authority justification, particularly in light of the statute's incorporation of substantive offenses codified in statutory provisions that from all indications were intended to incorporate recognized justifications and excuses.

It is true that here the target of the contemplated operations would be a U.S. citizen. But we do not believe al-Aulaqi's citizenship provides a basis for concluding that section 1119 would fail to incorporate the established public authority justification for a killing in this case. As we have explained, section 1119 incorporates the federal murder and manslaughter statutes, and thus its prohibition extends only to "unlawful" killings, 18 U.S.C. §§ 1111, 1112, a category that was intended to include,

19

---

[23] Courts have interpreted other federal homicide statutes to apply extraterritorially despite the absence of an express provision for extraterritorial application. *See, e.g.*, 18 U.S.C. § 1114 (criminalizing unlawful killings of federal officers and employees); *United States v. Al Kassar*, 582 F. Supp. 2d 488, 497 (S.D.N.Y. 2008) (construing 18 U.S.C. § 1114 to apply extraterritorially).

from all of the evidence of legislative intent we can find, only those kill-ings that may not be permissible in light of traditional justifications for such action. At the time the predecessor versions of sections 1111 and 1112 were enacted, it was understood that killings undertaken in accord with the public authority justification were not "unlawful" because they were justified. There is no indication that, because section 1119(b) pro-scribes the unlawful killing abroad of U.S. nationals by U.S. nationals, it silently incorporated all justifications for killings *except* that public authority justification.

III.

Given that section 1119 incorporates the public authority justifi-cation, we must next analyze whether the contemplated DoD and CIA operations would be encompassed by that justification. In particular, we must analyze whether that justification would apply even though the target of the contemplated operations is a United States citizen. We conclude that it would—a conclusion that depends in part on our deter-mination that each operation would accord with any potential consti-tutional protections of the United States citizen in these circumstances *(see infra* part VI). In reaching this conclusion, we do not address other cases or circumstances, involving different facts. Instead, we emphasize the sufficiency of the facts that have been represented to us here, with-out determining whether such facts would be necessary to the conclu-sion we reach.[24]

A.

20

We begin with the contemplated DoD operation. We need not attempt here to identify the minimum conditions that might establish a public authority justification for that operation. In light of the combina-tion of circumstances that we understand would be present, and which we describe below, we conclude that the justification would be available

---

[24] In light of our conclusion that section 1119 and the statutes it cross-references incorporate this justification, and that the operations here would be cov-ered by that justification, we need not and thus do not address whether other grounds might exist for concluding that the operations would be lawful.

because the operation would constitute the "lawful conduct of war"—a well-established variant of the public authority justification.[25]

As one authority has explained by example, "if a soldier intentionally kills an enemy combatant in time of war and within the rules of warfare, he is not guilty of murder," whereas, for example, if that soldier intentionally kills a prisoner of war—a violation of the laws of war—"then he commits murder." 2 LaFave, *Substantive Criminal Law* § 10.2(c), at 136; *see also State v. Gut,* 13 Minn. 341, 357 (1868) ("That it is legal to kill an alien enemy in the heat and exercise of war, is undeniable; but to kill such an enemy after he laid down his arms, and especially when he is confined in prison, is murder."); Perkins & Boyce, *Criminal Law* at 1093 ("Even in time of war an alien enemy, may not be killed needlessly after he has been disarmed and securely imprisoned").[26]

---

[25] *See. e.g.,* 2 Paul H. Robinson, *Criminal Law Defenses* § 148(a), at 208 (1984) (conduct that would violate a criminal statute is justified and thus not unlawful "[w]here the exercise of military authority relies upon the law governing the armed forces or upon the conduct of war"); 2 LaFave, *Substantive Criminal Law* § 10.2(c), at 136 ("another aspect of the public duty defense is where the conduct was required or authorized by 'the law governing the armed services or the lawful conduct of war'") (internal citation omitted); Perkins & Boyce, *Criminal Law* at 1093 (noting that a "typical instance[] in which even the extreme act of taking human life is done by public authority" involves "the killing of an enemy as an act of war and within the rules of war"); *Frye,* 10 Cal. Rptr. 2d at 221 n.2 (identifying "homicide done under a valid public authority, such as execution of a death sentence or killing an enemy in a time of war," as one example of a justifiable killing that would not be "unlawful" under the California statute describing murder as an "unlawful" killing); *State v. Gut,* 13 Minn. 341, 357 (1868) ("that it is legal to kill an alien enemy in the heat and exercise of war, is undeniable"); *see also* Model Penal Code § 3.03(2)(b) (proposing that criminal statutes expressly recognize a public authority justification for a killing that "occurs in the lawful conduct of war," notwithstanding the Code recommendation that the use of deadly force generally should be justified only if expressly prescribed by law); *see also id* at 25 n.7 (collecting representative statutes reflecting this view enacted prior to Code's promulgation); 2 Robinson, *Criminal Law Defenses* § 148(b), at 210–11 nn. 8–9 (collecting post-Model Code state statutes expressly recognizing such a defense).

[26] *Cf. Public Committee Against Torture in Israel v. Government of Israel,* HCJ 769/02 ¶ 19, 46 I.L.M. 375, 382 (Israel Supreme Court sitting as the High Court of Justice, 2006) ("When soldiers of the Israel Defense Forces act pursuant to the laws of armed conflict, they are acting 'by law', and they have a good justification defense [to criminal culpability]. However, if they act contrary to the laws of armed conflict they may be, *inter alia,* criminally liable for their actions."); *Calley v. Callaway,* 519 F.2d 184, 193 (5th Cir. 1975) ("an order to kill unresisting Vietnamese would be an illegal order, and . . . if [the defendant] knew the order was illegal or should have known it was illegal, obedience to an order was not a legal defense").

Moreover, without invoking the public authority justification by terms, our Office has relied on the same notion in an opinion addressing the intended scope of a federal criminal statute that concerned the use of possibly lethal force. *See United States Assistance to Countries that Shoot Down Civil Aircraft Involved in Drug Trafficking,* 18 Op. O.L.C. 148, 164 (1994) *("Shoot Down Opinion")* (concluding that the Aircraft Sabotage Act of 1984, 18 U.S.C. § 32(b)(2), which prohibits the willful destruction of a civil aircraft and otherwise applies to U.S. government conduct, should not be construed to have "the surprising and almost certainly unintended effect of criminalizing actions by military personnel that are lawful under international law and the laws of armed conflict").

In applying this variant of the public authority justification to the contemplated DoD operation, we note as an initial matter that DoD would undertake the operation pursuant to Executive war powers that Congress has expressly authorized. *See Youngstown Sheet & Tube Co. v. Sawyer,* 343 U.S. 579, 635 (1952) (Jackson, J., concurring) ("When the President acts pursuant to an express or implied authorization of Congress, his authority is at its maximum, for it includes all that he possesses in his own right plus all that Congress can delegate."). By authorizing the use of force against "organizations" that planned, authorized, and committed the September 11th attacks, Congress clearly authorized the President's use of "necessary and appropriate" force against al-Qaida forces, because al-Qaida carried out the September 11th attacks. *See* Authorization for Use of Military Force ("AUMF"), Pub. L. No. 107-40, 115 Stat. 224, §2(a) (2001) (providing that the President may "use all necessary and appropriate force against those nations, organizations, or persons he determines planned, authorized, committed or aided the terrorist attacks that occurred on September 11, 2001, or harbored such organizations or persons, in order to prevent any future acts of international terrorism against the United States by such nations, organizations, or persons.").[27] And, as we have explained, *supra* at 9, a decision-maker could reasonably conclude that this leader of AQAP

---

[27] We emphasize this point not in order to suggest that statutes such as the AUMF have superseded or implicitly repealed or amended section 1119, but instead as one factor that helps to make particularly clear why the operation contemplated here would be covered by the public authority justification that section 1119 (and section 1111) itself incorporates.

forces is part of al-Qaida forces. Alternatively, and as we have further explained, *supra* at 10 n.5, the AUMF applies with respect to forces "associated with" al-Qaida that are engaged in hostilities against the U.S. or its coalition partners, and a decision-maker could reasonably conclude that the AQAP forces of which al-Aulaqi is a leader are "associated with" al Qaida forces for purposes of the AUMF. On either view, DoD would carry out its contemplated operation against a leader of an organization that is within the scope of the AUMF, and therefore DoD would in that respect be operating in accord with a grant of statutory authority.

Based upon the facts represented to us, moreover, the target of the contemplated operation has engaged in conduct as part of that organization that brings him within the scope of the AUMF. High-level government officials have concluded, on the basis of al-Aulaqi's activities in Yemen, that al-Aulaqi is a leader of AQAP whose activities in Yemen pose a "continued and imminent threat" of violence to United States persons and interests. Indeed, the facts represented to us indicate that al-Aulaqi has been involved, through his operational and leadership roles within AQAP, in an abortive attack within the United States and continues to plot attacks intended to kill Americans from his base of operations in Yemen. The contemplated DoD operation, therefore, would be carried out against someone who is within the core of individuals against whom Congress has authorized the use of necessary and appropriate force.[28]

22   Al-Aulaqi is a United States citizen, however, and so we must also

---

[28] *See Hamlily*, 616 F. Supp. at 75 (construing AUMF to reach individuals who "function[] or participate[] within or under the command structure of [al-Qaida]"); *Gherebi v. Obama*, 609 F. Supp. 2d 43, 68 (D.D.C. 2009); *see also al-Marri v. Pucciarelli*, 534 F.3d 213, 325 (4th Cir. 2008) (en banc) (Wilkinson, J., dissenting in part) (explaining that the ongoing hostilities against al-Qaida permit the Executive to use necessary and appropriate force under the AUMF against an "enemy combatant," a term Judge Wilkinson would have defined as a person who is (1) "a member of" (2) "an organization or nation against whom Congress has declared war or authorized the use of military force," and (3) who "knowingly plans or engages in conduct that harms or aims to harm persons or property for the purpose of furthering the military goals of the enemy nation or organization"), *vacated and remanded sub nom. al-Marri v. Spagone*, 129 S. Ct. 1545 (2009); Government March 13th *Guantánamo Bay Detainee* Brief at 1 (arguing that AUMF authorizes detention of individuals who were "part of, or substantially supported, Taliban or al-Qaida forces or associated forces that are engaged in hostilities against the United States or its coalition partners, in-

consider whether his citizenship precludes the AUMF from serving as the source of lawful authority for the contemplated DoD operation. There is no precedent directly addressing the question in circumstances such as those present here; but the Supreme Court has recognized that, because military detention of enemy forces is "by 'universal agreement and practice,' [an] 'important incident[] of war,'" *Hamdi v. Rumsfeld*, 542 U.S. 507, 518 (2004) (plurality opinion) (quoting *Ex parte Quirin*, 317 U.S. 1, 28, 30 (1942)), the AUMF authorized the President to detain a member of Taliban forces who was captured abroad in an armed conflict against the United States on a traditional battlefield. *See id.* at

---

cluding any person who has committed a belligerent act, or has directly supported hostilities, in aid of such enemy armed forces").

Several of the Guantánamo habeas petitioners, as well as some commentators, have argued that in a non-international conflict of this sort, the laws of war and/or the AUMF do not permit the United States to treat persons who are part of al-Qaida as analogous to members of an enemy's armed forces in a traditional international armed conflict, but that the United States instead must treat all such persons as civilians, which (they contend) would permit targeting those persons only when they are directly participating in hostilities. *Cf. also al-Marri*, 534 F.3d at 237–47 (Motz, J. concurring in the judgment, and writing for four of nine judges) (arguing that the AUMF and the Constitution, as informed by the laws of war, do not permit military detention of an alien residing in the United States whom the government alleged was "closely associated with" al-Qaida, and that such individual must instead be treated as a civilian, because that person is not affiliated with the military arm of an enemy nation); Philip Alston, *Report of the Special Rapporteur on extrajudicial, summary or arbitrary executions* ¶ 58, at 19 (United Nations Human Rights Council, Fourteenth Session, Agenda Item 3, May 28, 2010) ("*Report of the Special Rapporteur*") (reasoning that because "[u]nder the [international humanitarian law] applicable to non-international armed conflict, there is no such thing as a 'combatant'"—i.e., a non-state actor entitled to the combatant's privilege—it follows that "States are permitted to attack only civilians who 'directly participate in hostilities'"). Primarily for the reasons that Judge Walton comprehensively examined in the *Gherebi* case, *see* 609 F. Supp. 2d at 62–69, we do not think this is the proper understanding of the laws of war in a non-international armed conflict, or of Congress's authorization under the AUMF. *Cf. also* International Committee of the Red Cross, *Interpretive Guidance on the Notion of Direct Participation in Hostilities Under International Humanitarian Law* 28, 34 (2009) (even if an individual is otherwise a "citizen" for purposes of the laws of war, a member of a non-state armed group can be subject to targeting by virtue of having assumed a "continuous combat function" on behalf of that group); Alston, *supra*, ¶ 65, at 30–31 (acknowledging that under the ICRC view, if armed group members take on a continuous command function, they can be targeted anywhere and at any time); *infra* at 37–38 (explaining that al-Aulaqi is continually and "actively" participating in hostilities and thus not protected by Common Article 3 of the Geneva Conventions).

23 | 517–19 (plurality opinion).[29] In addition, the Court held in *Hamdi* that this authorization applied even though the Taliban member in question was a U.S. citizen. *Id.* at 519–24; *see also Quirin,* 317 U.S. at 37–38 ("[c]itizens who associate themselves with the military arm of the enemy government, and with its aid, guidance and direction enter [the United States] bent on hostile acts," may be treated as "enemy belligerents" under the law of war). Furthermore, lower federal courts have relied upon *Hamdi* to conclude that the AUMF authorizes DoD to detain individuals who are part of al-Qaida even if they are apprehended and transferred to U.S. custody while not on a traditional battlefield. *See, e.g., Bensayah v. Obama,* No. 08-5537, 2010 WL 2640626, at *1, *5, *8 (D.C. Cir. June 28, 2010) (concluding that the Department of Defense could detain an individual turned over to the U.S. in Bosnia if it demonstrates he was part of al-Qaida); *Al-Adahi v. Obama,* No. 09-5333 (D.C. Cir. July 13, 2010) (DoD has authority under AUMF to detain individual apprehended by Pakistani authorities in Pakistan and then transferred to U.S.); *Anam v. Obama,* 2010 WL 58965 (D.D.C. 2010) (same); *Razak Ali v. Obama,* 2009 WL 4030864 (D.D.C. 2009) (same); *Sliti v. Bush,* 592 F. Supp. 2d 46 (D.D.C. 2008) (same).

In light of these precedents, we believe the AUMF's authority to use lethal force abroad also may apply in appropriate circumstances to a United States citizen who is part of the forces of an enemy organization within the scope of the force authorization. The use of lethal force against such enemy forces, like military detention, is an "'important incident of war,'" *Hamdi,* 542 U.S. at 518 (plurality opinion) (quotation omitted). *See, e.g.,* General Orders No. 100: Instructions for the Government of Armies of the United States in the Field ¶15 (Apr. 24, 1863) (the "Lieber Code") ("[m]ilitary necessity admits of all direct destruc-

---

[29] *See also Al Odah v. Obama,* No. 09-5331, 2010 WL 2679752, at *1, and other D.C. Circuit cases cited therein (D.C. Cir. 2010) (AUMF gives United States the authority to detain a person who is "part of" al-Qaida or Taliban forces); *Hamlily,* 616 F. Supp. 2d at 74 (Bates, J.); *Gherebi,* 609 F. Supp. 2d at 67 (Walton, J.); *Mattan v. Obama,* 618 F. Supp. 2d 24, 26 (D.D.C. 2009) (Lamberth, C. J.); *Al Mutairi v. United States,* 644 F. Supp. 2d 78, 85 (D.D.C. 2009) (Kollar-Kotelly, J.); *Awad v. Obama,* 646 F. Supp. 2d 20, 23 (D.D.C. 2009) (Robertson, J.); *Anam v. Obama,* 653 F. Supp. 2d 62, 64 (D.D.C. 2009) (Hogan, J.); *Hatim v. Obama,* 677 F. Supp. 2d 1, 7, (D.D.C. 2009) (Urbina, J.); *Al-Adahi v. Obama,* No. 05-280, 2009 WL 2584685 (D.D.C. Aug. 21, 2009) (Kessler, J.), *rev'd on other grounds.* No. 09-5333 (D.C. Cir. July 13, 2010).

tion of life or limb of armed enemies"); International Committee of the Red Cross, *Commentary on the Additional Protocols of 8 June 1977 to the Geneva Conventions of 12 Aug. 1949 and Relating to the Protection of Victims of Non-International Armed Conflicts (Additional Protocol II)* § 4789 (1987); Yoram Dinstein. *The Conduct of Hostilities Under the Law of International Armed Conflict* 94 (2004) ("*Conduct of Hostilities*") ("When a person takes up arms or merely dons a uniform as a member of the armed forces, he automatically exposes himself to enemy attack."). And thus, just as the AUMF authorizes the military detention of a U.S. citizen captured abroad who is part of an armed force within the scope of the AUMF, it also authorizes the use of "necessary and appropriate" lethal force against a U.S. citizen who has joined such an armed force. Moreover, as we explain further in Part VI, DoD would conduct the operation in a manner that would not violate any possible constitutional protections that al-Aulaqi enjoys by reason of his citizenship. Accordingly, we do not believe al-Aulaqi's citizenship provides a basis for concluding that he is immune from a use of force abroad that the AUMF otherwise authorizes.

In determining whether the contemplated DoD operation would constitute the "lawful conduct of war," LaFave, *Substantive Criminal Law* § 10.2(c), at 136, we next consider whether that operation would comply with the international law rules to which it would be subject—a question that also bears on whether the operation would be authorized by the AUMF. *See* Response for Petition for Rehearing and Rehearing En Banc, *Al Bihani v. Obama*, No. 09-5051 at 7 (D.C. Cir.) (May 13, 2010) (AUMF "should be construed, if possible, as consistent with international law") (citing *Murray v. Schooner Charming Betsy*, 6 U.S. (2 Cranch) 64, 118 (1804) ("an act of Congress ought never to be construed to violate the law of nations, if any other possible construction remains")); *see also F. Hoffman-La Roche Ltd. v. Empagran S.A.*, 542 U.S. 155, 164 (2004) (customary international law is "law that (we must assume) Congress ordinarily seeks to follow"). Based on the combination of facts presented [24] to us, we conclude that DoD would carry out its operation as part of the non-international armed conflict between the United States and al-Qaida, and thus that on those facts the operation would comply with international law so long as DoD would conduct it in accord with the applicable laws of war that govern targeting in such a conflict.

In *Hamdan v. Rumsfeld*, the Supreme Court held that the United States is engaged in a non-international armed conflict with al-Qaida. 548 U.S. 557, 628–31 (2006). In so holding, the Court rejected the argument that non-international armed conflicts are limited to civil wars and other internal conflicts between a state and an internal non-state armed group that are confined to the territory of the state itself; it held instead that a conflict between a transnational non-state actor and a nation, occurring outside that nation's territory, is an armed conflict "not of an international character" (quoting Common Article 3 of the Geneva Conventions) because it is not a "clash between nations." *Id.* at 630.

Here, unlike in *Hamdan*, the contemplated DoD operation would occur in Yemen, a location that is far from the most active theater of combat between the United States and al-Qaida. That does not affect our conclusion, however, that the combination of facts present here would make the DoD operation in Yemen part of the non-international armed conflict with al-Qaida.[30] To be sure, *Hamdan* did not directly address the geographic scope of the non-international armed conflict between the United States and al-Qaida that the Court recognized, other than to implicitly hold that it extended to Afghanistan, where Hamdan was apprehended. *See* 548 U.S. at 566; *see also id.* at 641–42 (Kennedy, J., concurring in part) (referring to Common Article 3 as "applicable to our Nation's armed conflict with al Qaeda in Afghanistan"). The Court did, however, specifically reject the argument that non-international armed conflicts are necessarily limited to internal conflicts. The Common Article 3 term "conflict not of an international character," the Court explained, bears its "literal meaning"—namely, that it is a conflict that "does not involve a clash between nations." *Id.* at 630 (majority opinion). The Court referenced the statement in the 1949 ICRC Commentary on the Additional Protocols to the Geneva Conventions that a non-international armed conflict "is distinct from an international armed conflict *because of the legal status of the entities opposing each other,*" *id.* at 631 (emphasis added). The Court explained that this

---

[30] Our analysis is limited to the circumstances presented here, regarding the contemplated use of lethal force in Yemen. We do not address issues that a use of force in other locations might present. *See also supra* note 1.

interpretation—that the nature of the conflict depends at least in part on the status of the parties, rather than simply on the locations in which they fight—in turn accords with the view expressed in the commentaries to the Geneva Conventions that "the scope of application" of Common Article 3, which establishes basic protections that govern conflicts not of an international character, "must be as wide as possible." *Id.*[31]

Invoking the principle that for purposes of international law an armed conflict generally exists only when there is "protracted armed violence between governmental authorities and armed groups," Decision on the Defence Motion for Interlocutory Appeal on Jurisdiction, *Prosecutor v. Tadic*, Case No. IT-94-1AR72, 70 (ICTY App. Chamber Oct. 2, 1995) ("*Tadic* Jurisdictional Decision"), some commentators have suggested that the conflict between the United States and al-Qaida cannot extend to nations outside Afghanistan in which the level of hostilities is less intense or prolonged than in Afghanistan itself. *See, e.g.,* Mary Ellen O'Connell, *Combatants and the Combat Zone*, 43 U. Rich. L. Rev. 845, 857–59 (2009); *see also* Philip Alston, *Report of the Special Rapporteur on extrajudicial, summary or arbitrary executions* ¶ 54, at 18 (United Nations Human Rights Council, Fourteenth Session, Agenda Item 3, May 28, 2010) (acknowledging that a non-international armed conflict can be transnational and "often does" exist "across State borders," but explaining that the duration and intensity of attacks in a particular nation is also among the "cumulative factors that must be con-

[25]

---

[31] We think it is noteworthy that the AUMF itself does not set forth an express geographic limitation on the use of force it authorizes, and that nearly a decade after its enactment, none of the three branches of the United States Government has identified a strict geographical limit on the permissible scope of the authority the AUMF confers on the President with respect to this armed conflict. *See, e.g.,* Letter from the President to the Speaker of the House of Representatives and the President Pro Tempore of the Senate (June 15, 2010) (reporting, "consistent with . . . the War Powers Resolution," that the armed forces, with the assistance of numerous international partners, continue to conduct operations "against al-Qa'ida terrorists," and that the United States has "deployed combat-equipped forces to a number of locations in the U.S. Central . . . Command area[] of operation in support of those [overseas counter-terrorist] operations"); Letter for the Speaker of the House of Representatives and the President Pro Tempore of the Senate, from President Barack Obama (Dec. 16, 2009) (similar); *DoD May 18 Memorandum for OLC*, at 2 (explaining that U.S. armed forces have conducted ███████████████ AQAP targets in Yemen since December 2009, and that DoD has reported such strikes to the appropriate congressional oversight committees).

sidered for the objective existence of an armed conflict"). There is little judicial or other authoritative precedent that speaks directly to the question of the geographic scope of a non-international armed conflict in which one of the parties is a transnational, non-state actor and where the principal theater of operations is not within the territory of the nation that is a party to the conflict. Thus, in considering this issue, we must look to principles and statements from analogous contexts, recognizing that they were articulated without consideration of the particular factual circumstances of the sort of conflict at issue here.

In looking for such guidance, we have not come across any authority for the proposition that when one of the parties to an armed conflict plans and executes operations from a base in a new nation, an operation to engage the enemy in that location can never be part of the original armed conflict—and thus subject to the laws of war governing that conflict—unless and until the hostilities become sufficiently intensive and protracted within that new location. That does not appear to be the rule, or the historical practice, for instance, in a traditional international conflict. *See* John R. Stevenson, Legal Adviser, Department of State, *United States Military Action in Cambodia: Questions of International Law* (address before the Hammarskjold Forum of the Association of the Bar of the City of New York, May 28, 1970), *in* 3 *The Vietnam War and International Law: The Widening Context* 23, 28–30 (Richard A. Falk, ed. 1972) (arguing that in an international armed conflict, if a neutral state has been unable for any reason to prevent violations of its neutrality by the troops of one belligerent using its territory as a base of operations, the other belligerent has historically been justified in attacking those enemy forces in that state). Nor do we see any obvious reason why that more categorical, nation-specific rule should govern in analogous circumstances in this sort of non-international armed conflict.[32] Rather, we think the determination of whether a particular operation would be part of an ongoing armed conflict for purposes of international law requires consideration of the particular facts and circumstances present in each case. Such an inquiry may be particularly appro-

26

---

[32] In the speech cited above, Legal Adviser Stevenson was referring to cases in which the government of the nation in question is unable to prevent violations of its neutrality by belligerent troops.

priate in a conflict of the sort here, given that the parties to it include transnational non-state organizations that are dispersed and that thus may have no single site serving as their base of operations.[33]

We also find some support for this view in an argument the United States made to the International Criminal Tribunal for Yugoslavia (ICTY) in 1995. To be sure, the United States was there confronting a question, and a conflict, quite distinct from those we address here. Nonetheless, in that case the United States argued that in determining *which* body of humanitarian law applies in a particular conflict, "the conflict must be considered as a whole," and that "it is artificial and improper to attempt to divide it into isolated segments, either geographically or chronologically, in an attempt to exclude the application of [the relevant] rules." Submission of the Government of the United States of America Concerning Certain Arguments Made by Counsel for the Accused in the Case of *The Prosecutor of the Tribunal v. Dusan Tadic*, Case No. IT-94-1AR72 (ICTY App. Chamber) at 27–28 (July 1995) ("U.S. *Tadic* Submission"). Likewise, the court in *Tadic*—although not addressing a conflict that was transnational in the way the U.S. conflict with al-Qaida is—also concluded that although "the definition of 'armed conflict' varies depending on whether the hostilities are international or internal . . . the scope of both internal and international armed conflicts *extends beyond the exact time and place of hostilities.*" *Tadic* Jurisdictional Decision ¶ 67 (emphasis added); *see also* International Committee of the Red Cross, *International Humanitarian Law and the Challenges of Contemporary Armed Conflicts* 18 (2003) (asserting that in order to assess whether an armed conflict exists it is necessary to determine "whether the totality of the violence taking place between states and transnational networks can be deemed to be armed conflict in the legal sense"). Although the basic approach that the United States proposed in *Tadic,* and that the ICTY may be understood to have endorsed, was advanced without the current conflict between the U.S. and al-

---

[33] The fact that the operation occurs in a new location might alter the way in which the military must apply the relevant principles of the laws of war—for example, requiring greater care in some locations in order to abide by the principles of distinction and proportionality that protect civilians from the use of military force. But that possible distinction should not affect the question of whether the laws of war govern the conflict in that new location in the first instance.

Qaida in view, that approach reflected a concern with ensuring that the laws of war, and the limitations on the use of force they establish, should be given an appropriate application.[34] And that same consideration, reflected in *Hamdan* itself, *see supra* at 24, suggests a further reason for skepticism about an approach that would categorically deny that an operation is part of an armed conflict absent a specified level and intensity of hostilities in the particular location where it occurs.

For present purposes, in applying the more context-specific approach to determining whether an operation would take place within the scope of a particular armed conflict, it is sufficient that the facts as they have been represented to us here, in combination, support the judgment that DoD's operation in Yemen would be conducted as part of the non-international armed conflict between the United States and al-Qaida. Specifically, DoD proposes to target a leader of AQAP, an organized enemy force[35] that is either a component of al-Qaida or that is a co-belligerent of that central party to the conflict and engaged in hostilities against the United States as part of the same comprehensive armed conflict, in league with the principal enemy. *See supra* at 9–10 & n.5. Moreover, DoD would conduct the operation in Yemen, where, according to the facts related to us, AQAP has a significant and orga-

---

[34] *See also* Geoffrey S. Corn & Eric Talbot Jensen, *Untying the Gordian Knot: A Proposal for Determining Applicability of the Laws of War to the War on Terror,* 81 Temp. L. Rev. 787, 799 (2008) ("If . . . the ultimate purpose of the drafters of the Geneva Conventions was to prevent 'law avoidance' by developing de facto law triggers—a purpose consistent with the humanitarian foundation of the treaties—then the myopic focus on the geographic nature of an armed conflict in the context of transnational counterterrorist combat operations serves to frustrate that purpose."); *cf. also* Derek Jinks, *September 11 and the Laws of War,* 28 Yale J. Int'l L. 1, 40–41 (2003) (arguing that if Common Article 3 applies to wholly internal conflicts, then it "applies a fortiori to armed conflicts with international or transnational dimensions," such as to the United States's armed conflict with al-Qaida).

[35] *Cf. Prosecutor v. Haradnizaj,* No IT-04-84-T 60 (ICTY Trial Chamber I, 2008) ("an armed conflict can exist only between parties that are sufficiently organized to confront each other with military means—a condition that can be evaluated with respect to non-state groups by assessing "several indicative factors, none of which are, in themselves, essential to establish whether the 'organization' criterion is fulfilled," including, among other things, the existence of a command structure, and disciplinary rules and mechanisms within the group, the ability of the group to gain access to weapons, other military equipment, recruits and military training, and its ability to plan, coordinate, and carry out military operations).

nized presence, and from which AQAP is conducting terrorist training in an organized manner and has executed and is planning to execute attacks against the United States. Finally, the targeted individual himself, on behalf of that force, is continuously planning attacks from that Yemeni base of operations against the United States, as the conflict with al-Qaida continues. *See supra* at 7–9. Taken together, these facts support the conclusion that the DoD operation would be part of the non-international armed conflict the Court recognized in *Hamdan*.[36]

There remains the question whether DoD would conduct its

28

---

[36] We note that the Department of Defense, which has a policy of compliance with the law of war "during all armed conflicts, however such conflicts are characterized, *and in all other military operations*," Chairman of the Joint Chiefs of Staff, Instruction 5810.0 ID, *Implementation of the DoD Law of War Program* ¶ 4.a, at 1 (Apr. 30, 2010) (emphasis added), has periodically used force—albeit in contexts different from a conflict such as this—in situations removed from "active battlefields," in response to imminent threats. *See, e.g.*, Nat'l Comm'n on Terrorist Attacks Upon the United States, *The 9/11 Commission Report* 116–17 (2004) (describing 1998 cruise missile attack on al-Qaida encampments in Afghanistan following al-Qaida bombings of U.S. embassies in East Africa); W. Hays Parks, *Memorandum of Law: Executive Order 12333 and Assassination*, Army Lawyer, at 7 (Dep't of Army Pamphlet 27-50-204) (Dec. 1989) (*"Assassination"*) at 7 n.8 (noting examples of uses of military force in "[s]elf defense against a continuing threat," including "the U.S. Navy air strike against Syrian military objections in Lebanon on 4 December 1983, following Syrian attacks on U.S. Navy F-14 TARPS flights supporting the multinational peacekeeping force in Beirut the preceding day," and "air strikes against terrorist-related targets in Libya on the evening of 15 April 1986"); *see also id* at 7 ("A national decision to employ military force in self defense against a legitimate terrorist or related threat would not be unlike the employment of force in response to a threat by conventional forces; only the nature of the threat has changed, rather than the international legal right of self defense. The terrorist organizations envisaged as appropriate to necessitate or warrant an armed response by U.S. forces are well-financed, highly-organized paramilitary structures engaged in the illegal use of force."); Advisory Opinion of 8 July 1996 on the Legality of the Threat or Use of Nuclear Weapons ¶ 42, 1996 I.C.J. 226, 245 ("Nuclear Weapons Advisory Opinion") (fundamental law-of-war norms are applicable even where military force might be employed outside the context of an armed conflict, such as when using powerful weapons in an act of national self-defense); *cf also 9/11 Commission Report* at 116–17 (noting the Clinton Administration position—with respect to a presidential memorandum authorizing CIA assistance to an operation that could result in the killing of Usama Bin Ladin "if the CIA and the tribals judged that capture was not feasible"—that "under the law of armed conflict, killing a person who posed an imminent threat to the United States would be an act of self-defense, not an assassination"). As we explain below, DoD likewise would conduct the operation contemplated here in accord with the laws of war and would direct its lethal force against an individual whose activities have been determined to pose a "continued and imminent threat" to U.S. persons and interests.

operation in accord with the rules governing targeting in a non-international armed conflict—namely, international humanitarian law, commonly known as the laws of war. *See* Dinstein, *Conduct of Hostilities* at 17 (international humanitarian law "takes a middle road, allowing belligerent States much leeway (in keeping with the demands of military necessity) and yet circumscribing their freedom of action (in the name of humanitarianism").[37] The 1949 Geneva Conventions to which the United States is a party do not themselves directly impose extensive restrictions on the conduct of a non-international armed conflict—with the principal exception of Common Article 3, *see Hamdan*, 548 U.S. at 630–31. But the norms specifically described in those treaties "are not exclusive, and the laws and customs of war also impose limitations on the conduct of participants in non-international armed conflict." U.S. *Tadic* Submission at 33 n.53; *see also, e.g.*, Convention Respecting the Laws and Customs of War on Land, Oct. 18, 1907, Preamble ("Hague Convention (IV)"), 36 Stat. 2277, 2280 (in cases "not included" under the treaty, "the inhabitants and the belligerents remain under the protection and the rule of the principles of the law of nations, as they result from the usages among civilized peoples, from the laws of humanity, and the dictates of the public conscience").

In particular, the "fundamental rules" and "intransgressible principles of international customary law," Advisory Opinion of 8 July 1996 on the Legality of the Threat or Use of Nuclear Weapons ¶ 79, 1996

---

[37] *Cf.* Nuclear Weapons Advisory Opinion ¶ 25, 1996 *I.C.J.* at 240 (explaining that the "test" of what constitutes an "arbitrary" taking of life under international human rights law, such as under article 6(1) of the International Covenant of Civil and Political Rights (ICCPR), must be determined by "the law applicable in armed conflict which is designed to regulate the conduct of hostilities," and "can only be decided by reference to the law applicable in armed conflict and not deduced from terms of the Covenant itself"); Written Statement of the Government of the United States of America before the International Court of Justice, *Re: Request by the United Nations General Assembly for an Advisory Opinion on the Legality of the Threat or Use of Nuclear Weapons* at 44 (June 20, 1995) (ICCPR prohibition on arbitrary deprivation of life "was clearly understood by its drafters to exclude the lawful taking of human life," including killings "lawfully committed by the military in time of war"); Dinstein, *Conduct of Hostilities* at 23 (right to life under human rights law "does not protect persons from the ordinary consequences of hostilities"); *cf. also infra* Part VI (explaining that the particular contemplated operations here would satisfy due process and Fourth Amendment standards because, *inter alia*, capturing al-Aulaqi is currently infeasible).

I.C.J. 226, 257 ("Nuclear Weapons Advisory Opinion"), which apply to all armed conflicts, include the "four fundamental principles that are inherent to all targeting decisions"—namely, military necessity, humanity (the avoidance of unnecessary suffering), proportionality, and distinction. United States Air Force, *Targeting*, Air Force Doctrine Document 2-1.9, at 88 (June 8, 2006); *see also generally id.* at 88–92; Dinstein, *Conduct of Hostilities* at 16–20, 115–16, 119–23. Such fundamental rules also include those listed in the annex to the Fourth Hague Convention, *see* Nuclear Weapons Advisory Opinion 80, at 258, article 23 of which makes it "especially forbidden" to, inter alia, kill or wound treacherously, refuse surrender, declare a denial of quarter, or cause unnecessary suffering, 36 Stat. at 2301–02.

DoD represents that it would conduct its operation against al-Aulaqi in compliance with these fundamental law-of-war norms. *See* Chairman of the Joint Chiefs of Staff, Instruction 5810.01D, *Implementation of the DoD Law of War Program* ¶ 4.a, at 1 (Apr. 30, 2010) ("It is DOD policy that . . . [m]embers of the DOD Components comply with the law of war during all armed conflicts, however such conflicts are characterized, and in all other military operations."). In particular, the targeted nature of the operation would help to ensure that it would comply with the principle of distinction, and DoD has represented to us that it would make every effort to minimize civilian casualties and that the officer who launches the ordnance would be required to abort a strike if he or she concludes that civilian casualties will be disproportionate or that such a strike will in any other respect violate the laws of war. *See DoD May 18 Memorandum for OLC*, at 1 ("Any official in the chain of command has the authority and duty to abort" a strike "if he or she concludes that civilian casualties will be disproportionate or that such a strike will otherwise violate the laws of war.").

Moreover, although DoD would specifically target al-Aulaqi, and would do so without advance warning, such characteristics of the contemplated operation would not violate the laws of war and, in particular, would not cause the operation to violate the prohibitions on treachery and perfidy—which are addressed to conduct involving a breach of confidence by the assailant. *See, e.g.*, Hague Convention IV, Annex, art. 23(b), 36 Stat. at 2301–02 ("[I]t is especially forbidden . . . to kill or wound treacherously individuals belonging to the hostile nation or

29

army"); *cf. also* Protocol Additional to the Geneva Conventions of 12 August 1949, and Relating to the Protection of Victims of International Armed Conflicts, art. 37(1) (prohibiting the killing, injuring or capture of an adversary in an international armed conflict by resort to acts "inviting the confidence of [the] adversary . . . with intent to betray that confidence," including feigning a desire to negotiate under truce or flag of surrender; feigning incapacitation; and feigning noncombatant status).[38] Those prohibitions do not categorically preclude the use of stealth or surprise, nor forbid military attacks on identified, individual soldiers or officers, *see* U.S. Army Field Manual 27-10, ¶ 31 (1956) (article 23(b) of the Annex to the Hague Convention IV does not "preclude attacks on individual soldiers or officers of the enemy whether in the zone of hostilities, occupied territory, or else-where"), and we are not aware of any other law-of-war grounds precluding the use of such tactics. *See* Dinstein, *Conduct of Hostilities* at 94–95, 199; Abraham D. Sofaer, *Terrorism, The Law, and the National Defense*, 126 Mil. L. Rev. 89, 120–21 (1989).[39] Relatedly, "there is no prohibition under the laws of war on the use of technologically advanced weapons systems in armed conflict—such as pilotless aircraft or so-called smart bombs—as long as they are employed in conformity with applicable laws of war." Koh, *The Obama Administration and International Law*. DOD also informs us that if al-Aulaqi offers to surrender, DoD would accept such an offer.[40]

---

[38] Although the United States is not a party to the First Protocol, the State Department has announced that "we support the principle that individual combatants not kill, injure, or capture enemy personnel by resort to perfidy." Remarks of Michael J, Matheson, Deputy Legal Adviser, Department of State, *The Sixth Annual American Red Cross-Washington College of Law Conference on International Humanitarian Law: A Workshop on Customary International Law and the 1977 Protocols Additional to the 1949 Geneva Conventions*, 2 Am. U. J. of Int'l L. & Pol'y 415, 425 (1987).

[39] There is precedent for the United States targeting attacks against particular commanders. *See, e.g.*, Patricia Zengel, *Assassination and the Law of Armed Conflict*, 134 Mil. L. Rev. 123, 136–37 (1991) (describing American warplanes' shoot-down during World War II of plane carrying Japanese Admiral Isoroku Yamamoto); *see also* Parks, *Assassination*, Army Lawyer at 5.

[40] *See* Geneva Conventions Common Article 3(1) (prohibiting "violence to life and person, in particular murder of all kinds," with respect to persons "taking no active part in the hostilities" in a non-international armed conflict, "including members of armed forces who have laid down their arms"); *see also* Hague Convention IV, Annex, art. 23(c), 37 Stat. at 2301–02 ("it is especially forbidden . . . [t]o kill or wound

In light of all these circumstances, we believe DoD's contemplated operation against al-Aulaqi would comply with international law, including the laws of war applicable to this armed conflict, and would fall within Congress's authorization to use "necessary and appropriate force" against al-Qaida. In consequence, the operation should be understood to constitute the lawful conduct of war and thus to be encompassed by the public authority justification. Accordingly, the contemplated attack, if conducted by DoD in the manner described, would not result in an "unlawful" killing and thus would not violate section 1119(b).

B.

We next consider whether the CIA's contemplated operation against al-Aulaqi in Yemen would be covered by the public authority justification. We conclude that it would be; and thus that operation, too, would not result in an "unlawful" killing prohibited by section 1119. As with our analysis of the contemplated DoD operation, we rely on the sufficiency of the particular factual circumstances of the CIA operation as they have been represented to us, without determining that the presence of those specific circumstances would be necessary to the

---

an enemy who, having laid down his arms, or having no longer means of defence, has surrendered at discretion"); *id.* art. 23(d) (forbidding a declaration that no quarter will be given); 2 William Winthrop, *Military Law and Precedents 788* (1920) ("The time has long passed when 'no quarter' was the rule on the battlefield, or when a prisoner could be put to death simply by virtue of his capture.").

conclusion we reach.

31

32

We explain in Part VI why the Constitution would impose no bar to the CIA's contemplated operation under these circumstances, based on the facts as they have been represented to us. There thus remains the question whether that operation would violate any statutory restrictions, which in turn requires us to consider whether 18 U.S.C. § 1119 would apply to the contemplated CIA operation.[42] Based on the combination of circumstances that we understand would be present, we conclude that the public authority justification that section 1119 incorporates— and that would prevent the contemplated DoD operation from violating section 1119(b)—would also encompass the contemplated CIA operation.[43]

---

[42] We address potential restrictions imposed by two other criminal laws—18 U.S.C. §§ 956(a) and 2441—in Parts IV and V of this opinion.

[43] We note, in addition, that the "lawful conduct of war" variant of the public authority justification, although often described with specific reference to operations

Specifically, we understand that the CIA, like DoD, would carry [33] out the attack against an operational leader of an enemy force, as part of the United States's ongoing non-international armed conflict with al-Qaida.

the CIA

would conduct the operation in a manner that accords with the rules of international humanitarian law governing this armed conflict, and in circumstances  *See supra* at 10–11.[44]

---

conducted by the armed forces, is not necessarily limited to operations by such forces; some descriptions of that variant of the justification, for example, do not imply such a limitation. *See, e.g., Frye*, 10 Cal. Rptr. 2d at 221 n.2 ("homicide done under a valid public authority, such as execution of a death sentence or killing an enemy in a time of war"); Perkins & Boyce, *Criminal Law* at 1093 ("the killing of an enemy as an act of war and within the rules of war").

44

If the killing by a member of the armed forces would comply with the law of war and otherwise be lawful, actions of CIA officials facilitating that killing should also not be unlawful. *See, e.g., Shoot Down Opinion* at 165 n.33 ("[O]ne cannot be prosecuted for aiding and abetting the commission of an act that is not itself a crime.") (citing *Shuttlesworth v. City of Birmingham*, 373 U.S. 262 (1963)).

Nor would the fact that CIA personnel would be involved in the operation itself cause the operation to violate the laws of war. It is true that CIA personnel, by virtue of their not being part of the armed forces, would not enjoy the immunity from prosecution under the domestic law of the countries in which they act for their conduct in targeting and killing enemy forces in compliance with the laws of war— an immunity that the armed forces enjoy by virtue of their status. *See Report of the Special Rapporteur* ¶ 71, at 22; *see also* Dinstein, *Conduct of Hostilities*, at 31. Nevertheless, lethal activities conducted in accord with the laws of war, and undertaken in the course of lawfully authorized hostilities, do not violate *the laws of war* by virtue of the fact that they are carried out in part by government actors who are not entitled to the combatant's privilege. The contrary view "arises . . . from a fundamental confusion between acts punishable under international law and acts with respect to which international law affords no protection." Richard R. Baxter, *So-Called "Unprivileged Belligerency": Spies, Guerillas, and Saboteurs*, 28 Brit. Y.B. Int'l L. 323, 342

34   Nothing in the text or legislative history of section 1119 indicates
that Congress intended to criminalize such an operation. Section 1119
incorporates the traditional public authority justification, and did not
impose any special limitation on the scope of that justification. As we
have explained, *supra* at 17–19, the legislative history of that criminal
prohibition revealed Congress's intent to close a jurisdictional loophole
that would have hindered prosecutions of murders carried out by private persons abroad. It offers no indication that Congress intended to
prohibit the targeting of an enemy leader during an armed conflict in a
manner that would accord with the laws of war when performed by a
duly authorized government agency. Nor does it indicate that Congress,

---

(1951) ("the law of nations has not ventured to require of states that they . . . refrain
from the use of secret agents or that these activities upon the part of their military
forces or civilian population be punished"). *Accord* Yoram Dinstein, *The Distinction
Between Unlawful Combatants and War Criminals*, in *International Law at a Time
of Perplexity: Essays in Honour of Shabtai Rosenne* 103–16 (Y. Dinstein ed. 1989);

Statements in the Supreme Court's decision in *Ex parte Quirin*, 317 U.S. 1
(1942), are sometimes cited for the contrary view. *See, e g., id.* at 36 n.12 (suggesting
that passing through enemy lines in order to commit "any hostile act" while not in
uniform "renders the offender liable to trial for violation of the laws of war"); *id.* at 31
(enemies who come secretly through the lines for purposes of waging war by destruction of life or property "without uniform" not only are "generally not to be entitled to
the status of prisoners of war," but also "to be offenders against the law of war subject
to trial and punishment by military tribunals"). Because the Court in *Quirin* focused
on conduct taken behind enemy lines, it is not clear whether the Court in these passages intended to refer only to conduct that would constitute perfidy or treachery.
To the extent the Court meant to suggest more broadly that any hostile acts performed by unprivileged belligerents are *for that reason* violations of the laws of war,
the authorities the Court cited (the Lieber Code and Colonel Winthrop's military
law treatise) do not provide clear support. *See* John C. Dehn, *The Hamdan Case and
the Application of a Municipal Offense*, 7. J. Int'l Crim. J., 63, 73–79 (2009); *see also*
Baxter, *So-Called "Unprivileged Belligerency,"* 28 Brit. Y.B. Int'l L. at 339–40; Michael
N. Schmitt, *Humanitarian Law and Direct Participation in Hostilities by Private Contractors or Civilian Employees*, 5 Chi. J. Int'l L. 511, 521 n.45 (2005); W. Hays Parks,
Special Forces' Wear of Non-Standard Uniforms, 4 Chic. J. Int'l L. 493, 510–11 n.31
(2003). We note in this regard that DoD's current Manual for Military Commissions
does not endorse the view that the commission of an unprivileged belligerent act,
without more, constitutes a violation of the international law of war. *See* Manual for
Military Commissions, Part IV, § 5(13), Comment, at IV–11 (2010 ed., Apr. 27, 2010)
(murder or infliction of serious bodily injury "committed while the accused did not
meet the requirements of privileged belligerency" can be tried by a military commission "even if such conduct does not violate the international law of war").

in closing the identified loophole, meant to place a limitation on the CIA that would not apply to DoD.

Thus, we conclude that just as Congress did not intend section 1119 to bar the particular attack that DoD contemplates, neither did it intend to prohibit a virtually identical attack on the same target, in the same authorized conflict and in similar compliance with the laws of war, that the CIA would carry out in accord with

35

45&46

See also infra at 38–41 (explaining that the CIA operation under the circumstances described to us would comply with constitutional due process and the Fourth Amendment's "reasonableness" test for the use of deadly force).

Accordingly, we conclude that, just as the combination of circumstances present here supports the judgment that the public authority justification would apply to the contemplated operation by the armed forces, the combination of circumstances also supports the judgment that the CIA's operation, too, would be encompassed by that justification. The CIA's contemplated operation, therefore, would not result in an "unlawful" killing under section 1111 and thus would not violate section 1119.

---

[45] As one example, the Senate Report pointed to the Department of Justice's conclusion that the Neutrality Act, 18 U.S.C. § 960, prohibits conduct by private parties but is not applicable to the CIA and other government agencies. *Id.* The Senate Report assumed that the Department's conclusion about the Neutrality Act was premised on the assertion that in the case of government agencies, there is an "absence of the mens rea necessary to the offense." *Id.* In fact, however, this Office's conclusion about that Act was not based on questions of mens rea, but instead on a careful analysis demonstrating that Congress did not intend the Act, despite its words of general applicability, to apply to the activities of government officials acting within the course and scope of their duties as officers of the United States. *See Application of Neutrality Act to Official Government Activities*, 8 Op. O.L.C. 58 (1984).

[46] *Cf. also VISA Fraud Investigation*, 8 Op. O.L.C. at 287 (applying similar analysis in evaluating the effect of criminal prohibitions on certain otherwise authorized law enforcement operations, and explaining that courts have recognized it may be lawful for law enforcement agents to disregard otherwise applicable laws "when taking action that is necessary to attain the permissible law enforcement objective, when the action is carried out in a reasonable fashion"); *id.* at 288 (concluding that issuance of an otherwise unlawful visa that was necessary for undercover operation to proceed, and done in circumstances—"for a limited purpose and under close supervision"—that were "reasonable," did not violate federal statute).

IV.

For similar reasons, we conclude that the contemplated DoD and CIA operations would not violate another federal criminal statute dealing with "murder" abroad, 18 U.S.C. § 956(a). That law makes it a crime to conspire within the jurisdiction of the United States "to commit at any place outside the United States an act that would constitute the offense of murder, kidnapping, or maiming if committed in the special maritime and territorial jurisdiction of the United States" if any conspirator acts within the United States to effect any object of the conspiracy.

Like section 1119(b), section 956(a) incorporates by reference the [36] understanding of "murder" in section 1111 of title 18. For reasons we explained earlier in this opinion, *see supra* at 12–14, section 956(a) thus incorporates the traditional public authority justification that section 1111 recognizes. As we have further explained both the CIA and DoD operations, on the facts as they have been represented to us, would be covered by that justification. Nor do we believe that Congress's reference in section 956(a) to "the special maritime and territorial jurisdiction of the United States" reflects an intent to transform such a killing into a "murder" in these circumstances—notwithstanding that our analysis of the applicability of the public authority justification is limited for present purposes to operations conducted abroad. A contrary conclusion would require attributing to Congress the surprising intention of criminalizing through section 956(a) an otherwise lawful killing of an enemy leader that another statute specifically prohibiting the murder of U.S. nationals abroad does not prohibit.

The legislative history of section 956(a) further confirms our conclusion that that statute should not be so construed. When the provision was first introduced in the Senate in 1995, its sponsors addressed and rejected the notion that the conspiracy prohibited by that section would apply to "duly authorized" actions undertaken on behalf of the federal government. Senator Biden introduced the provision at the behest of the President, as part of a larger package of antiterrorism legislation. *See* 141 Cong. Rec. 4491 (1995) (statement of Sen. Biden). He explained that the provision was designed to "fill[] a void in the law," because section 956 at the time prohibited only U.S.-based conspiracies to commit certain property crimes abroad, and did not address crimes against persons. *Id.* at 4506. The amendment was designed to cover an offense "committed by terrorists" and was "intended to ensure that the government is able to punish those persons who use the United States as a base in which to plot such a crime to be carried out outside the jurisdiction of the United States." *Id.* Notably, the sponsors of the new legislation deliberately declined to place the new offense either within chapter 19 of title 18, which is devoted to "Conspiracy," or within chapter 51, which collects "Homicide" offenses (including those established in sections 1111, 1112, 1113 and 1119). Instead, as Senator Biden explained, "[s]ection 956 is contained in chapter 45 of title 18, United States Code, relating to interference with the foreign relations of the United States," and thus was intended to "cover[] those individuals who, without appropriate governmental authorization, engage in prohibited conduct that is harmful to the foreign relations of the United States." *Id.* at 4507. Because, as Senator Biden explained, the provision was designed, like other provisions of chapter 45, to prevent private interference with U.S. foreign relations, "[i]t is not intended to apply to duly authorized actions undertaken on behalf of the United States Government." *Id.; see also* 8 Op. O.L.C. 58 (1984) (concluding that section 5 of the Neutrality Act, 18 U.S.C. § 960, which is also in chapter 45 and which forbids the planning of, or participation in, military or naval expeditions to be carried on from the United States against a foreign state with which the United States is at peace, prohibits only persons acting in their private capacity from engaging in such conduct, and does not proscribe activities undertaken by government officials acting within the course and scope of their duties as United States officers). Senator Daschle expressed this same understanding when he introduced the identical provision in a different version of the anti-terrorism legislation a few months later. *See* 141 Cong. Rec. 11,960 (1995) (statement of Sen. Daschle). Congress enacted the new section 956(a) the following year, as part of the Antiterrorism and Effective Death Penalty Act, Pub. L. No. 104-132, tit. VII, § 704(a), 110 Stat. 1214, 1294–95 (1996). As far as we have been able to determine, the legislative history contains nothing to contradict the construction of section 956(a) described by Senators Biden and Daschle.

| 37 |

Accordingly, we do not believe section 956(a) would prohibit the contemplated operations.

V.

We next consider the potential application of the War Crimes Act, 18 U.S.C. § 2441, which makes it a federal crime for a member of the Armed Forces or a national of the United States to "commit[] a war crime." *Id.* § 2441(a). Subsection 2441(c) defines a "war crime" for purposes of the statute to mean any conduct (i) that is defined as a grave breach in any of the Geneva Conventions (or any Geneva protocol to which the U.S. is a party); (ii) that is prohibited by four specified articles of the Fourth Hague Convention of 1907; (iii) that is a "grave breach" of Common Article 3 of the Geneva Conventions (as defined elsewhere in section 2441) when committed "in the context of and in association with an armed conflict not of an international character"; or (iv) that is a willful killing or infliction of serious injury in violation of the 1996 Protocol on Prohibitions or Restrictions on the Use of Mines, Booby-Traps and Other Devices. Of these, the only subsection potentially applicable here is that dealing with Common Article 3 of the Geneva Conventions. [47]

In defining what conduct constitutes a "grave breach" of Common Article 3 for purposes of the War Crimes Act, subsection 2441(d) includes "murder," described in pertinent part as "[t]he act of a person who intentionally kills, or conspires or attempts to kill . . . one or more persons taking no active part in the hostilities, including those placed out of combat by sickness, wounds, detention, or any other cause." 18 U.S.C. § 2441(d)(1)(D). This language derives from Common Article 3(1) itself, which prohibits certain acts (including murder) against "[p]ersons taking no active part in the hostilities, including members of armed forces who have laid down their arms and those placed '*hors de combat*' by sickness, wounds, detention, or any other cause." *See, e.g.,* Geneva Convention Relative to the Treatment of Prisoners of War, Aug. 12, 1949, [1955], art. 3(1), 6 U.S.T. 3316, 3318–20. Although Common

---

[47] The operations in question here would not involve conduct covered by the Land Mine Protocol. And the articles of the Geneva Conventions to which the United States is currently a party *other than* Common Article 3, as well as the relevant provisions of the Annex to the Fourth Hague Convention, apply by their terms only to armed conflicts between two or more of the parties to the Conventions. *See, e.g.,* Geneva Convention Relative to the Treatment of Prisoners of War, Aug. 12, 1949, [1955], art. 2, 6 U.S.T, 3316, 3406.

Article 3 is most commonly applied with respect to persons within a belligerent party's control, such as detainees, the language of the article is not so limited—it protects all "[p]ersons taking no active part in the hostilities" in an armed conflict not of an international character.

Whatever might be the outer bounds of this category of covered persons, we do not think it could encompass al-Aulaqi. Common Article 3 does not alter the fundamental law-of-war principle concerning a belligerent party's right in an armed conflict to target individuals who are part of an enemy's armed forces. *See supra* at 23. The language of Common Article 3 "makes clear that members of such armed forces [of both the state and non-state parties to the conflict] . . . are considered as 'taking no active part in the hostilities' only once they have disengaged from their fighting function ('have laid down their arms') or are placed *hors de combat*; mere suspension of combat is insufficient." International Committee of the Red Cross, *Interpretive Guidance on the Notion of Direct Participation in Hostilities Under International Humanitarian Law* 28 (2009); *cf. also id.* at 34 ("individuals whose continuous function involves the preparation, execution, or command of acts or operations amounting to direct participation in hostilities are assuming a continuous combat function," in which case they can be deemed to be members of a non-state armed group subject to continuous targeting); *accord Gherebi v. Obama*, 609 F. Supp. 2d 43, 65 (D.D.C. 2009) ("the fact that 'members of armed forces who have laid down their arms and those placed *hors de combat*' are not 'taking [an] active part in the hostilities' necessarily implies that 'members of armed forces' who have not surrendered or been incapacitated are 'taking [an] active part in the hostilities' simply by virtue of their membership in those armed forces"); *id.* at 67 ("Common Article 3 is not a suicide pact; it does not provide a free pass for the members of an enemy's armed forces to go to or fro as they please so long as, for example, shots are not fired, bombs are not exploded, and planes are not hijacked"). Al-Aulaqi, an active, high-level leader of an enemy force who is continually involved in planning and recruiting for terrorist attacks, can on that basis fairly be said to be taking "an active part in hostilities." Accordingly, targeting him in the circumstances posited to us would not violate Common Article 3 and therefore would not violate the War Crimes Act.

38

VI.

We conclude with a discussion of potential constitutional limitations on the contemplated operations due to al-Aulaqi's status as a U.S. citizen, elaborating upon the reasoning in our earlier memorandum discussing that issue. Although we have explained above why we believe that neither the DoD or CIA operation would violate sections 1119(b), 956(a) and 2441 of title 18 of the U.S. Code, the fact that al-Aulaqi is a United States citizen could raise distinct questions under the Constitution. As we explained in our earlier memorandum, Barron Memorandum at 5–7, we do not believe that al-Aulaqi's U.S. citizenship imposes constitutional limitations that would preclude the contemplated lethal action under the facts represented to us by DoD, the CIA and the Intelligence Community.

Because al-Aulaqi is a U.S. citizen, the Fifth Amendment's Due Process Clause, as well as the Fourth Amendment, likely protects him in some respects even while he is abroad. *See Reid v. Covert*, 354 U.S. 1, 5–6 (1957) (plurality opinion); *United States v. Verdugo-Urquidez*, 494 U.S. 259, 269–70 (1990); *see also In re Terrorist Bombings of U.S. Embassies in East Africa*, 552 F.3d 157, 170 n.7 (2d Cir. 2008).

39

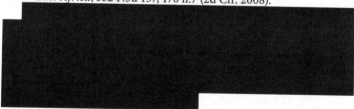

In *Hamdi*, a plurality of the Supreme Court used the *Mathews v. Eldridge* balancing test to analyze the Fifth Amendment due process rights of a U.S. citizen captured on the battlefield in Afghanistan and detained in the United States who wished to challenge the government's assertion that he was a part of enemy forces, explaining that "the process due in any given instance is determined by weighing 'the private interest that will be affected by the official action' against the Government's asserted interest, 'including the function involved' and the burdens the Government would face in providing greater process." 542 U.S. at 529 (plurality opinion) (quoting *Mathews v. Eldridge*, 424 U.S. 319, 335 (1976)).

We believe similar reasoning supports the constitutionality of the contemplated operations here. As explained above, on the facts represented to us, a decision-maker could reasonably decide that the threat posed by al-Aulaqi's activities to United States persons is "continued" and "imminent"

40

In addition to the nature of the threat posed by al-Aulaqi's activities, both agencies here have represented that they intend to capture rather than target al-Aulaqi if feasible; yet we also understand that an operation by either agency to capture al-Aulaqi in Yemen would be infeasible at this time.

Cf., e.g., Public Committee Against Torture in Israel v. Government of Israel, HCJ 769/02 40, 46 I.L.M. 375, 394 (Israel Supreme Court sitting as the High Court of Justice, 2006) (although arrest, investigation and trial "might actually be particularly practical under the conditions of belligerent occupation, in which the army controls the area in which the operation takes place," such alternatives "are not means which can always be used," either because they are impossible or because they involve a great risk to the lives of soldiers).

Although in the "circumstances of war," as the *Hamdi* plurality observed, "the risk of erroneous deprivation of a citizen's liberty in the absence of sufficient process . . . is very real," 542 U.S. at 530, the plurality also recognized that "the realities of combat" render certain uses of force "necessary and appropriate," including against U.S. citizens who have become part of enemy forces—and that "due process analysis need not blink at those realities," *id.* at 531. ▮▮▮▮▮▮▮▮▮ we conclude that at least where, as here, the target's activities pose a "continued and imminent threat of violence or death" to U.S. persons, "the highest officers in the Intelligence Community have reviewed the factual basis" for the lethal operation, and a capture operation would be infeasible—and where the CIA and DoD "continue to monitor whether changed circumstances would permit such an alternative," ▮▮▮▮ ▮▮▮▮▮▮ *see also DoD May 18 Memorandum for OLC* at 2—the "realities of combat" and the weight of the government's interest in using an authorized means of lethal force against this enemy are such that the Constitution would not require the government to provide further process to the U.S. person before using such force. *Cf Hamdi* 542 U.S. at 535 (noting that Court "accord[s] the greatest respect and consideration to the judgments of military authorities in matters relating to the actual prosecution of war, and . . . the scope of that discretion necessarily is wide") (plurality opinion).

41

Similarly, assuming that the Fourth Amendment provides some protection to a U.S. person abroad who is part of al-Qaida and that the operations at issue here would result in a "seizure" within the meaning of that Amendment, ████████████████████████████ ██ The Supreme Court has made clear that the constitutionality of a seizure is determined by "balanc[ing] the nature and quality of the intrusion on the individual's Fourth Amendment interests against the importance of the governmental interests alleged to justify the intrusion." *Tennessee v. Garner*, 471 U.S. 1, 8 (1985) (internal quotation marks omitted); *accord Scott v. Harris*, 550 U.S. 372, 383 (2007). Even in domestic law enforcement operations, the Court has noted that "[w]here the officer has probable cause to believe that the suspect poses a threat of serious physical harm, either to the officer or to others, it is not constitutionally unreasonable to prevent escape by using deadly force." *Garner*, 471 U.S. at 11. Thus, "if the suspect threatens the officer with a weapon or there is probable cause to believe that he has committed a crime involving the infliction or threatened infliction of serious physical harm, deadly force may be used if necessary to prevent escape and if, where feasible, some warning has been given." *Id.* at 11–12.

The Fourth Amendment "reasonableness" test is situation-dependent. *Cf. Scott*, 550 U.S. at 382 (*Garner* "did not establish a magical on/off switch that triggers rigid preconditions whenever an officer's actions constitute 'deadly force'"). What would constitute a reasonable use of lethal force for purposes of domestic law enforcement operations will be very different from what would be reasonable in a situation like such as that at issue here. In the present circumstances, as we understand the facts, the U.S. citizen in question has gone overseas and become part of the forces of an enemy with which the United States is engaged in an armed conflict; that person is engaged in continual planning and direction of attacks upon U.S. persons from one of the enemy's overseas bases of operations; the U.S. government does not know precisely when such attacks will occur; and a capture operation would be infeasible ███████████████████ at least where high-level government officials have determined that a capture operation overseas is infeasible and that the targeted person is part of a dangerous enemy force and is engaged in activities that pose a continued and imminent threat to U.S. persons or interests ████████████████ the use of lethal force would not violate the Fourth Amendment. ████████████████████ ██████████████████ and thus that the intrusion on any Fourth Amendment interests would be outweighed by "the importance of the governmental interests [that] justify the intrusion," *Garner*, 471 U.S. at 8, based on the facts that have been represented to us.

Please let us know if we can be of further assistance.

David J. Barron
Acting Assistant Attorney General

3

Remarks of Harold Hongju Koh, Legal
Adviser, U.S. Department of State

Annual Meeting of the American Society of
International Law, Washington, D.C.

March 25, 2010

"The Obama Administration and International Law"

Initially, the Obama administration defended its targeted-killing policies mainly through anonymous leaks to the media. But the revelation
that the government was targeting Anwar al-Aulaqi, an American,
sparked a debate, and some officials felt strongly that the administration should defend its policies publicly. Harold Koh, the State Department's legal adviser, delivered these remarks at the annual meeting of
the American Society of International Law. Before joining the administration, Koh had been a prominent international-law scholar and
advocate of human rights. Consequently, the importance of this speech
derived in part from the fact that it was Koh who delivered it.

The document from which this text was transcribed is posted at:
www.ACLU.org/TDM/KohSpeech.

Thank you, Dean Areen, for that very generous introduction, and very special thanks to my good friends President Lucy Reed and Executive Director Betsy Andersen for the extraordinary work you do with the American Society of International Law. It has been such a great joy in my new position to be able to collaborate with the Society on so many issues.

* * *

Since this is my first chance to address you as Legal Adviser, I thought I would speak to three issues. First, the nature of my job as Legal Adviser. Second, to discuss the strategic vision of international law that we in the Obama Administration are attempting to implement. Third and finally, to discuss particular issues that we have grappled with in our first year in a number of high-profile areas: the International Criminal Court, the Human Rights Council, and what I call The Law of 9/11: detentions, use of force, and prosecutions.

* * *

III. Current Legal Challenges

* * *

B. The Law of 9/11

Let me focus the balance of my remarks on that aspect of my job that I call "The Law of 9/11." In this area, as in the other areas of our work, we believe, in the President's words, that "living our values doesn't make us weaker, it makes us safer and it makes us stronger."

We live in a time, when, as you know, the United States finds itself engaged in several armed conflicts. As the President has noted, one conflict, in Iraq, is winding down. He also reminded us that the conflict in Afghanistan is a "conflict that America did not seek, one in which we are joined by forty-three other countries . . . in an effort to defend ourselves and all nations from further attacks." In the conflict occurring in Afghanistan and elsewhere, we continue to fight the perpetrators of 9/11: a non-state actor, al-Qaeda (as well as the Taliban forces that harbored al-Qaeda).

Everyone here at this meeting is committed to international law. But as President Obama reminded us, "the world must remember that it was not simply international institutions—not just treaties and declarations—that brought stability to a post-World War II world. . . . [T]he instruments of war do have a role to play in preserving the peace."

With this background, let me address a question on many of your minds: how has this Administration determined to conduct these armed conflicts and to defend our national security, consistent with its abiding commitment to international law? *Let there be no doubt: the Obama Administration is firmly committed to complying with all applicable law, including the laws of war, in all aspects of these ongoing armed conflicts.* As the President reaffirmed in his Nobel Prize Lecture, "Where force is necessary, we have a moral and strategic interest in binding ourselves to certain rules of conduct . . . [E]ven as we confront a vicious adversary that abides by no rules . . . the United States of America must remain a standard bearer in the conduct of war. That is what makes us different from those whom we fight. That is the source of our strength." We in the Obama Administration have worked hard since we entered office to ensure that we conduct all aspects of these armed conflicts—in particular, detention operations, targeting, and prosecution of terrorist suspects—in a manner consistent not just with the applicable laws of war, but also with the Constitution and laws of the United States.

Let me say a word about each: detention, targeting, and prosecution.

* * *

B. Use of Force

In the same way, in all of our operations involving the *use of force*, including those in the armed conflict with al-Qaeda, the Taliban and associated forces, the Obama Administration is committed by word and deed to conducting ourselves in accordance with all applicable law. With respect to the subject of targeting, which has been much commented upon in the media and international legal circles, there are obviously limits to what I can say publicly. What I can say *is that it is the considered view of this Administration—and it has certainly been my experience during my time as Legal Adviser—that U.S. targeting practices, including lethal operations conducted with the use of unmanned aerial vehicles, comply with all applicable law, including the laws of war.*

The United States agrees that it must conform its actions to all applicable law. As I have explained, as a matter of international law, the United States is in an armed conflict with al-Qaeda, as well as the Taliban and associated forces, in response to the horrific 9/11 attacks, and may use force consistent with its inherent right to self-defense under international law. As a matter of domestic law, Congress authorized the use of all necessary and appropriate force through the 2001 Authorization for Use of Military Force (AUMF). These domestic and international legal authorities continue to this day.

As recent events have shown, al-Qaeda has not abandoned its intent to attack the United States, and indeed continues to attack us. Thus, in this ongoing armed conflict, the United States has the authority under international law, and the responsibility to its citizens, to use force, including lethal force, to defend itself, including by targeting persons such as high-level al-Qaeda leaders who are planning attacks. As you know, this is a conflict with an organized terrorist enemy that does not have conventional forces, but that plans and executes its attacks against us and our allies while hiding among civilian populations. That behavior simultaneously makes the application of international law more difficult and more critical for the protection of innocent civilians. Of course, whether a particular individual will be targeted in a particular location will depend upon considerations specific to each case, including those related to the imminence of the threat, the sovereignty of the other states involved, and the willingness and ability of those states to suppress the threat the target poses. In particular, this Administration has carefully reviewed the rules governing targeting operations to ensure that these operations are conducted consistently with law of war principles, including:

- First, the principle of *distinction*, which requires that attacks be limited to military objectives and that civilians or civilian objects shall not be the object of the attack; and
- Second, the principle of *proportionality*, which prohibits attacks that may be expected to cause incidental loss of civilian life, injury to civilians, damage to civilian objects, or a combination thereof, that would be excessive in relation to the concrete and direct military advantage anticipated.

In U.S. operations against al-Qaeda and its associated forces —including lethal operations conducted with the use of unmanned aerial vehicles—great care is taken to adhere to these principles in both planning and execution, to ensure that only legitimate objectives are targeted and that collateral damage is kept to a minimum.

Recently, a number of legal objections have been raised against U.S. targeting practices. While today is obviously not the occasion for a detailed legal opinion responding to each of these objections, let me briefly address four:

First, some have suggested that the *very act of targeting* a particular leader of an enemy force in an armed conflict must violate the laws of war. But individuals who are part of such an armed group are belligerents and, therefore, lawful targets under international law. During World War II, for example, American aviators tracked and shot down the airplane carrying the architect of the Japanese attack on Pearl Harbor, who was also the leader of enemy forces in the Battle of Midway. This was a lawful operation then, and would be if conducted today. Indeed, targeting particular individuals serves to narrow the focus when force is employed and to avoid broader harm to civilians and civilian objects.

Second, some have challenged *the very use of advanced weapons systems*, such as unmanned aerial vehicles, for lethal operations. But the rules that govern targeting do not turn on the type of weapon system used, and there is no prohibition under the laws of war on the use of technologically advanced weapons systems in armed conflict—such as pilotless aircraft or so-called smart bombs—so long as they are employed in conformity with applicable laws of war. Indeed, using such advanced technologies can ensure both that the best intelligence is available for planning operations, and that civilian casualties are minimized in carrying out such operations.

Third, some have argued that the use of lethal force against specific individuals fails to provide adequate process and thus constitutes *unlawful extrajudicial killing*. But a state that is engaged in an armed conflict or in legitimate self-defense is not required to provide targets with legal process before the state may use lethal force. Our procedures and practices for identifying lawful targets are extremely robust, and advanced technologies have helped to make our targeting even more precise. In my experience, the principles of distinction and proportionality that the United States applies are not just recited at meetings. They are implemented rigorously throughout the planning and execution of lethal operations to ensure that such operations are conducted in accordance with all applicable law.

Fourth and finally, some have argued that our targeting practices violate *domestic law,* in particular, the long-standing *domestic ban on assassinations.* But under domestic law, the use of lawful weapons systems—consistent with the applicable laws of war—for precision targeting of specific high-level belligerent leaders when acting in self-defense or during an armed conflict is not unlawful, and hence does not constitute "assassination."

In sum, let me repeat: as in the area of detention operations, this Administration is committed to ensuring that the targeting practices that I have described are lawful.

* * *

IV. CONCLUSION
In closing, in the last year, this Administration has pursued principled engagement with the ICC and the Human Rights Council, and has reaffirmed its commitment to international law with respect to all three aspects of the armed conflicts in which we find ourselves: detention, targeting and prosecution. While these are not all we want to achieve, neither are they small accomplishments. As the President said in his Nobel Lecture, "I have reaffirmed America's commitment to abide by the Geneva Conventions. We lose ourselves when we compromise the very ideals that we fight to defend. And we honor ideals by upholding them not when it's easy, but when it is hard." As President Obama went on to say, even in this day and age war is sometimes justified, but "this truth," he said, "must coexist with another—that no matter how justified, war promises human tragedy. The soldier's courage and sacrifice is full of glory. . . . But war itself is never glorious, and we must never trumpet it as such. So part of our challenge is reconciling these two seemingly irreconcilable truths—that war is sometimes necessary, and war at some level is an expression of human folly."

Although it is not always easy, I see my job as an international lawyer in this Administration as reconciling these truths around a thoroughgoing commitment to the rule of law. That is the commitment I made to the President and the Secretary when I took this job with an oath to uphold the Constitution and laws of the United States. That is a commitment that I make to myself every day that I am a government lawyer. And that is a commitment that I make to each of you, as a lawyer deeply committed—as we all are—to the goals and aspirations of this American Society of International Law.

Thank you.

4

Justice Department White Paper

May 25, 2011

"Legality of a Lethal Operation by the Central Intelligence Agency Against a U.S. Citizen ██████████████"

After Judge John Bates's December 2010 dismissal of Nasser al-Aulaqi's first lawsuit against the U.S. government, Senator Ron Wyden and other members of the Senate Intelligence Committee asked the Obama administration for an explanation of its legal basis for targeting an American citizen. Attorney General Eric Holder directed the Office of Legal Counsel to prepare a white paper for the committee. A heavily redacted version of the classified white paper was released to the ACLU in 2014 in connection with litigation under the Freedom of Information Act. The document closely tracks the OLC's July 2010 legal memo (Document 2 in this volume). It addresses the implications of certain domestic criminal statutes, as well as "possible constitutional limitations" on the CIA's authority to carry out the killing of American citizens.

The document from which this text was transcribed is posted at: www.ACLU.org/TDM/WhitePaper1.

This white paper sets forth the legal basis upon which the Central Intelligence Agency ("CIA") could use lethal force in Yemen against a United States citizen who senior officials reasonably determined was a senior leader of al-Qaida or an associated force of al-Qaida.

███████████████████████████ Furthermore, 18 U.S.C. § 1119(b), which criminalizes the murder abroad of a United States national by another U.S. national, does not prohibit such use of lethal force. The text and legislative history of the relevant statutes, precedents of the Office of Legal Counsel ("OLC"), and ordinary principles of statutory construction support the conclusion that section 1119 imposes no bar to operations against a senior leader of al-Qaida or an associated force who nevertheless is a U.S. citizen. Section 1119(b) bars only "unlawful" killings (cross-referencing 18 U.S.C. §§ 1111, 1112, 1113), and, in light of the circumstances outlined below, the killing would not be "unlawful" because it would fall within the traditional justification for conduct undertaken pursuant to "public authority." Here, the authority to use lethal force in national self-defense, as recognized by congressional enactments, would make this kind of operation lawful, and section 1119 would not be violated. ████████████████

Nor would such an operation violate either 18 U.S.C. § 956(a)—which makes it a crime to conspire within the jurisdiction of the United States "to commit at any place outside the United States an act that would constitute the offense of murder, kidnapping, or maiming if committed in the special maritime and territorial jurisdiction of the United States" if any conspirator acts within the United States to effect any object of the conspiracy—or the War Crimes Act, 18 U.S.C. § 2441. Finally, an operation, under the circumstances outlined below, would not transgress any possible constitutional limitations—a conclusion that is also relevant to the judgment that a CIA operation would be performed pursuant to public authority and thus would not violate either section 1119(b) or section 956(a).[1] █████████████
████████████████████

---

[1] This white paper addresses exclusively the use of force abroad, in the circumstances described herein. It does not address legal issues that the use of force in different circumstances or in any nation other than Yemen might present. ████

I.

A.

Furthermore, according to the CIA, although there may be no occasion for surrender in light of the means by which such an operation would be carried out, the CIA would prefer to capture this target, and if a potential target offers to surrender, such surrender would be accepted, if feasible. This would include any targets in Yemen, although the CIA assesses that a capture in Yemen would not be feasible at this time. *See infra* at 20–21. The CIA has further represented that this sort of operation would not be undertaken in a perfidious or treacherous manner.

Finally, any U.S. citizen targeted in such an operation would be an individual with an operational and senior leadership role in al-Qaida or one of its associated forces. Moreover, the individual would be one who had previously participated in operational planning for attempted attacks on the United States and who has expressed interest in conducting additional terrorist attacks in the United States.

B.

4

5

II.

Subsection 1119(b) of title 18 provides that "[a] person who, being a national of the United States, kills or attempts to kill a national of the United States while such national is outside the United States but within the jurisdiction of another country shall be punished as provided under sections 1111, 1112, and 1113." 18 U.S.C. § 1119(b).[4] In light of the nature of the operation described above, and the fact that its target would be a "national of the United States" who is outside the United States, it might be suggested that section 1119(b) would prohibit such an operation. Section 1119, however, bars only unlawful killings and the United

---

[4] *See also* 18 U.S.C. § 1119(a) (providing that "national of the United States" has the meaning stated in section 101(a)(32) of the Immigration and Nationality Act, 8 U.S.C. § 1101 (a)(22)).

States' use of lethal force in national self-defense is not an unlawful killing. Section 1119 is best construed to incorporate the public authority
justification, which can render lethal action carried out by a governmental official lawful in some circumstances, and this public authority
justification would apply to such a CIA operation. ██████████████

A.

Although section 1119(b) refers only to the "punish[ments]" provided under sections 1111, 1112, and 1113, courts have construed section 1119(b) to incorporate the substantive elements of these cross-
referenced provisions of title 18. *See e.g., United States v. Wharton*, 320
F.3d 526, 533 (5th Cir. 2003); *United States v. White*, 51 F. Supp. 2d 1008,
1013–14 (E.D. Ca. 1997). Section 1111 of title 18 sets forth criminal penalties for "murder," and provides that "[m]urder is the unlawful killing
of a human being with malice aforethought." *Id.* § 1111(a). Section 1112
similarly provides criminal sanctions for "manslaughter," and states
that "[m]anslaughter is the unlawful killing of a human being without
malice." *Id.* § 1112. Section 1113 provides criminal penalties for
"attempts to commit murder or manslaughter." *Id* § 1113. It is therefore
clear that section 1119(b) bars only "unlawful killings."[5]

This limitation on section 1119(b)'s scope is significant, as the legislative history to the underlying offenses that the section incorporates
makes clear. The provisions section 1119(b) incorporates derive from
sections 273 and 274 of the Act of March 4, 1909, ch. 321, 35 Stat. 1088,
1143. The 1909 Act codified and amended the penal laws of the United
States. Section 273 of the enactment defined murder as "the unlawful killing of a human being with malice aforethought," and section
274 defined manslaughter as "the unlawful killing of a human being

---

[5] Section 1119 itself also expressly imposes various procedural limitations
on prosecution. Subsection 1119(c)(1) requires that any prosecution be authorized
in writing by the Attorney General, the Deputy Attorney General, or an Assistant
Attorney General, and precludes the approval of such an action "if prosecution has
been previously undertaken by a foreign country for the same conduct." In addition, subsection 1119(c)(2) provides that "[n]o prosecution shall be approved under
this section unless the Attorney General, in consultation with the Secretary of State,
determines that the conduct took place in a country in which the person is no longer
present, and the country lacks the ability to lawfully secure the person's return"—a
determination that "is not subject to judicial review," *id.*

without malice." 35 Stat. 1143.[6] In 1948, Congress codified the federal murder and manslaughter provisions at sections 1111 and 1112 of title 18 and retained the definitions of murder and manslaughter in nearly identical form, *see* Act of June 25, 1948, ch. 645, 62 Stat. 683, 756, including the references to "unlawful killing" that remain in the statutes today—references that track similar formulations in some state murder statutes.[7]

---

[6] A 1908 joint congressional committee report on the Act explained that "[u]nder existing law [i.e., prior to the 1909 Act], there [had been] no statutory definition of crimes of murder or manslaughter." Report by the Special Joint Comm. on the Revision of the Laws, Revision and Codification of the Laws, Etc., H.R. Rep. No 2. 60th Cong. 1st Sess. at 12 (Jan. 6, 1908) ("Joint Committee Report"). The 1878 edition of the Revised Statutes, however, did contain a definition for manslaughter (but not murder): "Every person who, within any of the places or upon any of the waters [within the exclusive jurisdiction of the United States] unlawfully and willingly, but without malice, strikes, stabs, wounds, or shoots at, otherwise injures another, of which striking, stabbing, wounding, shooting, or other injury such other person dies, either on land or sea, within or without the United States, is guilty of the crime of manslaughter." Revised Statutes § 5341 (1878 ed.) (quoted in *United States v. Alexander*, 47) F.2d 923, 944–45 n.54 (D.C. Cir. 1972)). With respect to murder, the 1908 report noted that the legislation "enlarges the common-law definition, and is similar in terms to the statutes defining murder in a large majority of the States." Joint Committee Report at 24; *see also Revision of the Penal Laws: Hearings on S. 2982 Before the Senate as a Whole.* 60th Cong. 1st Sess. 1184, 1185 (1908) (statement of Senator Heyburn) (same). With respect to manslaughter, the report states that "[w]hat is said with respect to (the murder provision) is true as to this section, manslaughter being defined and classified in language similar to that to be found in the statutes of a large majority of the States." Joint Committee Report at 24.

[7] *See e.g.*, Cal. Penal Code § 187(a) (West 2009) ("Murder is the unlawful killing of a human being, or a fetus, with malice aforethought."); Fla. Stat. § 782.04(1)(a) (West 2009) (including "unlawful killing of a human being" as an element or murder); Idaho Code Ann. § 18-4001 (West 2009) ("Murder is the unlawful killing of a human being"); Nev. Rev. Stat. Ann. § 200.010 (West 2008) (including "unlawful killing of a human being" as an element of murder); R.I. Gen. Laws § 11.23.1 (West 2008) ("The unlawful killing of a human being with malice aforethought is murder"); Tenn. Code Ann. § 39-13-201 (West 2009) ("Criminal homicide is the unlawful killing of another person"). Such statutes, in turn, reflect the view often expressed in the common law of murder that the crime requires an "unlawful" killing. *See e.g.*, Edward Coke, *The Third Part of the Institutes of Laws of England* 47 (London, W. Clarke & Sons 1809) ("Murder is when a man of sound memory, and of the age of discretion, unlawfully killeth within any county of the realm any reasonable creature *in rerum natura* under the king's peace, with malice fore-thought, either expressed by the party, or implied by law, so as the party wounded, or hurt, &c. die of the wound, or hurt, &c. within a year and a day after the same."); 4 William Blackstone, *Commentaries on the Laws of England* 195 (Oxford 1769) (same); *see also A Digest of Opin-*

7

As this legislative history indicates, guidance as to the meaning of what constitutes an "unlawful killing" in sections 1111 and 1112—and thus for purposes of section 1119(b)—can be found in the historical understanding of murder and manslaughter. That history shows that states have long recognized justifications and excuses to statutes criminalizing "unlawful" killings.[8] One state court, for example, in construing that state's murder statute explained that "the word 'unlawful' is a term of art" that "connotes a homicide with the absence of factors of excuse or justification," *People v. Frye*, 10 Cal. Rptr. 2d 217, 221 (Cal. App. 1992). That court further explained that the factors of excuse or justification in question include those that have traditionally been recognized. *Id.* at 221 n.2. Other authorities support the same conclusion. *See, e.g., Mullaney v. Wilbur*, 421 U.S. 684, 685 (1975) (requirement of "unlawful" killing in Maine murder statute meant that killing was "neither justifiable nor excusable"); *cf. also* Rollin M. Perkins & Ronald N. Boyce, *Criminal Law* 56 (3d ed. 1982) ("Innocent homicide is of two kinds, (1) justifiable and (2) excusable."). Accordingly, section 1119 does not proscribe killings covered by a justification traditionally recognized, such as under the common law or state and federal murder stat-

---

ions of the Judge Advocates General of the Army 1074 n.3 (1912) ("Murder, at common law, is the unlawful killing of a person by a person of sound memory and discretion, of any reasonable creature in being and under the peace of the State, which malice aforethought either express or implied") (internal quotation marks omitted).

[8] The same is true with respect to other statutes, including federal laws, that modify a prohibited act other than murder or manslaughter with the term "unlawfully." *See, e.g., Territory v. Gonzales*, 89 P. 250, 252 (N.M. Terr. 1907) (construing the term "unlawful" in statute criminalizing assault with a deadly weapon as "clearly equivalent" to "without excuse or justification"). For example, 18 U.S.C. § 2339C makes it unlawful, *inter alia*, to "unlawfully and willfully provide [] or collect [] funds" with the intention that they be used (or knowledge they are to be used) to carry out an act that is an offense within certain specified treaties, or to engage in certain other terrorist acts. The legislative history of section 2339C makes clear that "[t]he term 'unlawfully' is intended to embody common law defenses." H.R. Rep. No. 107-307, at 12 (2001). Similarly, the Uniform Code of Military Justice makes it unlawful for members of the armed forces to, "without justification or excuse, unlawfully kill [] a human being" under certain specified circumstances. 10 U.S.C. § 918. Notwithstanding that the statute already expressly requires lack of justification or excuse, it is the longstanding view of the armed forces that "[k]illing a human being is *unlawful*" for purposes of this provision "when done without justification or excuse." Manual for Courts-Martial United States (2008 ed.) at IV–63. art. 118, comment (c) (1) (emphasis added).

utes. *See White*, 51 F. Supp. 2d at 1013 ("Congress did not intend [section 1119] to criminalize justifiable or excusable killings.").

B.

Before one such recognized justification—the justification of "public authority"—can be analyzed in the context of a potential CIA operation, it is necessary to explain why section 1119(b) incorporates that particular justification. ████████████████

The public authority justification, generally understood, is well-accepted, and it is clear it may be available even in cases where the particular criminal statute at issue does not expressly refer to a public authority justification.[9] Prosecutions where such a "public authority" justification is invoked are understandably rare, *see* American Law Institute, Model Penal Code and Commentaries § 3.03 Comment 1, at 24 (1985); *cf Visa Fraud Investigation*, 8 Op. O.L.C. 284, 285 n.2. 286 (1984), and thus there is little case law in which courts have analyzed the scope of the justification with respect to the conduct of government officials.[10] Nonetheless, discussions in the leading treatises and in the

|8|

---

[9] Where a federal criminal statute incorporates the public authority justification, and the government conduct at issue is within the scope of that justification, there is no need to examine whether the criminal prohibition has been repealed, impliedly or otherwise, by some other statute that might potentially authorize the governmental conduct, including by the authorizing statute that might supply the predicate for the assertion of the public authority justification itself. Rather, in such cases, the criminal prohibition simply does not apply to the particular governmental conduct at issue in the first instance because Congress intended that prohibition to be qualified by the public authority justification that it incorporates. Conversely, where another statute expressly authorizes the government to engage in the *specific* conduct in question, then there would be no need to invoke the more general public authority justification doctrine, because in such a case the legislature itself has, in effect, carved out a specific exception permitting the executive to do what the legislature has otherwise generally forbidden. Such a circumstance is not addressed in this white paper.

[10] The question of a "public authority" justification is much more frequently litigated in cases where a private party charged with a crime interposes the defense that he relied upon authority that a public official allegedly conferred upon him to engage in the challenged conduct. *See generally* United States Attorneys' Manual tit. 9, Criminal Resource Manual § 2055 (describing and discussing three different such defenses of "governmental authority"): National Comm'n on Reform of Federal Criminal Laws, A Proposed New Federal Criminal Code § 602(2); Model Penal Code § 3.03(3)(b); *see also United States v. Fulcher*, 250 F.3d 244, 253 (4th Cir. 2001); *United States v. Rosenthal*, 793 F.2d 1214, 1235–36 (11th Cir. 1986); *United States v. Duggan*,

Model Penal Code demonstrate its legitimacy. *See* 2 Wayne R. LaFave, *Substantive Criminal Law* § 10.2(b), at 135 (2d ed. 2003); Perkins & Boyce, *Criminal Law* at 1093 ("Deeds which otherwise would be criminal, such as taking or destroying property, taking hold of a person by force and against his will, placing him in confinement, or even taking his life, are not crimes if done with proper public authority."); *see also* Model Penal Code § 3.03 (1)(a), (d), (e), at 22–23 (proposing codification of justification where conduct is "required or authorized by," inter alia, "the law defining the duties or functions of a public officer. . ."; "the law governing the armed services or the lawful conduct of war"; or "any other provision of law imposing a public duty"); National Comm'n on Reform of Federal Criminal Laws, A Proposed New Federal Criminal Code § 602(1) ("Conduct engaged in by a public servant in the course of his official duties is justified when it is required or authorized by law."). And OLC has invoked analogous rationales when it has analyzed whether Congress intended a particular criminal statute to prohibit specific conduct that otherwise falls within a government agency's authorities.[11]

The public authority justification does not excuse all conduct of public officials from all criminal prohibitions. The legislature may design some criminal prohibitions to place bounds on the kinds of governmental conduct that can be authorized by the Executive. Or the legislature may enact a criminal prohibition in order to delimit the scope of the conduct that the legislature has otherwise authorized the Executive to

9

---

743 F.2d 59, 83–84 (2d Cir. 1984); Fed. R. Crim. P. 12.3 (requiring defendant to notify government if he intends to invoke such a public authority defense). Such cases are not addressed in this white paper, and the discussion of the "public authority" justification is limited to the question of whether a particular criminal law applies to specific conduct undertaken by *government agencies* pursuant to their authorities.

[11] *See, e.g., Visa Fraud Investigation*, 8 Op. O.L.C. at 287–88 (concluding that civil statute prohibiting issuance of visa to an alien known to be ineligible did not prohibit State Department from issuing such a visa where "necessary" to facilitate important Immigration and Naturalization Service undercover operation carried out in a "reasonable" fashion).

undertake pursuant to another statute.[12] But the recognition that a federal criminal statute may incorporate the public authority justification reflects the fact that it would not make sense to attribute to Congress the intent with respect to each of its criminal statutes to prohibit all covered activities undertaken by public officials in the legitimate exercise of their otherwise lawful authorities, even if Congress has clearly intended to make those same actions a crime when committed by persons who are not acting pursuant to such public authority. In some instances, therefore, the better view of a criminal prohibition may well be that Congress meant to distinguish those persons who are acting pursuant to public authority, at least in some circumstances, from those who are not, even if the statute by terms does not make that distinction express. *Cf. Nardone v. United States*, 302 U.S. 379, 384 (1937) (federal criminal statutes should be construed to exclude authorized conduct of public officers where such a reading "would work obvious absurdity as, for example, the application of a speed law to a policeman pursuing a criminal or the driver of a fire engine responding to an alarm").[13]

Here, in the case of a federal murder statute, there is no general bar to applying the public authority justification to criminal prohibition. For example, with respect to prohibitions on the unlawful use of deadly force, the Model Penal Code recommended that legislatures should make the public authority (or "public duty") justification available, though only where the use of such force is covered by a more particular justification (such as defense of others or the use of deadly force by law enforcement), where the use of such force "is otherwise expressly authorized by law," or where such force "occurs in the lawful conduct of war." Model Penal Code 3.03(2)(b), at 22; *see also id.* Comment 3, at 26. Some

---

[12] *See, e.g., Nardone v. United States*, 302 U.S. 379, 384 (1937) (government wiretapping was proscribed by federal statute).

[13] Each potentially applicable statute must be carefully and separately examined to discern Congress's intent in this respect—such as whether it imposes a less qualified limitation than section 1119 imposes. *See generally, e.g., United States Assistance to Countries that Shoot Down Civil Aircraft Involved in Drug Trafficking*, 18 Op. O.L.C. 143 (1994); *Application of Neutrality Act to Official Government Activities*, 8 Op. O.L.C. 58 (1984).

states proceeded to adopt the Model Penal Code recommendation.[14] Other states, although not adopting that precise formulation, have enacted specific statutes dealing with the question of when public officials are justified in using deadly force, which often prescribe that an officer acting in the performance of his official duties must reasonably have believed that such force was "necessary."[15] Other states have more broadly provided that the public authority defense is available where the government officer engages in a "reasonable exercise" of his official functions.[16] There is, however, no federal statute that is analogous, and neither section 1119 nor any of the incorporated title 18 provisions setting forth the substantive elements of the section 1119(b) offense, provide any express guidance as to the existence or scope of this justification.

Against this background, the touchstone for the analysis of whether section 1119 incorporates not only justifications generally, but also the public authority justification in particular, is the legislative intent underlying this criminal statute. Here, the statute should be read to exclude from its prohibitory scope killings that are encompassed by traditional justifications, which include the public authority justification. There are no indications that Congress had a contrary intention. Nothing in the text or legislative history of sections 1111–1113 of title 18 suggests that Congress intended to exclude the established public authority justification from those that Congress otherwise must be understood to have imported through the use of the modifier "unlawful" in those statutes (which, as explained above, establish the substantive scope of

---

[14] *See, e.g.,* Neb. Rev. Stat. § 28-1408(2)(b); Pa. C.S.A. § 504(b)(2); Tex. Penal Code tit. 2 § 9.21(c).

[15] *See, e.g.,* Ariz Rev. Stat. § 13-410C; Maine Rev. Stat. Ann. Tit. 17 § 102.2.

[16] *See, e.g.,* Ala. Stat. § 13A-3-22; N.Y. Penal Law § 35.05(1); LaFave, *Substantive Criminal Law* § 10.2(b), at 135 n.15; *see also* Robinson, *Criminal Law Defenses* § 149(a), at 215 (proposing that the defense should be available only if the actor engages in the authorized conduct "when and to the extent necessary to protect or further the interest protected or furthered by the grant of authority" and where it "is reasonable in relation to the gravity of the harms or evils threatened and the importance of the interests to be furthered by such exercise of authority"); *id.* § 149(c), at 218–20.

section 1119(b)).[17] Nor is there anything in the text or legislative history of section 1119 itself to suggest that Congress intended to abrogate or otherwise affect the availability under that statute of this traditional justification for killings. On the contrary, the relevant legislative materials indicate that in enacting section 1119 Congress was merely closing a gap in a field dealing with entirely different kinds of conduct than that at issue here.

The origin of section 1119 was a bill entitled the "Murder of United States Nationals Acts of 1991," which Senator Thurmond introduced during the 102d Congress in response to the murder of an American in South Korea who had been teaching at a private school there. *See* 137 Cong. Rec. 8675–77 (1991) (statement of Sen. Thurmond). Shortly after the murder, another American teacher at the school accused a former colleague (who was also a U.S. citizen) of having committed the murder, and also confessed to helping the former colleague cover up the crime. The teacher who confessed was convicted in a South Korean court of destroying evidence and aiding the escape of a criminal suspect, but the individual she accused of murder had returned to the United States before the confession. *Id.* at 8675. The United States did not have an extradition treaty with South Korea that would have facilitated prosecution of the alleged murderer and therefore, under then-existing law, "the Federal Government ha[d] no jurisdiction to prosecute a person residing in the United States who ha[d] murdered an American abroad except in limited circumstances, such as a terrorist murder or the murder of a Federal official." *Id.*

To close the "loophole under Federal law which permits persons who murder Americans in certain foreign countries to go punished," *id.*, the Thurmond bill would have added a new section to title 18 providing that "[w]hoever kills or attempts to kill a national of the United States while such national is outside the United States but within the jurisdiction of another country shall be punished as provided under

---

[17] The argument that the use of the term "unlawful" supports the conclusion that section 1119 incorporates the public authority justification does not suggest that the absence of such a term would require a contrary conclusion regarding the intended application of a criminal statute to otherwise authorized government conduct in other cases. Each statute must be considered on its own terms to determine the relevant congressional intent. *See supra* note 13.

sections 1111, 1112, and 1113 of this title." S. 861, 102d Cong. (incorporated in S. 1241, 102d Cong. §§ 3201–03 (1991)). The proposal also contained a separate provision amending the procedures for extradition "to
provide the executive branch with the necessary authority, in the
absence of an extradition treaty, to surrender to foreign governments
those who commit violent crimes against U.S. nationals." 137 Cong.
Rec. 8676 (1991) (statement of Sen. Thurmond) (discussing S. 861, 102d
Cong., § 3).[18] The Thurmond proposal was incorporated into an omnibus crime bill that both the House and Senate passed, but that bill did
not become law.

In the 103d Congress, a revised version of the Thurmond bill was
included as part of the Violent Crime Control and Law Enforcement
Act of 1994, H.R. 3355 § 60009, 103d Cong. (1994). The new legislation
differed from the previous bill in two key respects. First, it prescribed
criminal jurisdiction only where both the perpetrator and the victim
were U.S. nationals, whereas the original Thurmond bill would have
extended jurisdiction to all instances in which the victim was a U.S.
national (based on so-called "passive personality" jurisdiction[19]). Second, the revised legislation did not include the separate provision from
the earlier Thurmond legislation that would have amended the procedures for extradition. Congress enacted the revised legislation in 1994
as part of Public Law No. 103-322, and it was codified as section 1119
of title 18. *See* Pub. L. No. 103-322, § 60009, 108 Stat. 1796, 3972 (1994).

Thus, section 1119 was designed to close a jurisdictional
loophole—exposed by a murder that had been committed abroad by a
private individual—to ensure the possibility of prosecuting U.S. nationals who murdered other U.S. nationals in certain foreign countries that

---

[18] The Thurmond proposal also contained procedural limitations on prosecution virtually identical to these that Congress ultimately enacted and codified at 18
U.S.C. § 1119(c). *See* S. 861, 102d Cong. § 2.

[19] *See* Geoffrey R. Watson, *The Passive Personality Principle*, 28 Tex. Int'l. L.J.
1, 13 (1993); 137 Cong. Rec. 8677 (1991) (letter for Senator Ernest F. Hollings, from Janet G. Mullins, Assistant Secretary, Legislative Affairs, U.S. State Department (Dec.
26, 1989), submitted for the record during floor debate on the Thurmond bill) (S4752)
("The United States has generally taken the position that the exercise of extraterritorial criminal jurisdiction based solely on the nationality of the victim interferes
unduly with the application of local law by local authorities.").

lacked the ability to lawfully secure the perpetrator's appearance at trial. This loophole had nothing to do with the sort of ███████████ ████ CIA counterterrorism operation at issue here. Indeed, prior to the enactment of section 1119, the only federal statute expressly making it a crime to kill U.S. nationals abroad, at least outside the special and maritime jurisdiction of the United States, reflected what appears to have been a particular concern with protection of Americans from terrorist attacks. See 18 U.S.C. § 2332(a), (d) (criminalizing unlawful killings of U.S. nationals abroad where the Attorney General or his subordinate certifies that the "offense was intended to coerce, intimidate, or retaliate against a government or a civilian population").[20] It therefore would be anomalous to now read section 1119's closing of a limited jurisdictional gap as having been intended to jettison important applications of the established public authority justification, particularly in light of the statute's incorporation of substantive offenses codified in statutory provisions that from all indications were intended to incorporate recognized justifications and excuses.

| 12 |

It is true that here the target may be a U.S. citizen. Nevertheless, U.S. citizenship does not provide a basis for concluding that section 1119 would fail to incorporate the established public authority justification for a killing in this case. As explained above, section 1119 incorporates the federal murder and manslaughter statutes, and thus its prohibition extends only to "unlawful" killings, 18 U.S.C. §§ 1111, 1112, a category that was intended to include, from all of the evidence of legislative intent, only those killings that may not be permissible in light of traditional justifications for such action. At the time the predecessor versions of sections 1111 and 1112 were enacted, it was understood that killings undertaken in accord with the public authority justification were not "unlawful" because they were justified. There is no indication that, because section 1119(b) proscribes the unlawful killing abroad of U.S. nationals by U.S. nationals, it silently incorporated

---

[20] Courts have interpreted other federal homicide statutes to apply extraterritorially despite the absence of an express provision for extraterritorial application. See, e.g., 18 U.S.C. § 1114 (criminalizing unlawful killings of federal officers and employees); United States v. Al Kassar, 582 F. Supp. 2d 488, 497 (S.D.N.Y. 2008) (construing 18 U.S.C. § 1114 to apply extraterritorially).

all justifications for killings *except* that public authority justification. ███████████████████████

III.

Given that section 1119 incorporates the public authority justifi-cation, the next question is whether a potential CIA operation would be encompassed by that justification and, in particular, whether that justification would apply even when the target is a United States citi-zen. The analysis leads to the conclusion that it would—a conclusion that depends in part on the further determination that this kind of operation would accord with any potential constitutional protections of a United States citizen in these circumstances (*see infra* part VI). In reaching this conclusion, this white paper does not address other cir-cumstances involving different facts. The facts addressed here would be sufficient to establish the justification, whether or not any particular fact is necessary to the conclusion."[21] ████████████████

A.

The frame of reference here is that the United States is currently in the midst of an armed conflict, *see* Authorization for Use of Military Force ("AUMF"), Pub. L. No, 107-40, 115 Stat. 224, § 2(a) (2001), and the public authority justification would encompass an operation such as this one were it conducted by the military consistent with the laws of war. As one legal commentator has explained by example, "if a soldier intentionally kills an enemy combatant in time of war and within the rules of warfare, he is not guilty of murder," whereas, for example, if that soldier intentionally kills a prisoner of war—a violation of the laws of war—"then he commits murder," 2 LaFave, *Substantive Criminal Law* § 10.2(c), at 136; *see also State v. Gut*, 13 Minn. 341, 357 (1868) ("That it is legal to kill an alien enemy in the heat and exercise of war, is undeniable; but to kill such an enemy after he laid down his arms, and especially when he is confined in prison, is murder."): Perkins & Boyce, *Criminal Law* at 1093 ("Even in time of war an alien enemy may not be

---

[21] In light of the conclusion that section 1119 and the statutes it cross-references incorporate this justification, and that the justification would cover an operation of the sort discussed here, this discussion does not address whether other grounds might exist for concluding that such an operation would be lawful.

killed needlessly after he has been disarmed and securely imprisoned").[22]
Moreover, without invoking the public authority justification by terms,
OLC has relied on the same notion in an opinion addressing the intended scope of a federal criminal statute that concerned the use of possibly
lethal force. *See United States Assistance to Countries that Shoot Down
Civil Aircraft Involved in Drug Trafficking*, 18 Op. O.L.C. 148, 164 (1994)
(*"Shoot Down Opinion"*) (concluding that the Aircraft Sabotage Act of
1984, 18 U.S.C. § 32(b)(2), which prohibits the willful destruction of a
civil aircraft and otherwise applies to U.S. government conduct, should
not be construed to have "the surprising and almost certainly unintended effect of criminalizing actions by military personnel that are
lawful under international law and the laws of armed conflict").

As explained above, an operation of this sort would be targeted at a
senior leader al-Qaida or its associated forces who participated in operational planning for attempted attacks on the United States on behalf
of such forces and who continues to plan such attacks. *See supra* at 2.
Such an individual would have engaged in conduct bringing him within
the scope of the AUMF. Any military operation against such a person,
therefore, would be carried out against someone who is within the core
of individuals against whom Congress has authorized line use of necessary and appropriate force.

This sort operation would also be consistent with the laws of war
applicable, to a non-international armed conflict[23] if carried out by mili-

---

[22] *Cf. Public Committee Against Torture in Israel v. Government of Israel*, HCJ
769/02 ¶ 19, 46 L.L. M. 375, 382 (Israel Supreme Court sitting as the High Court of
Justice, 2006) ("When soldiers of the Israel Defense Forces act pursuant to the laws of
armed conflict, they are acting 'by law', and they have a good justification defense [to
criminal culpability]. However, if they act contrary to the laws of armed conflict they
may be, *inter alia*, criminally liable for their actions"); *Caller v. Callaway*, 519 F.2d
184, 193 (5th Cir. 1975) ("an order to kill unresisting Vietnamese would be an illegal
order, and . . . if [the defendant] knew the order was illegal or should have known it
was illegal, obedience to an order was not a legal defense").

[23] The rules of non-international armed conflict are relevant because the Supreme Court has held that the United States is engaged in a non-international armed
conflict with al-Qaida. *Hamdan v. Rumsfeld*, 548 U.S. 557, 628–31 (2006). Although
an operation of the kind discussed here would occur in Yemen, a location that is far
from the most active theater of combat between the United States and al-Qaida, that
does not affect the conclusion. There appears to be no authority for the proposition

14 tary personnel. Any military member responsible for such a strike
would likely have an obligation to abort a strike if he or she concluded
that civilian casualties would be disproportionate or that such a strike
would in any other respect violate the laws of war. *See* Chairman of the
Joint Chiefs of Staff, Instruction 5810.01D, *Implementation of the DoD
Law of War Program* ¶ 4.a. at 1 (Apr. 30, 2010) ("It is DOD policy that . . .
[m]embers of the DOD Components comply with the law of war during
all armed conflicts, however such conflicts are characterized, and in all
other military operations."). Moreover, the targeted nature of this sort
of operation would help to ensure that it would comply with the principle of distinction. *See, e.g.*, United States Air Force, *Targeting*, Air
Force Doctrine Document 2-1.9, at 88 (June 8, 2006) (explaining that
the "four fundamental principles that are inherent to all targeting decisions" are military necessity, humanity (the avoidance of unnecessary
suffering), proportionality, and distinction). Further, while such an
operation would be conducted without warning, it would not violate the
prohibitions on treachery and perfidy—which are addressed to conduct
involving a breach of confidence by the assailant. *See, e.g.*, Hague Convention IV, Annex, art. 23.3(b), 36 Stat, at 2301–02 ("[I]t is especially
forbidden . . . to kill or wound treacherously individuals belonging to
the hostile nation or army"); *cf. also* Protocol Additional to the Geneva

---

that when one of the parties to an armed conflict plans and executes operations from
a base in a new nation, an operation to engage the enemy in that location can never
be part of the original armed conflict—and thus subject to the laws of war governing that conflict—unless and until the hostilities become sufficiently intensive and
protracted within that new location. Nor is there any obvious reason why that more
categorical, nation-specific rule should govern in a non-international armed conflict.
Rather, the determination of whether a particular operation would be part of an ongoing armed conflict for purposes of international law requires consideration of the
particular facts and circumstances present in each case.

Here, any potential operation would target a senior leader of al-Qaida or its
associated forces. Moreover, such an operation would be conducted in Yemen, where
a co-belligerent of al-Qaida, engaged in hostilities against the United States as part
of the same comprehensive armed conflict and in league with the principal enemy,
has a significant and organized presence, and from which it is conducting terrorist
training in an organized manner and has executed and is planning to execute attacks
against the United States. Finally, the target of such an operation would be someone
continuously planning attacks from that Yemeni base of operations against the United States, as the conflict with al-Qaida continues. These facts in combination support
the judgment that this sort of operation in Yemen would be conducted as part of the
non-international armed conflict between the United States and al-Qaida.

Conventions of 12 August 1949, and Relating to the Protection of Victims of International Armed Conflicts, art. 37(1) (prohibiting the killing, injuring or capture of an adversary in an international armed conflict by resort to acts "inviting the confidence of [the] adversary . . . with intent to betray that confidence," including feigning a desire to negotiate under truce or flag of surrender; feigning incapacitation; and feigning noncombatant status).[24]

In light of all these circumstances, a military operation against the sort of individual described above would comply with international law, including the laws of war applicable to this armed conflict, and would fall within Congress's authorization to use "necessary and appropriate force" against al-Qaida. Consequently, the potential attack, if conducted under military authority in the manner described, should be understood to constitute the lawful conduct of war and thus to be encompassed by the public authority justification.

B.

Given the assessment that an analogous operation carried out pursuant to the AUMF would fall within the scope of the public authority justification, there is no reason to reach a different conclusion for a CIA operation.[25] As discussed above, such an operation would consist of an

15

---

[24] Although the United States is not a party to the First Protocol, the State Department has announced that "we support the principle that individual combatants not kill, injure, or capture enemy personnel by resort to perfidy." Remarks of Michael J. Matheson, Deputy Legal Adviser, Department of State, *The Sixth Annual American Red Cross-Washington College of Law Conference on International Humanitarian Law. A Workshop on Customary International Law and the 1977 Protocols Additional to the 1949 Geneva Conventions*, 2 Am. U. J. of Int'l L. & Pol'y 415, 425 (1987).

[25] The potential restrictions imposed by two other criminal laws—18 U.S.C. §§ 956(a) and 2441—are addressed in Parts IV and V of this white paper. Part VI explains why the Constitution would impose no bar to a potential CIA operation under these circumstances, based on the facts outlined above.

attack against an operational leader of the enemy force, as part of the United States's ongoing non-international armed conflict with al-Qaida.

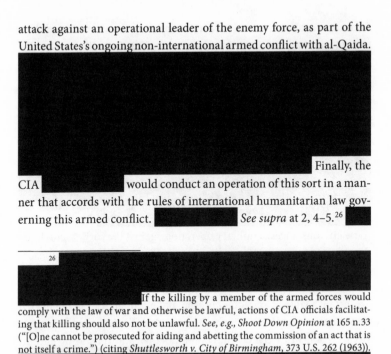

Finally, the CIA   would conduct an operation of this sort in a manner that accords with the rules of international humanitarian law governing this armed conflict.   *See supra* at 2, 4–5.[26]

---

[26]   If the killing by a member of the armed forces would comply with the law of war and otherwise be lawful, actions of CIA officials facilitating that killing should also not be unlawful. *See, e.g., Shoot Down Opinion* at 165 n.33 ("[O]ne cannot be prosecuted for aiding and abetting the commission of an act that is not itself a crime.") (citing *Shuttlesworth v. City of Birmingham*, 373 U.S. 262 (1963)).

Nor does the fact that CIA personnel would be involved in this sort of lethal operation itself cause it to violate the laws of war. It is true that CIA personnel, by virtue of their not being part of the armed forces, would not enjoy the immunity from prosecution under the domestic law of the countries in which they act for their conduct in targeting and killing enemy forces in compliance with the laws of war—an immunity that the armed forces enjoy by virtue of their status. *See* Philip Alston, *Report of the Special Rapporteur on extrajudicial, summary or arbitrary executions* ¶ 71, at 22 (United Nations Human Rights Council, Fourteenth Session, Agenda Item 3, May 28, 2010); *see also* Yoram Dinstein, *The Conduct of Hostilities Under the Law of International Armed Conflict* 31 (2004) ("*Conduct of Hostilities*"). Nevertheless, lethal activities conducted in accord with the laws of war, and undertaken in the course of lawfully authorized hostilities, do not violate *the laws of war* by virtue of the fact that they are carried out in part by government actors who are not entitled to the combatant's privilege. The contrary view "arises . . . from a fundamental confusion between acts punishable under international law and acts with respect to which international law affords no protection." Richard R. Baxter, *So-Called "Unprivileged Belligerency": Spies, Guerrillas, and Saboteurs*, 28 Brit. Y. B. Int'l L, 323, 342 (1951) ("the law of nations has not ventured to require of states that they . . . refrain from the use of secret agents or that these activities upon the part of their military forces or civilian population be punished"). *Accord* Yoram Dinstein, *The Distinction Between Unlawful Combatants and War Criminals*, in *International Law at a Time of Perplexity: Essays In*

Nothing in the text or legislative history of section 1119 indicates that Congress intended to criminalize such an operation. Section 1119 incorporates the traditional public authority justification, and did not impose any special limitation on the scope of that justification. As explained above, *supra* at 10–12, the legislative history of that criminal prohibition revealed Congress's intent to close a jurisdictional loophole that would have hindered prosecutions of murders carried out by private persons abroad. It offers no indication that Congress intended to prohibit the targeting of an enemy leader during an armed conflict in a manner that would accord with the laws of war when performed by a duly authorized government agency. Nor does it indicate that Congress,

---

Honour of Shabtai Rosenne 103–16 (Y. Dinstein ed. 1989). Statements in the Supreme Court's decision in *Ex parte Quirin*, 317 U.S. 1942, are sometimes cited for the contrary view. *See, e.g., id.* at 36 n.12 (suggesting that passing through enemy lines in order to commit "any hostile act" while not in uniform "renders the offender liable to trial for violation of the laws of war"); *id.* at 31 (enemies who come secretly through the lines for purposes of waging war by destruction of life or property "without uniform" not only are "generally not to be entitled to the status of prisoners of war," but also "to be offenders against the law of war subject to trial and punishment by military tribunals"). Because the Court in *Quirin* focused on conduct taken behind enemy lines, it is not clear whether the Court in these passages intended to refer only to conduct that would constitute perfidy or treachery. To the extent the Court meant to suggest more broadly that any hostile acts performed by unprivileged belligerents are *for that reason* violations of the law of war, the authorities the Court cited (the Lieber Code and Colonel Winthop's military law treatise) do not provide clear support. *See* John C. Dehn, *The Hamdan Case and the Application of a Municipal Offense*, 7 J. Int'l Crim. L. 63, 73–79 (2009); *see also* Baxter, *So-Called "Unprivileged Belligerency,"* 28 Brit. Y. B. Int'l L. at 339–40; Michael N. Schmitt, *Humanitarian Law and Direct Participation in Hostilities by Private Contractors or Civilian Employees*, 5 Chi. J. Int'l L. 511, 521 n.45 (2005); W. Hays Parks, *Special Forces Wear of Non-Standard Uniforms*, 4 Chi. J. Int'l L. 493, 510–11 n.31 (2003). DoD's current Manual for Military Commissions, however, does not endorse the view that the commission of an unprivileged belligerent act, without more, constitutes a violation of the international law of war. *See* Manual for Military Commissions, Part IV, § 5(13). Comment at IV–11 (2010 ed., Apr. 27, 2010) (murder or infliction of serious bodily injury "committed while the accused did not meet the requirements of privileged belligerency" can be tried by a military commission "even if such conduct does not violate the international law of war").

in closing the identified loophole, meant to place a limitation on the
CIA that would not apply to the armed forces.

[27] Thus, just as Congress would not have intended section
1119 to bar a military attack on the sort of individual described above,
neither would it have intended the provision to prohibit an attack on
the same target, in the same authorized conflict and in similar compliance with the laws of war, carried out by the CIA in accord with

Finally, there is no basis in prior OLC precedent for reaching a different conclusion. Outside the context of the use of deadly force, OLC has
had occasion to address whether particular criminal statutes should be
construed to criminalize otherwise authorized government activities,
notwithstanding the absence of an express exception to that effect. OLC's
opinions on such questions have not directly invoked the public authority justification, but they have engaged in the same basic, context-specific
inquiry concerning whether Congress intended the criminal statute at
issue to prohibit government activities in circumstances where the same

17

---

[27] As one example, the Senate Report pointed to the Department of Justice's
conclusion that the Neutrality Act, 18 U.S.C. § 960, prohibits conduct by private parties but is not applicable to the CIA and other government agencies. *Id.* The Senate
Report assumed that the Department's conclusion about the Neutrality Act was premised on the assertion that in the case of government agencies, there is an "absence of
the *mens rea* necessary to the offense." *Id.* In fact, however, the Department's conclusion about that Act was not based on questions of *mens rea*, but instead on a careful
analysis demonstrating that Congress did not intend the Act, despite its words of
general applicability, to apply to the activities of government officials acting within
the course and scope of their duties as officers of the United States. *See Application of
Neutrality Act to Official Government Activities*, 8 Op. O.L.C. 58 (1984).

conduct would be unlawful if performed by a private person. OLC concluded in one such opinion that a statutory prohibition on granting visas to aliens in sham marriages, 8 U.S.C. § 1201(g) (3), would not prohibit granting such a visa as part of an undercover operation. *Visa Fraud Investigation*, 8 Op. O.L.C. at 284. OLC explained that courts have recognized that it may be lawful for law enforcement agents to disregard otherwise applicable laws "when taking action that is necessary to attain the permissible law enforcement objective, when the action is carried out in a reasonable fashion." *Id.* at 287. The issuance of an otherwise unlawful visa that was necessary for the undercover operation to proceed, done in circumstances—"for a limited purpose and under close supervision"— that were "reasonable," did not violate the federal statute. *Id.* at 288. Given the combination of circumstances concerning such an operation, it plainly would meet this standard. *See also infra* at 19–22 (explaining that a CIA operation under the proposed circumstances would comply with constitutional due process and the Fourth Amendment's "reasonableness" test for the use of deadly force). ▮▮▮▮▮▮▮▮▮

Accordingly, the combination of circumstances present here supports the judgment that a CIA operation of this sort would be encompassed by the public authority justification. Such an operation, therefore, would not result in an "unlawful" killing under section 1111 and thus would not violate section 1119. ▮▮▮▮▮▮▮

IV.

For similar reasons, CIA operation of the kind discussed here, would not violate another federal criminal statute dealing with "murder" abroad, 18 U.S.C. § 956(a). That law makes it a crime to conspire within the jurisdiction of the United States "to commit at any place outside the United States an act that would constitute the offense of murder, kidnapping, or maiming if committed in the special maritime and territorial jurisdiction of the United States" if any conspirator acts within in the United States to effect any object of the conspiracy.

Like section 1119(b), section 956(a) bars only unlawful killings, and the United States' use of lethal force in national self-defense is not an unlawful killing. Section 956(a) incorporates by reference the understanding of "murder" in section 1111 of title 18. For reasons explained earlier in this white paper, *see supra* at 5–7, section 956(a) thus incorporates the traditional public authority justification that section 1111 recognizes. A CIA operation, on the facts outlined above, would be covered by that justification. Nor does Congress's reference in section 956(a) to "the special maritime and territorial jurisdiction of the United States" reflect an intent to transform such a killing into a "murder" in these circumstances—notwithstanding that the analysis of applicability of the public authority justification is limited for present purposes to operations conducted abroad. A contrary conclusion would require attributing to Congress the surprising intention of criminalizing through section 956(a) an otherwise lawful killing of an enemy leader that another statute specifically prohibiting the murder of U.S. nationals abroad does not prohibit. ████████████████

18   The legislative history of section 956(a) further confirms the conclusion that that statute should not be so construed. When the provision was first introduced in the Senate in 1995, its sponsors addressed and rejected the notion that the conspiracy prohibited by that section would apply to "duly authorized" actions undertaken on behalf of the federal government. Senator Biden introduced the provision at the behest of the President, as part of a larger package of anti-terrorism legislation. *See* 141 Cong. Rec. 4491 (1995) (statement of Sen. Biden). He explained that the provision was designed to "fill[] a void in the law," because section 956 at the time prohibited only U.S.-based conspiracies to commit certain property crimes abroad, and did not address crimes against persons. *Id.* at 4506. The amendment was designed to cover an offense "committed by terrorists" and was "intended to ensure that the government is able to punish those persons who use the United States as a base in which to plot such a crime to be carried out outside the jurisdiction of the United States." *Id.* Notably, the sponsors of the new legislation deliberately declined to place the new offense either within chapter 19 of title 18, which is devoted to "Conspiracy," or within chapter 51, which collects "Homicide" offenses (including those established in sections 1111, 1112, 1113 and 1119). Instead, as Senator Biden explained, "[s]ection 956 is contained in chapter 45 of title 18, United States Code, relating to interference with the foreign relations of the United States," and thus was intended to "cover[] those individuals who, without appropriate governmental authorization, engage in prohibited conduct

that is harmful to the foreign relations of the United States." *Id.* at 4507. Because, as Senator Biden explained, the provision was designed, like other provisions of chapter 45, to prevent private interference with U.S. foreign relations, "[i]t is not intended to apply to duly authorized actions undertaken on behalf of the United States Government." *Id.; see also* 8 Op. O.L.C. 58 (1984) (concluding that section 5 of the Neutrality Act, 18 U.S.C. § 960, which is also in chapter 45 and which forbids the planning of, or participation in, military or naval expedition to be carried on from the United States against a foreign state with which the United States is at peace, prohibits only persons acting in their private capacity from engaging in such conduct, and does not proscribe activities undertaken by government officials acting within the course and scope of their duties as United States officers). Senator Daschle expressed this same understanding when he introduced the identical provision in a different version of the anti-terrorism legislation a few months later. *See* 141 Cong. Rec. 11, 960 (1995) (statement of Sen. Daschle). Congress enacted the new section 956(a) the following year, as part of the Antiterrorism and Effective Death Penalty Act, Pub. L. No. 104–132, tit. VII, § 704(a), 110 Stat. 1214, 1294–95 (1996). The legislative history appears to contain nothing to contradict the construction of section 956(a) described by Senators Biden and Daschle.

Accordingly, section 956(a) would not prohibit an operation of the kind discussed here. █████████████████████████████████

V.

The War Crimes Act, 18 U.S.C. § 2441, which makes it a federal crime for a member of the Armed Forces or a national of the United States to "commit[] a war crime." *Id.* § 2441 (a). Subsection 2411(c) defines a "war crime" for purposes of the statute to mean any conduct (i) that is defined as a grave breach in any of the Geneva Conventions (or any Geneva protocol to which the U.S. is a party); (ii) that is prohibited by four specified articles of the Fourth Hague Convention of 1907; (iii) that is a "grave breach" of Common Article 3 of the Geneva Conventions (as defined elsewhere in section 2441) when committed "in the context of and in association with an armed conflict not of an international character"; or (iv) that is a willful killing or infliction of

19

serious injury in violation of the 1996 Protocol on Prohibitions or Restrictions on the Use of Mines, Booby-Traps and Other Devices. Of these, the only subsection potentially applicable here is that dealing with Common Article 3 of the Geneva Conventions.[28]

In defining what conduct constitutes a "grave breach" of Common Article 3 for purposes of the War Crimes Act, subsection 2441(d) includes "murder," described in pertinent part as "[t]he act of a person who intentionally kills, or conspires or attempts to kill . . . one or more persons taking no active part in the hostilities, including those placed out of combat by sickness, wounds, detention, or any other cause." 18 U.S.C. § 2441(d)(1)(D). This language derives from Common Article 3(1) itself, which prohibits certain acts (including murder) against "[p]ersons taking no active part in the hostilities, including members of armed forces who have laid down their arms and those placed 'hors de combat' by sickness, wounds, detention, or any other cause." See, e.g., Geneva Convention Relative to the Treatment of Prisoners of War, Aug. 12. 1949, [1955], art. 3(1). 6 U.S.T. 3316, 3318–20. Although Common Article 3 is most commonly applied with respect to persons within a belligerent party's control, such as detainees, the language of the article is not so limited—it protects all "[p]ersons taking no active part in the hostilities" in an armed conflict not of an international character.

Whatever might be the outer bounds of this category of covered persons, it could not encompass an individual of the sort considered here. Common Article 3 does not alter the fundamental law-of-war principle concerning a belligerent party's right in an armed conflict to target individuals who are part of an enemy's armed forces. The language of Common Article 3 "makes clear that members of such armed forces [of both the state and non-state parties to the conflict] . . . are considered as 'taking no active part in the hostilities only once they

---

[28] An operation of the kind in question here would not involve conduct covered by the Land Mine Protocol. And the articles of the Geneva Conventions to which the United States is currently a party other than Common Article 3, as well as the relevant provisions of the Annex to the Fourth Hague Convention, apply by their terms only to armed conflicts between two or more of the parties to the Conventions. See, e.g., Geneva Convention Relative to the Treatment of Prisoners of War, Aug. 12, 1949, [1955], art. 2, 6 U.S.T. 3316, 3406.

have disengaged from their fighting function ('have laid down their arms') or are placed *hors de combat*, mere suspension of combat is insufficient." International Committee of the Red Cross, *Interpretive Guidance on the Notion of Direct Participation in Hostilities Under International Humanitarian Law* 28 (2009); *cf. also id.* at 34 ("individuals whose continuous function involves the preparation, execution, or command of acts or operations amounting to direct participation in hostilities are assuming a continuous combat function," in which case they can be deemed to be members of a non-state armed group subject to continuous targeting); *accord Gherebi v. Obama*, 609 F. Supp. 2d 43, 65 (D.D.C. 2009) ("the fact that 'members of armed forces who have laid down their arms and those placed *hors de combat*' are not 'taking [an] active part in the hostilities' necessarily implies that 'members of armed forces' who have not surrendered or been incapacitated are 'taking [an] active part in the hostilities' simply by virtue of their membership in those armed forces"); *id.* at 67 ("Common Article 3 is not a suicide pact; it does not provide a free pass for the members of an enemy's armed forces to go to or fro as they please so long as, for example, shots are not fired, bombs are not exploded, and planes are not hijacked"). An active, high-level leader of an enemy force who is continually involved in planning and recruiting for terrorist attacks, can on that basis fairly be said to be taking "an active part in hostilities." Accordingly, targeting him in the circumstances discussed here would not violate Common Article 3 and therefore would not violate the War Crimes Act. ███████████

███████████

VI.

Although (as explained above) this sort of CIA operation would not violate sections 1119(b), 956(a) and 2441 of title 18 of the U.S. Code, the fact that such an operation may target a U.S. citizen could raise distinct questions under the Constitution. Nevertheless, on the facts outlined above, the Constitution would not preclude such a lethal action because of a target's U.S. citizenship. ███████████

The Fifth Amendment's Due Process Clause, as well as the Fourth Amendment, likely protects a U.S. citizen in some respects even while he is abroad. *See Reid v. Covert*, 354 U.S. 1, 5–6 (1957) (plurality opinion);

United States v. Verdugo-Urquidez, 494 U.S. 259, 269–70 (1990); *see also In re Terrorist Bombings of U.S. Embassies in East Africa*, 552 F.3d 157, 170 n.7 (2d Cir. 2008). The fact that a central figure in al-Qaida or its associated forces is a U.S. citizen, however, does not give that person constitutional immunity from attack. This conclusion finds support in Supreme Court case law addressing whether the military may constitutionally use certain types of military force against a U.S. citizen who is a part of enemy forces. *See Hamdi v. Rumsfeld*, 542 U.S. 507, 521–24 (2004) (plurality opinion): *Ex parte Quirin*, 317 U.S. 1, 37–38 (1942)).

In *Hamdi*, a plurality of the Supreme Court used the *Mathews v. Eldridge* balancing test to analyze the Fifth Amendment due process rights of a U.S. citizen captured on the battlefield in Afghanistan and detained in the United States who wished to challenge the assertion that he was a part of enemy forces, explaining that "the process due in any given instance is determined by weighing 'the private interest that will be affected by the official action' against the Government's asserted interest, 'including the function involved' and the burdens the Government would face in providing greater process." 542 U.S. at 529 (plurality opinion) (quoting *Mathews v. Eldridge*, 424 U.S. 319, 335 (1976)). Under this balancing test, at least in circumstances where the highest officers in the Intelligence Community have reviewed the factual basis for a lethal operation, and where the CIA has reviewed, and found infeasible, an operation to capture a targeted individual instead of killing him and continues to monitor whether changed circumstances would permit such an alternative, the Constitution does not require the government to provide further process to the U.S. person before using lethal force against him. *See Hamdi*, 542 U.S. at 534 (plurality opinion) ("[t]he parties agree that initial captures on the battlefield need not receive the process we discuss here; that process is due only when the determination is made to continue to hold those who have been seized"). On the battlefield, the Government's interests and burdens preclude offering a process to judge whether a detainee is truly an enemy combatant.

As explained above, such an operation would be carried out against an individual a decision-maker could reasonably decide poses a

"continued" and "imminent" ██████████████████████████████ ▢21
████████████████████ threat to the United States. Moreover, the CIA has represented that it would capture rather than target
an individual if feasible, but that such a capture operation in Yemen
would be infeasible at this time.

██
██
██
██
██████████████████████████████ *Cf., e.g., Public Committee Against Tor-*
ture in Israel v. Government of Israel, HCJ 769/02 ¶ 40, 46 I.L.M. 375,
394 (Israel Supreme Court sitting as the High Court of Justice, 2006)
(although arrest, investigation and trial "might actually be particularly
practical under the conditions of belligerent occupation, in which the
army controls the area in which the operation takes place," such alternatives "are not means which can always be used," either because they
are impossible or because they involve great risk to the lives of soldiers).
████████████████████████████

Although in the "circumstances of war," as the *Hamdi* plurality
observed, "the risk of erroneous deprivation of a citizen's liberty in the
absence of sufficient process . . . is very real," 542 U.S. at 530, the plurality also recognized that "the realities of combat" render certain uses of
force "necessary and appropriate," including against U.S. citizens who
have become part of enemy forces—and that "due process analysis need
not blink at those realities," *id.* at 531. Thus, at least where, as here, the
target's activities pose a "continued and imminent threat of violence or
death" to U.S. persons, the highest officers in the Intelligence Community have reviewed the factual basis for a lethal operation, and a capture
operation would be infeasible—and where the CIA continues to monitor whether changed circumstances would permit such an alternative—
the "realities of combat" and the weight of the government's interest in
using an authorized means of lethal force against this enemy are such
that the Constitution would not require the government to provide further process to the U.S. person before using such force. *Cf. Hamdi* 542

U.S. at 535 (noting that Court "accord[s] the greatest respect and consideration to the judgments of military authorities in matters relating to the actual prosecution of war, and . . . the scope of that discretion necessarily is wide") (plurality opinion). █████████████

Similarly, even assuming the Fourth Amendment provides some protection to a U.S. person abroad who is part of al-Qaida and that the sort of operation discussed here would result in a "seizure" within the meaning of that Amendment, such a lethal operation would not violate the Fourth Amendment. The Supreme Court has made clear that the constitutionality of a seizure is determined by "balanc[ing] the nature and quality of the intrusion on the individual's Fourth Amendment interests against the importance of the governmental interests alleged to justify the intrusion." *Tennessee v. Garner*, 471 U.S. 1, 8 (1985) (internal quotation marks omitted), *accord Scott v. Harris*, 550 U.S. 372, 383 (2007). Even in domestic law enforcement operations, the Court has noted that "[w]here the officer has probable cause to believe that the suspect poses a threat of serious physical harm either to the officer or to others, it is not constitutionally unreasonable to prevent escape by using deadly force." *Garner*, 471 U.S. at 11. Thus, "if the suspect threatens the officer with a weapon or there is probable cause to believe that he has committed a crime involving the infliction or threatened infliction of serious physical harm, deadly force may be used if necessary to prevent escape and if, where feasible, some warning has been given." *Id.* at 11–12. ██████████████

The Fourth Amendment "reasonableness" test is situation-dependent. *Cf. Scott*, 550 U.S. at 382 (Garner "did not establish a magical on/off switch that triggers rigid preconditions whenever an officer's actions constitute 'deadly force'"). What would constitute a reasonable use of lethal force for purposes of domestic law enforcement operations will be very different from what would be reasonable in the situation discussed here. At least where high-level government officials have determined that a capture operation overseas is infeasible and that the targeted person is part of a dangerous enemy force and is engaged in activities that pose a continued and imminent threat to U.S. persons or interests ████████████████████████ the use of lethal force would not violate the Fourth Amendment. Here, the intrusion on any Fourth Amendment interests

[22]

would be outweighed by "the importance of the governmental interests [that] justify the intrusion," *Garner*, 471 U.S. at 8, based on the facts outlined above.

5

Remarks of John O. Brennan, Assistant to
the President for Homeland Security and
Counterterrorism

Harvard Law School, Cambridge,
Massachusetts

September 16, 2011

"Strengthening Our Security by Adhering to Our Values and Laws"

John Brennan, who served as President Obama's chief counterterrorism
adviser from 2009 until 2013, and then as director of the CIA, was
reportedly the chief architect of the administration's targeted-killing
policies. In this speech, Brennan discusses, among other things, the geographic scope of the armed conflict against al-Qaeda and the breadth
of the U.S. government's authority to carry out strikes beyond "hot"
battlefields. Brennan argues here that the government has the authority
to use lethal force even in response to threats that are not "imminent"
in the conventional sense of the word.

The document from which this text was transcribed is posted at:
www.ACLU.org/TDM/BrennanSpeech1.

Good evening. Thank you, Dan, for your very kind introduction and for your service to our nation, in both the judicial and executive branches.* At the White House, Dan helped us navigate some of the most complex legal issues related to our efforts to keep the American people safe. I know that President Obama is grateful for his service. And I am grateful for having had the opportunity to sit through his many law tutorials during national security meetings in the White House Situation Room. I dare say that those tutorials were a tad less expensive than what some of you currently are paying for his pearls of wisdom.

* * *

Now, I am not a lawyer, despite Dan's best efforts. I am the President's senior advisor on counterterrorism and homeland security. And in this capacity—and during more than thirty years working in intelligence and on behalf of our nation's security—I've developed a profound appreciation for the role that our values, especially the rule of law, play in keeping our country safe. It's an appreciation of course, understood by President Obama, who, as you may know, once spent a little time here. That's what I want to talk about this evening—how we have strengthened, and continue to strengthen, our national security by adhering to our values and our laws.

Obviously, the death of Usama Bin Laden marked a strategic milestone in our effort to defeat al-Qa'ida. Unfortunately, Bin Laden's death, and the death and capture of many other al-Qa'ida leaders and operatives, does not mark the end of that terrorist organization or its efforts to attack the United States and other countries. Indeed, al-Qa'ida, its affiliates and its adherents remain the preeminent security threat to our nation.

The core of al-Qa'ida—its leadership based in Pakistan—though severely crippled, still retains the intent and capability to attack the United States and our allies. Al-Qa'ida's affiliates—in places like Pakistan, Yemen, and countries throughout Africa—carry out its murderous agenda. And al-Qa'ida adherents—individuals, sometimes with little or no contact with the group itself—have succumbed to its hateful

---

* [Ed.: Brennan was introduced by Daniel Julius Meltzer, a Harvard Law School professor who served as principal deputy counsel to President Obama from January 2009 to June 2010.]

ideology and work to facilitate or conduct attacks here in the United States, as we saw in the tragedy at Fort Hood.

Guiding principles
In the face of this ongoing and evolving threat, the Obama Administration has worked to establish a counterterrorism framework that has been effective in enhancing the security of our nation. This framework is guided by several core principles.

First, our highest priority is—and always will be—the safety and security of the American people. As President Obama has said, we have no greater responsibility as a government.

Second, we will use every lawful tool and authority at our disposal. No single agency or department has sole responsibility for this fight because no single department or agency possesses all the capabilities needed for this fight.

Third, we are pragmatic, not rigid or ideological—making decisions not based on preconceived notions about which action seems "stronger," but based on what will actually enhance the security of this country and the safety of the American people. We address each threat and each circumstance in a way that best serves our national security interests, which includes building partnerships with countries around the world.

Fourth—and the principle that guides all our actions, foreign and domestic—we will uphold the core values that define us as Americans, and that includes adhering to the rule of law. And when I say "all our actions," that includes covert actions, which we undertake under the authorities provided to us by Congress. President Obama has directed that all our actions—even when conducted out of public view—remain consistent with our laws and values.

For when we uphold the rule of law, governments around the globe are more likely to provide us with intelligence we need to disrupt ongoing plots, they're more likely to join us in taking swift and decisive action against terrorists, and they're more likely to turn over suspected terrorists who are plotting to attack us, along with the evidence needed to prosecute them.

When we uphold the rule of law, our counterterrorism tools are more likely to withstand the scrutiny of our courts, our allies, and the American people. And when we uphold the rule of law it provides a powerful alternative to the twisted worldview offered by al-Qa'ida. Where terrorists offer injustice, disorder and destruction, the United States and its allies stand for freedom, fairness, equality, hope, and opportunity.

In short, we must not cut corners by setting aside our values and flouting our laws, treating them like luxuries we cannot afford. Indeed, President Obama has made it clear—we must reject the false choice between our values and our security. We are constantly working to optimize both. Over the past two and a half years, we have put in place an approach—both here at home and abroad—that will enable this Administration and its successors, in cooperation with key partners overseas, to deal with the threat from al-Qa'ida, its affiliates, and its adherents in a forceful, effective and lasting way.

In keeping with our guiding principles, the President's approach has been pragmatic—neither a wholesale overhaul nor a wholesale retention of past practices. Where the methods and tactics of the previous administration have proven effective and enhanced our security, we have maintained them. Where they did not, we have taken concrete steps to get us back on course.

Unfortunately, much of the debate around our counterterrorism policies has tended to obscure the extraordinary progress of the past few years. So with the time I have left, I want to touch on a few specific topics that illustrate how our adherence to the rule of law advances our national security.

Nature and geographic scope of the conflict

First, our definition of the conflict. As the President has said many times, we are at war with al-Qa'ida. In an indisputable act of aggression, al-Qa'ida attacked our nation and killed nearly 3,000 innocent people. And as we were reminded just last weekend, al-Qa'ida seeks to attack us again. Our ongoing armed conflict with al-Qa'ida stems from our right—recognized under international law—to self defense.

An area in which there is some disagreement is the geographic scope of the conflict. The United States does not view our authority to use military force against al-Qa'ida as being restricted solely to "hot" battlefields like Afghanistan. Because we are engaged in an armed conflict with al-Qa'ida, the United States takes the legal position that—in accordance with international law—we have the authority to take action against al-Qa'ida and its associated forces without doing a separate self-defense analysis each time. And as President Obama has stated on numerous occasions, we reserve the right to take unilateral action if or when other governments are unwilling or unable to take the necessary actions themselves.

That does not mean we can use military force whenever we want, wherever we want. International legal principles, including respect for a state's sovereignty and the laws of war, impose important constraints on our ability to act unilaterally—and on the way in which we can use force—in foreign territories.

Others in the international community—including some of our closest allies and partners—take a different view of the geographic scope of the conflict, limiting it only to the "hot" battlefields. As such, they argue that, outside of these two active theatres, the United States can only act in self-defense against al-Qa'ida when they are planning, engaging in, or threatening an armed attack against U.S. interests if it amounts to an "imminent" threat.

In practice, the U.S. approach to targeting in the conflict with al-Qa'ida is far more aligned with our allies' approach than many assume. This Administration's counterterrorism efforts outside of Afghanistan and Iraq are focused on those individuals who are a threat to the United States, whose removal would cause a significant—even if only temporary—disruption of the plans and capabilities of al-Qa'ida and its associated forces. Practically speaking, then, the question turns principally on how you define "imminence."

We are finding increasing recognition in the international community that a more flexible understanding of "imminence" may be appropriate when dealing with terrorist groups, in part because threats posed by non-state actors do not present themselves in the ways that evidenced imminence in more traditional conflicts. After all, al-Qa'ida does not follow a traditional command structure, wear uniforms, carry its arms openly, or mass its troops at the borders of the nations it attacks. Nonetheless, it possesses the demonstrated capability to strike with little notice and cause significant civilian or military casualties. Over time, an increasing number of our international counterterrorism partners have begun to recognize that the traditional conception of what constitutes an "imminent" attack should be broadened in light of the modern-day capabilities, techniques, and technological innovations of terrorist organizations.

The convergence of our legal views with those of our international partners matters. The effectiveness of our counterterrorism activities depends on the assistance and cooperation of our allies—who, in ways public and private, take great risks to aid us in this fight. But their participation must be consistent with their laws, including their interpretation of international law. Again, we will never abdicate the security of the United States to a foreign country or refrain from taking action when appropriate. But we cannot ignore the reality that cooperative counterterrorism activities are a key to our national defense. The more our views and our allies' views on these questions converge, without constraining our flexibility, the safer we will be as a country.

* * *

As a people, as a nation, we cannot—and we must not—succumb to the temptation to set aside our laws and our values when we face threats to our security, including and especially from groups as depraved as al-Qa'ida. We're better than that. We're better than them. We're Americans.

Thank you all very much.

6

Justice Department White Paper

November 8, 2011

"Lawfulness of a Lethal Operation Directed Against a U.S. Citizen Who Is a Senior Operational Leader of Al-Qa'ida or an Associated Force"

The Justice Department shared this unclassified white paper with the Senate and House Judiciary Committees in June 2012. It was leaked to journalist Michael Isikoff and published by *Newsweek* on February 4, 2013, as the Senate was about to consider President Obama's nomination of John Brennan to the post of CIA director. (The government later released the document officially in response to a FOIA request filed by the journalist Jason Leopold.) The disclosure of the document in February 2013 provided the public with the first detailed look at some of the legal reasoning underlying the government's targeted-killing policies.

The document from which this text was transcribed is posted at: www.ACLU.org/TDM/WhitePaper2.

This white paper sets forth a legal framework for considering the circumstances in which the U.S. government could use lethal force in a foreign country outside the area of active hostilities against a U.S. citizen who is a senior operational leader of al-Qa'ida or an associated force[1] of al-Qa'ida—that is, an al-Qa'ida leader actively engaged in planning operations to kill Americans. The paper does not attempt to determine the minimum requirements necessary to render such an operation lawful; nor does it assess what might be required to render a lethal operation against a U.S. citizen lawful in other circumstances, including an operation against enemy forces on a traditional battlefield or an operation against a U.S. citizen who is not a senior operational leader of such forces. Here the Department of Justice concludes only that where the following three conditions are met, a U.S. operation using lethal force in a foreign country against a U.S. citizen who is a senior operational leader of al-Qa'ida or an associated force would be lawful: (1) an informed, high-level official of the U.S. government has determined that the targeted individual poses an imminent threat of violent attack against the United States; (2) capture is infeasible, and the United States continues to monitor whether capture becomes feasible; and (3) the operation would be conducted in a manner consistent with applicable law of war principles. This conclusion is reached with recognition of the extraordinary seriousness of a lethal operation by the United States against a U.S. citizen, and also of the extraordinary seriousness of the threat posed by senior operational al-Qa'ida members and the loss of life that would result were their operations successful.

The President has authority to respond to the imminent threat posed by al-Qa'ida and its associated forces, arising from his constitutional responsibility to protect the country, the inherent right of the United States to national self defense under international law, Congress's authorization of the use of all necessary and appropriate military force against this enemy, and the existence of an armed conflict with al-Qa'ida under international law. Based on these authorities, the President may use force against al-Qa'ida and its associated forces. As

---

[1] An associated force of al-Qa'ida includes a group that would qualify as a co-belligerent under the laws of war. *See Hamlily v. Obama*, 616 F. Supp. 2d 63, 74–75 (D.D.C. 2009) (authority to detain extends to "'associated forces,'" which "mean 'co-belligerents' as that term is understood under the laws of war").

detailed in this white paper, in defined circumstances, a targeted killing of a U.S. citizen who has joined al-Qa'ida or its associated forces would be lawful under U.S. and international law. Targeting a member of an enemy force who poses an imminent threat of violent attack to the United States is not unlawful. It is a lawful act of national self defense. Nor would it violate otherwise applicable federal laws barring unlawful killings in Title 18 or the assassination ban in Executive Order No. 12333. Moreover, a lethal operation in a foreign nation would be consistent with international legal principles of sovereignty and neutrality if it were conducted, for example, with the consent of the host nation's government or after a determination that the host nation is unable or unwilling to suppress the threat posed by the individual targeted.   2

Were the target of a lethal operation a U.S. citizen who may have rights under the Due Process Clause and the Fourth Amendment, that individual's citizenship would not immunize him from a lethal operation. Under the traditional due process balancing analysis of *Mathews v. Eldridge*, we recognize that there is no private interest more weighty than a person's interest in his life. But that interest must be balanced against the United States' interest in forestalling the threat of violence and death to other Americans that arises from an individual who is a senior operational leader of al-Q'aida or an associated force of al-Q'aida and who is engaged in plotting against the United States.

The paper begins with a brief summary of the authority for the use of force in the situation described here, including the authority to target a U.S. citizen having the characteristics described above with lethal force outside the area of active hostilities. It continues with the constitutional questions, considering first whether a lethal operation against such a U.S. citizen would be consistent with the Fifth Amendment's Due Process Clause, U.S. Const, amend. V. As part of the due process analysis, the paper explains the concepts of "imminence," feasibility of capture, and compliance with applicable law of war principles. The paper then discusses whether such an operation would be consistent with the Fourth Amendment's prohibition on unreasonable seizures, U.S. Const. amend. IV. It concludes that where certain conditions are met, a lethal operation against a U.S. citizen who is a senior operational leader of al-Qa'ida or its associated forces—a terrorist organization engaged in constant plotting against the United States, as well as an

enemy force with which the United States is in a congressionally authorized armed conflict—and who himself poses an imminent threat of
violent attack against the United States, would not violate the Constitution. The paper also includes an analysis concluding that such an operation would not violate certain criminal provisions prohibiting the killing of U.S. nationals outside the United States; nor would it constitute
either the commission of a war crime or an assassination prohibited by
Executive Order 12333.

I.

The United States is in an armed conflict with al-Qa'ida and its associated forces, and Congress has authorized the President to use all necessary and appropriate force against those entities. *See* Authorization
for Use of Military Force ("AUMF"), Pub. L. No. 107-40, § 2(a), 115 Stat.
224, 224 (2001). In addition to the authority arising from the AUMF,
the President's use of force against al-Qa'ida and associated forces is
lawful under other principles of U.S. and international law, including
the President's constitutional responsibility to protect the nation and
the inherent right to national self-defense recognized in international
law *(see, e.g.,* U.N. Charter art. 51). It was on these bases that the United States responded to the attacks of September 11, 2001, and "[t]hese
domestic and international legal authorities continue to this day." Harold Hongju Koh, Legal Adviser, U.S. Department of State, Address to
the Annual Meeting of the American Society of International Law: The
Obama Administration and International Law (Mar. 25, 2010) ("2010
Koh ASIL Speech").

Any operation of the sort discussed here would be conducted in a
foreign country against a senior operational leader of al-Qa'ida or its
associated forces who poses an imminent threat of violent attack against
the United States. A use of force under such circumstances would be
justified as an act of national self-defense. In addition, such a person
would be within the core of individuals against whom Congress has
authorized the use of necessary and appropriate force. The fact that
such a person would also be a U.S. citizen would not alter this conclusion. The Supreme Court has held that the military may constitutionally
use force against a U.S. citizen who is a part of enemy forces. *See Hamdi,*
542 U.S. 507, 518 (2004) (plurality opinion); *id.* at 587, 597 (Thomas, J.,

dissenting); *Ex Parte Quirin*, 317 U.S. at 37–38. Like the imposition of military detention, the use of lethal force against such enemy forces is an "important incident of war." *Hamdi*, 542 U.S. at 518 (plurality opinion) (quotation omitted). *See, e.g.*, General Orders No. 100: *Instructions for the Government of Armies of the United States in the Field* ¶ 15 (Apr. 24, 1863) ("[m]ilitary necessity admits of all direct destruction of life or limb of armed enemies") (emphasis omitted); International Committee of the Red Cross, *Commentary on the Additional Protocols of 8 June 1977 to the Geneva Conventions of 12 Aug. 1949 and Relating to the Protection of Victims of Non-International Armed Conflicts* (Additional Protocol II) § 4789 (1987) ("Those who belong to armed forces or armed groups may be attacked at any time."); Yoram Dinstein, *The Conduct of Hostilities Under the Law of International Armed Conflict* 94 (2004) ("When a person takes up arms or merely dons a uniform as a member of the armed forces, he automatically exposes himself to enemy attack."). Accordingly, the Department does not believe that U.S. citizenship would immunize a senior operational leader of al-Qa'ida or its associated forces from a use of force abroad authorized by the AUMF or in national self-defense.

In addition, the United States retains its authority to use force against al-Qa'ida and associated forces outside the area of active hostilities when it targets a senior operational leader of the enemy forces who is actively engaged in planning operations to kill Americans. The United States is currently in a non-international armed conflict with al-Qa'ida and its associated forces. *See Hamdan v. Rumsfeld*, 548 U.S. 557, 628–31 (2006) (holding that a conflict between a nation and a transnational non-state actor, occurring outside the nation's territory, is an armed conflict "not of an international character" (quoting Common Article 3 of the Geneva Conventions) because it is not a "clash between nations"). Any U.S. operation would be part of this non-international armed conflict, even if it were to take place away from the zone of active hostilities. *See* John O. Brennan, Assistant to the President for Homeland Security and Counterterrorism, Remarks at the Program on Law and Security, Harvard Law School: Strengthening Our Security by Adhering to Our Values and Laws (Sept. 16, 2011) ("The United States does not view our authority to use military force against al-Qa'ida as being restricted solely to 'hot' battlefields like Afghanistan."). For example, the AUMF itself does not set forth an express geographic limitation on the use of force it authorizes. *See Hamdan*, 548 U.S. at 631 (Kennedy, J., concurring) (what makes a non-international armed conflict distinct from an international armed conflict is "the legal status of the entities opposing each other"). None of the three branches of the U.S. Government has identified a strict geographical limit on the permissible scope of the AUMF's authorization. *See, e.g.,* Letter for the Speaker of the House of Representatives and the President Pro Tempore of the Senate from the President (June 15, 2010) (reporting that the armed forces, with the assistance of numerous international partners, continue to conduct operations "against al-Qa'ida terrorists," and that the United States has "deployed combat-equipped forces to a number of locations in the U.S. Central . . . Command area[] of operation in support of those [overseas counter-terrorist] operations"); *Bensayah v. Obama*, 610 F.3d 718, 720, 724–25, 727 (D.C. Cir. 2010) (concluding that an individual turned over to the United States in Bosnia could be detained if the government demonstrates he was part of al-Qa'ida); *al-Adahi v. Obama*, 613 F.3d 1102, 1003, 1111 (D.C. Cir. 2010) (noting authority under AUMF to detain individual apprehended by Pakistani authorities in Pakistan and then transferred to U.S. custody).

Claiming that for purposes of international law, an armed conflict generally exists only when there is "protracted armed violence between governmental authorities and organized armed groups," *Prosecutor v. Tadic*, Case No. IT-94-1 AR72, Decision on the Defence Motion for Interlocutory Appeal on Jurisdiction, ¶ 70 (Int'l Crim. Trib. for the Former Yugoslavia, App. Chamber Oct. 2, 1995), some commenters have suggested that the conflict between the United States and al-Qa'ida cannot lawfully extend to nations outside Afghanistan in which the level of hostilities is less intense or prolonged than in Afghanistan itself. *See, e.g.,* Mary Ellen O'Connell, *Combatants and the Combat Zone*, 43 U. Rich. L. Rev. 845, 857–59 (2009). There is little judicial or other authoritative precedent that speaks directly to the question of the geographic scope of a non-international armed conflict in which one of the parties is a transnational, non-state actor and where the principal theater of operations is not within the territory of the nation that is a party to the conflict. Thus, in considering this potential issue, the Department looks to principles and statements from analogous contexts.

The Department has not found any authority for the proposition that when one of the parties to an armed conflict plans and executes operations from a base in a new nation, an operation to engage the enemy in that location cannot be part of the original armed conflict, and thus subject to the laws of war governing that conflict, unless the hostilities become sufficiently intense and protracted in the new location. That does not appear to be the rule of the historical practice, for instance, even in a traditional international conflict. *See* John R. Stevenson, Legal Adviser, Department of State, United States Military Action in Cambodia: Questions of International Law, Address before the Hammarskjold Forum of the Association of the Bar of the City of New York (May 28, 1970), *in* 3 *The Vietnam War and International Law: The Widening Context* 23, 28–30 (Richard A. Falk, ed. 1972) (arguing that in an international armed conflict, if a neutral state has been unable for any reason to prevent violations of its neutrality by the troops of one belligerent using its territory as a base of operations, the other belligerent has historically been justified in attacking those enemy forces in that state). Particularly in a non-international armed conflict, where terrorist organizations may move their base of operations from one country to another, the determination of whether a particular operation would be part of an ongoing armed conflict would require consideration of the particular facts and circumstances in each case, including the fact that transnational non-state organizations such as al-Qa'ida may have no single site serving as their base of operations. *See also, e.g.*, Geoffrey S. Com & Eric Talbot Jensen, *Untying the Gordian Knot: A Proposal for Determining Applicability of the Laws of War to the War on Terror*, 81 Temp. L. Rev. 787, 799 (2008) ("If . . . the ultimate purpose of the drafters of the Geneva Conventions was to prevent 'law avoidance' by developing de facto law triggers—a purpose consistent with the humanitarian foundation of the treaties—then the myopic focus on the geographic nature of an armed conflict in the context of transnational counterterrorist combat operations serves to frustrate that purpose.").[2]

5

---

[2] *See Prosecutor v. Tadic*, Case No. IT-94-1 AR72, Submission of the Government of the United States of America Concerning Certain Arguments Made by Counsel for the Accused, at 27–28 (Int'l Crim. Trib. For the Former Yugoslavia, App. Chamber July 17, 1995) (in determining which body of law applies in a particular conflict, "the conflict must be considered as a whole," and "it is artificial and

If an operation of the kind discussed in this paper were to occur in a location where al-Qa'ida or an associated force has a significant and organized presence and from which al-Qa'ida or an associated force, including its senior operational leaders, plan attacks against U.S. persons and interests, the operation would be part of the non-international armed conflict between the United States and al-Qa'ida that the Supreme Court recognized in *Hamdan*. Moreover, such an operation would be consistent with international legal principles of sovereignty and neutrality if it were conducted, for example, with the consent of the host nation's government or after a determination that the host nation is unable or unwilling to suppress the threat posed by the individual targeted. In such circumstances, targeting a U.S. citizen of the kind described in this paper would be authorized under the AUMF and the inherent right to national self-defense. Given this authority, the question becomes whether and what further restrictions may limit its exercise.

II.

The Department assumes that the rights afforded by Fifth Amendment's Due Process Clause, as well as the Fourth Amendment, attach to a U.S. citizen even while he is abroad. *See Reid v. Covert*, 354 U.S. 1, 5–6 (1957) (plurality opinion); *United States v. Verdugo-Urquidez*, 494 U.S. 259, 269–70 (1990); *see also In re Terrorist Bombings of U.S. Embassies in East Africa*, 552 F.3d 157, 170 n.7 (2d Cir. 2008). The U.S. citizenship of a leader of al-Qa'ida or its associated forces, however, does not give that person constitutional immunity from attack. This paper next considers whether and in what circumstances a lethal operation would violate any possible constitutional protections of a U.S. citizen.

A.

The Due Process Clause would not prohibit a lethal operation of the sort contemplated here. In *Hamdi*, a plurality of the Supreme Court used the *Mathews v. Eldridge* balancing test to analyze the Fifth Amendment due process rights of a U.S. citizen who had been captured on the battlefield

---

improper to attempt to divide it into isolated segments, either geographically or chronologically").

in Afghanistan and detained in the United States, and who wished to challenge the government's assertion that he was part of enemy forces. The Court explained that the "process due in any given instance is determined by weighing 'the private interest that will be affected by the official action against the Government's asserted interest, 'including the function involved' and the burdens the Government would face in providing greater process." *Hamdi*, 542 U.S. at 529 (plurality opinion) (quoting *Mathews v. Eldridge*, 424 U.S. 319, 335 (1976)). The due process balancing analysis applied to determine the Fifth Amendment rights of a U.S. citizen with respect to law-of-war detention supplies the framework for assessing the process due a U.S. citizen who is a senior operational leader of an enemy force planning violent attacks against Americans before he is subjected to lethal targeting.

In the circumstances considered here, the interests on both sides would be weighty. *See Hamdi*, 542 U.S. at 529 (plurality opinion) ("It is beyond question that substantial interests lie on both sides of the scale in this case."). An individual's interest in avoiding erroneous deprivation of his life is "uniquely compelling." *See Ake v. Oklahoma*, 470 U.S. 68, 178 (1985) ("The private interest in the accuracy of a criminal proceeding that places an individual's life or liberty at risk is almost uniquely compelling."). No private interest is more substantial. At the same time, the government's interest in waging war, protecting its citizens, and removing the threat posed by members of enemy forces is also compelling. *Cf Hamdi*, 542 U.S. at 531 (plurality opinion) ("On the other side of the scale are the weighty and sensitive governmental interests in ensuring that those who have in fact fought with the enemy during a war do not return to battle against the United States."). As the *Hamdi* plurality observed, in the "circumstances of war," "the risk of erroneous deprivation of a citizen's liberty in the absence of sufficient process . . . is very real," *id*. at 530 (plurality opinion), and, of course, the risk of an erroneous deprivation of a citizen's life is even more significant. But, "the realities of combat" render certain uses of force "necessary and appropriate," including force against U.S. citizens who have joined enemy forces in the armed conflict against the United States and whose activities pose an imminent threat of violent attack against the United States—and "due process analysis need not blink at those realities." *Id*. at 531 (plurality opinion). These same realities must also be considered in assessing "the burdens the Government would face in providing greater process" to a member of enemy forces. *Id*. at 529, 531 (plurality opinion).

In view of these interests and practical considerations, the United States would be able to use lethal force against a U.S. citizen, who is located outside the United States and is an operational leader continually planning attacks against U.S. persons and interests, in at least the following circumstances: (1) where an informed, high-level official of the U.S. government has determined that the targeted individual poses an imminent threat of violent attack against the United States; (2) where a capture operation would be infeasible—and where those conducting the operation continue to monitor whether capture becomes feasible; and (3) where such an operation would be conducted consistent with applicable law of war principles. In these circumstances, the "realities" of the conflict and the weight of the government's interest in protecting its citizens from an imminent attack are such that the Constitution would not require the government to provide further process to such a U.S. citizen before using lethal force. *Cf. Hamdi*, 542 U.S. at 535 (plurality opinion) (noting that the Court "accord[s] the greatest respect and consideration to the judgments of military authorities in matters relating to the actual prosecution of war, and . . . the scope of that discretion necessarily is wide"); *id*. at 534 (plurality opinion) ("The parties agree that initial captures on the battlefield need not receive the process we have discussed here; that process is due only when the determination is made to continue to hold those who have been seized.") (emphasis omitted).

Certain aspects of this legal framework require additional explication. *First*, the condition that an operational leader present an "imminent" threat of violent attack against the United States does not require the United States to have clear evidence that a specific attack on U.S. persons and interests will take place in the immediate future. Given the nature of, for example, the terrorist attacks on September 11, in which civilian airliners were hijacked to strike the World Trade Center and the Pentagon, this definition of imminence, which would require the United States to refrain from action until preparations for an attack are concluded, would not allow the United States sufficient time to defend itself. The defensive options available to the United States may be reduced or eliminated if al-Qa'ida operatives disappear and cannot be found when the time of their attack approaches. Consequently, with respect to al-Qa'ida leaders who are continually planning attacks, the United States is likely to have only a limited window of opportunity within which to defend Americans in a manner that has both a high likelihood of success and sufficiently reduces the probabilities of civilian causalities. *See* Michael N. Schmitt, *State-Sponsored Assassination in International and Domestic Law*, 17 Yale J. Int'l L. 609, 648 (1992). Furthermore, a "terrorist 'war' does not consist of a massive attack across an international border, nor does it consist of one isolated incident that occurs and is then past. It is a drawn out, patient, sporadic pattern of attacks. It is very difficult to know when or where the next incident will occur." Gregory M. Travalio, *Terrorism, International Law, and the Use of Military Force*, 18 Wis. Int'l L.J. 145, 173 (2000); *see also* Testimony of Attorney-General Lord Goldsmith, 660 Hansard. H.L. (April 21, 2004) 370 (U.K.), *available at* http://www.publications. parliament.uk/pa/ld200304/ldhansrd/vo040421/text/40421-07.htm (what constitutes an imminent threat "will develop to meet new circumstances and new threats. . . . It must be right that states are able to act in self-defense in circumstances where there is evidence of further imminent attacks by terrorist groups, even if there is no specific evidence of where such an attack will take place or of the precise nature of the attack."). Delaying action against individuals continually planning to kill Americans until some theoretical end stage of the planning for a particular plot would create an unacceptably high risk that the action would fail and that American casualties would result.

By its nature, therefore, the threat posed by al-Qa'ida and its associated forces demands a broader concept of imminence in judging when a person continually planning terror attacks presents an imminent threat, making the use of force appropriate. In this context, imminence must incorporate considerations of the relevant window of opportunity, the possibility of reducing collateral damage to civilians, and the likelihood of heading off future disastrous attacks on Americans. Thus, a decision maker determining whether an al-Qa'ida operational leader presents an imminent threat of violent attack against the United States must take into account that certain members of al-Qa'ida (including any potential target of lethal force) are continually plotting attacks

8

against the United States; that al-Qa'ida would engage in such attacks regularly to the extent it were able to do so; that the U.S. government may not be aware of all al-Qa'ida plots as they are developing and thus cannot be confident that none is about to occur; and that, in light of these predicates, the nation may have a limited window of opportunity within which to strike in a manner that both has a high likelihood of success and reduces the probability of American casualties.

With this understanding, a high-level official could conclude, for example, that an individual poses an "imminent threat" of violent attack against the United States where he is an operational leader of al-Qa'ida or an associated force and is personally and continually involved in planning terrorist attacks against the United States. Moreover, where the al-Qa'ida member in question has recently been involved in activities posing an imminent threat of violent attack against the United States, and there is no evidence suggesting that he has renounced or abandoned such activities, that member's involvement in al-Qa'ida's continuing terrorist campaign against the United States would support the conclusion that the member poses an imminent threat.

Second, regarding the feasibility of capture, capture would not be feasible if it could not be physically effectuated during the relevant window of opportunity or if the relevant country were to decline to consent to a capture operation. Other factors such as undue risk to U.S. personnel conducting a potential capture operation also could be relevant. Feasibility would be a highly fact-specific and potentially time-sensitive inquiry.

Third, it is a premise here that any such lethal operation by the United States would comply with the four fundamental law-of-war principles governing the use of force: necessity, distinction, proportionality, and humanity (the avoidance of unnecessary suffering). *See, e.g.*, United States Air Force, Targeting, Air Force Doctrine Document 2-1.9, at 88 (June 8, 2006); Dinstein, *Conduct of Hostilities* at 16–20, 115–16, 119–23; *see also 2010 Koh ASIL Speech*. For example, it would not be consistent with those principles to continue an operation if anticipated civilian casualties would be excessive in relation to the anticipated military advantage. Chairman of the Joint Chiefs of Staff Instruction 5810.01D, Implementation of the DoD Law of War Program ¶ 4.a, at 1 (Apr. 30, 2010). An operation consistent with the laws of war could not violate the prohibitions against treachery and perfidy, which address a breach of confidence by the assailant. *See, e.g.*, Hague Convention IV, Annex, art. 23(b), Oct. 18, 1907, 36 Stat 2277, 2301–02 ("[I]t is especially forbidden . . . [t]o kill or wound treacherously individuals belonging to the hostile nation or army. . . . "). These prohibitions do not, however, categorically forbid the use of stealth or surprise, nor forbid attacks on identified individual soldiers or officers. *See* U.S. Army Field Manual 27-10, *The Law of Land Warfare*, ¶ 31 (1956) (article 23(b) of the Annex to the Hague Convention IV does not "preclude attacks on individual soldiers or officers of the enemy whether in the zone of hostilities, occupied territory, or else-where"). And the Department is not aware of any other law-of-war grounds precluding use of such tactics. *See* Dinstein, *Conduct of Hostilities* at 94–95, 199; Abraham D. Sofaer, *Terrorism, the Law, and the National Defense*, 126 Mil. L. Rev. 89, 120–21 (1989). Relatedly, "there is no prohibition under the laws of war on the use of technologically advanced weapons systems in armed conflict—such as pilotless aircraft or so-called smart bombs—as long as they are employed in conformity with applicable laws of war." *2010 Koh ASIL Speech*. Further, under this framework, the United States would also be required to accept a surrender if it were feasible to do so.

| | 9 |

In sum, an operation in the circumstances and under the constraints described above would not result in a violation of any due process rights.

B.

Similarly, assuming that a lethal operation targeting a U.S. citizen abroad who is planning attacks against the United States would result in a "seizure" under the Fourth Amendment, such an operation would not violate that Amendment in the circumstances posited here. The Supreme Court has made clear that the constitutionality of a seizure is determined by "balanc[ing] the nature and quality of the intrusion on the individual's Fourth Amendment interests against the importance of the governmental interests alleged to justify the intrusion." *Tennessee v. Garner*, 471 US. 1, 8 (1985) (internal quotation marks omitted); *accord Scott v. Harris*, 550 U.S. 372, 383 (2007). Even in domestic law enforcement operations, the Court has noted that "[w]here the officer has probable cause to believe that the suspect poses a threat of serious physical harm, either to the officer or to others, it is not constitutionally unreasonable to prevent escape by using deadly force." *Garner*, 471 U.S. at 11. Thus, "if the suspect threatens the officer with a weapon or there is probable cause to believe that he has committed a crime involving the infliction or threatened infliction of serious physical harm, deadly force may be used if necessary to prevent escape, and if, where feasible, some warning has been given." *Id.* at 11–12.

The Fourth Amendment "reasonableness" test is situation-dependent. *Cf. Scott*, 550 U.S. at 382 ("*Garner* did not establish a magical on/off switch that triggers rigid preconditions whenever an officer's actions constitute 'deadly force.'"). What would constitute a reasonable use of lethal force for purposes of domestic law enforcement operations differs substantially from what would be reasonable in the situation and circumstances discussed in this white paper. But at least in circumstances where the targeted person is an operational leader of an enemy force and an informed, high-level government official has determined that he poses an imminent threat of violent attack against the United States, and those conducting the operation would carry out the operation only if capture were infeasible, the use of lethal force would not violate the Fourth Amendment. Under such circumstances, the intrusion on any Fourth Amendment interests would be outweighed by the "importance of the governmental interests [that] justify the intrusion," *Garner*, 471 U.S. at 8—the interests in protecting the lives of Americans.

C.

Finally, the Department notes that under the circumstances described in this paper, there exists no appropriate judicial forum to evaluate these constitutional considerations. It is well-established that "[m]atters intimately related to foreign policy and national security are rarely proper subjects for judicial intervention," *Haig v. Agee*, 453 U.S. 280, 292 (1981), because such matters "frequently turn on standards that defy judicial application," or "involve the exercise of a discretion demonstrably committed to the executive or legislature," *Baker v. Carr*, 369 U.S. 186, 211 (1962). Were a court to intervene here, it might be required inappropriately to issue an ex ante command to the President and officials responsible for operations with respect to their specific tactical judgment to mount a potential lethal operation against a senior operational leader of al-Qa'ida or its associated forces. And judicial enforcement of such orders would require the Court to supervise inherently predictive judgments by the President and his national security advisors as to when and how to use force against a member of an enemy force against which Congress has authorized the use of force.

III.

Section 1119(b) of title 18 provides that a "person who, being a national of the United States, kills or attempts to kill a national of the United States while such national is outside the United States but within the jurisdiction of another country shall be punished as provided under sections 1111, 1112, and 1113." 18 U.S.C. § 1119(b) (2006).[3] Because the person who would be the target of the kind of operation discussed here would be a U.S. citizen, it might be suggested that section 1119(b) would prohibit such an operation. Section 1119, however, incorporates the federal murder and manslaughter statutes, and thus its prohibition extends only to "unlawful killing[s]," 18 U.S.C. §§1111(a), 1112(a) (2006). Section 1119 is best construed to incorporate the "public authority" justification, which renders lethal action carried out by a government official lawful in some circumstances. As this paper explains below, a lethal operation of the kind discussed here would fall within the public authority exception under the circumstances and conditions posited because it would be conducted in a manner consistent with applicable law of war principles governing the non-international conflict between the United States and al-Qa'ida and its associated forces. It therefore would not result in an unlawful killing.[4]

A.

Although section 1119(b) refers only to the "punish[ments]" provided under sections 1111, 1112, and 1113, courts have held that section

11

---

[3] See also 18 U.S.C. § 1119(a) (2006) (providing that "'national of the United States' has the meaning stated in section 101(a)(22) of the Immigration and Nationality Act," 8 U.S.C. § 1101(a)(22)(2006)).

[4] In light of the conclusion that section 1119 and the statutes it cross-references incorporate this justification, and that the justification would cover an operation of the sort discussed here, this discussion does not address whether an operation of this sort could be lawful on any other grounds.

1119(b) incorporates the substantive elements of those cross-referenced provisions of title 18. *See, e.g., United States v. Wharton*, 320 F.3d 526, 533 (5th Cir. 2003); *United States v. White*, 51 F. Supp. 2d 1008, 1013–14 (E.D. Cal. 1997). Section 1111 of title 18 sets forth criminal penalties for "murder," and provides that "[m]urder is the unlawful killing of a human being with malice aforethought." 18 U.S.C. § 1111(a). Section 1112 similarly provides criminal sanctions for "[m]anslaughter," and states that "[m]anslaughter is the unlawful killing of a human being without malice." *Id.* § 1112(a). Section 1113 provides criminal penalties for "attempts to commit murder or manslaughter." *Id.* § 1113. It is therefore clear that section 1119(b) bars only "unlawful killing."

Guidance as to the meaning of the phrase "unlawful killing" in sections 1111 and 1112—and thus for purposes of section 1119(b)—can be found in the historical understandings of murder and manslaughter. That history shows that states have long recognized justifications and excuses to statutes criminalizing "unlawful" killings.[5] One state court, for example, in construing that state's murder statute, explained that "the word 'unlawful' is a term of art" that "connotes a homicide with the absence of factors of excuse or justification." *People v. Frye*, 10 Cal. Rptr. 2d 217, 221 (Cal. Ct. App. 1992). That court further explained that the factors of excuse or justification in question include those that have traditionally been recognized. *Id.* at 221 n.2. Other authorities support the same conclusion. *See, e.g., Mullaney v. Wilbur*, 421 U.S. 684, 685 (1975) (requirement of "unlawful" killing in Maine murder statute meant that killing was "neither justifiable nor excusable"); *cf. also* Rollin M. Perkins & Ronald N. Boyce, *Criminal Law* 56 (3d ed. 1982) ("Innocent homicide is of two kinds, (1) justifiable and (2) excusable."). Accordingly, section

---

[5] The same is true with respect to other statutes, including federal laws, that modify a prohibited act other than murder or manslaughter with the term "unlawfully." *See, e.g., Territory v. Gonzales*, 89 P. 250, 252 (N.M. 1907) (construing the term "unlawful" in statute criminalizing assault with a deadly weapon as "clearly equivalent" to "without excuse or justification"). For example, 18 U.S.C. § 2339C(a) (1) (2006) makes it unlawful, *inter alia*, to "unlawfully and willfully provide[] or collect[] funds" with the intention that they may be used (or knowledge they are to be used) to carry out an act that is an offense within certain specified treaties, or to engage in certain other terrorist acts. The legislative history of section 2339C makes clear that "[t]he term 'unlawfully' is intended to embody common law defenses." H.R. Rep. No. 107-307, at 12 (2001).

1119 does not proscribe killings covered by a justification traditionally recognized under the common law or state and federal murder statutes. "Congress did not intend [section 1119] to criminalize justifiable or excusable killings." *White*, 51 F. Supp. 2d at 1013.

B.

The public authority justification is well-accepted, and it may be available even in cases where the particular criminal statute at issue does not expressly refer to a public authority justification. Prosecutions where such a "public authority" justification is invoked are understandably rare, *see* American Law Institute Model Penal Code and Commentaries § 3.03 Comment 1, at 23–24 (1985); *cf. Visa Fraud Investigation*, 8 Op. O.L.C. 284, 285 n.2, 286 (1984), and thus there is little case law in which courts have analyzed the scope of the justification with respect to the conduct of government officials. Nonetheless, discussions in the leading treatises and in the Model Penal Code demonstrate its legitimacy. *See* 2 Wayne R. LaFave, *Substantive Criminal Law* § 10.2(b), at 135 (2d ed. 2003); Perkins & Boyce, *Criminal Law* at 1093 ("Deeds which otherwise would be criminal, such as taking or destroying property, taking hold of a person by force and against his will, placing him in confinement, or even taking his life, are not crimes if done with proper public authority."); *see also* Model Penal Code § 3.03(1)(a), (d), (e), at 22–23 (proposing codification of justification where conduct is "required or authorized by," *inter alia*, "the law defining the duties or functions of a public officer," "the law governing the armed services or the lawful conduct of war," or "any other provision of law imposing a public duty"); National Commission on Reform of Federal Criminal Laws, *A Proposed New Federal Criminal Code* § 602(1) (1971) ("Conduct engaged in by a public servant in the course of his official duties is justified when it is required or authorized by law."). And the Department's Office of Legal Counsel ("OLC") has invoked analogous rationales when it has analyzed whether Congress intended a particular criminal statute to prohibit specific conduct that otherwise falls within a government agency's authorities. *See, e.g, Visa Fraud Investigation*, 8 Op. O.L.C. at 287–88 (concluding that a civil statute prohibiting issuance of visa to an alien known to be ineligible did not prohibit State Department from issuing such a visa where "necessary" to facilitate an important Immigration and Naturalization Service undercover operation carried out in a "reasonable" fashion).

The public authority justification would not excuse all conduct of public officials from all criminal prohibitions. The legislature may design some criminal prohibitions to place bounds on the kinds of governmental conduct that can be authorized by the Executive. Or the legislature may enact a criminal prohibition in order to limit the scope of the conduct that the legislature has otherwise authorized the Executive to undertake pursuant to another statute. *See, e.g, Nardone v. United States*, 302 U.S. 379, 384 (1937) (federal statute proscribed government wiretapping). But the generally recognized public authority justification reflects that it would not make sense to attribute to Congress the intent to criminalize all covered activities undertaken by public officials in the legitimate exercise of their otherwise lawful authorities, even if Congress clearly intends to make those same actions a crime when committed by persons not acting pursuant to public authority. In some instances, therefore, the best interpretation of a criminal prohibition is that Congress intended to distinguish persons who are acting pursuant to public authority from those who are not, even if the statute does not make that distinction express. *Cf. id.* at 384 (federal criminal statutes should be construed to exclude authorized conduct of public officers where such a reading "would work obvious absurdity as, for example, the application of a speed law to a policeman pursuing a criminal or the driver of a fire engine responding to an alarm").[6]

The touchstone for the analysis whether section 1119 incorporates not only justifications generally, but also the public authority justification in particular, is the legislative intent underlying this statute. Here, the statute should be read to exclude from its prohibitory scope killings that are encompassed by traditional justifications, which include the public authority justification. The statutory incorporation of two other criminal statutes expressly referencing "unlawful" killings is one indication. *See supra* at 10–11. Moreover, there are no indications that

---

[6] Each potentially applicable statute must be carefully and separately examined to discern Congress's intent in this respect. *See generally, e.g, Nardone*, 302 U.S. 379; *United States Assistance to Countries that Shoot Down Civil Aircraft Involved in Drug Trafficking*, 18 Op. O.L.C. 148 (1994); *Application of Neutrality Act to Official Government Activities*, 8 Op. O.L.C. 58 (1984).

Congress had a contrary intention. Nothing in the text or legislative history of sections 1111–1113 of title 18 suggests that Congress intended to exclude the established public authority justification from those justifications that Congress otherwise must be understood to have imported through the use of the modifier "unlawful" in those statutes. Nor is there anything in the text or legislative history of section 1119 itself to suggest that Congress intended to abrogate or otherwise affect the availability of this traditional justification for killings. On the contrary, the relevant legislative materials indicate that, in enacting section 1119, Congress was merely closing a gap in a field dealing with entirely different kinds of conduct from that at issue here.[7]

The Department thus concludes that section 1119 incorporates the public authority justification.[8] This paper turns next to the question whether a lethal operation could be encompassed by that justification

14

---

[7] Section 1119 was designed to close a jurisdictional loophole—exposed by a murder that had been committed abroad by a private individual—to ensure the possibility of prosecuting U.S. nationals who murdered other U.S. nationals in certain foreign countries that lacked the ability to lawfully secure the perpetrator's appearance at trial. *See* 137 Cong. Rec. 8675–76 (1991) (statement of Sen. Thurmond). This loophole is unrelated to the sort of authorized operation at issue here. Indeed, prior to the enactment of section 1119, the only federal statute expressly making it a crime to kill U.S. nationals abroad (outside the United States' special and maritime jurisdiction) reflected what appears to have been a particular concern with the protection of Americans from terrorist attacks. *See* 18 U.S.C. § 2332(a), (d) (2006) (criminalizing unlawful killings of U.S. nationals abroad where the Attorney General or his subordinate certifies that the "offense was intended to coerce, intimidate, or retaliate against a government or a civilian population").

[8] 18 U.S.C. § 956(a)(1) (2006) makes it a crime to conspire within the jurisdiction of the United States "to commit at any place outside the United States an act that would constitute the offense of murder, kidnapping, or maiming if committed in the special maritime and territorial jurisdiction of the United States" if any conspirator acts within the United States to effect any object of the conspiracy. Like section 1119(b), section 956(a) incorporates the public authority justification. In addition, the legislative history of section 956(a) indicates that the provision was "not intended to apply to duly authorized actions undertaken on behalf of the United States Government." 141 Cong. Rec. 4491, 4507 (1995) (section-by-section analysis of bill submitted by Sen. Biden, who introduced the provision at the behest of the President); *see also id.* at 11,960 (section-by-section analysis of bill submitted by Sen. Daschle, who introduced the identical provision in a different version of the anti-terrorism legislation a few months later). Thus, for the reasons that section 1119(b) does not prohibit the United States from conducting a lethal operation against a U.S. citizen, section 956(a) also does not prohibit such an operation.

and, in particular, whether that justification would apply when the target is a U.S. citizen. The analysis here leads to the conclusion that it would.

C.

A lethal operation against an enemy leader undertaken in national self-defense or during an armed conflict that is authorized by an informed, high-level official and carried out in a manner that accords with applicable law of war principles would fall within a well established variant of the public authority justification and therefore would not be murder. *See, e.g.,* 2 Paul H. Robinson, *Criminal Law Defenses* § 148(a), at 208 (1984) (conduct that would violate a criminal statute is justified and thus not unlawful "[w]here the exercise of military authority relies upon the law governing the armed forces or upon the conduct of war"); 2 LaFave, *Substantive Criminal Law* § 10.2(c) at 136 ("another aspect of the public duty defense is where the conduct was required or authorized by 'the law governing the armed services or the lawful conduct of war'"); Perkins & Boyce, *Criminal Law* at 1093 (noting that a "typical instance[] in which even the extreme act of taking human life is done by public authority" involves "the killing of an enemy as an act of war and within the rules of war").[9]

The United States is currently in the midst of a congressionally authorized armed conflict with al-Qa'ida and associated forces, and may act in national self-defense to protect U.S. persons and interests who are under continual threat of violent attack by certain al-Qa'ida operatives planning operations against them. The public authority justification would apply to a lethal operation of the kind discussed in this paper if it were conducted in accord with applicable law of war principles. As one legal commentator has explained, "if a soldier intentionally kills an enemy combatant in time of war and within the rules of warfare, he is not guilty of murder," whereas, for example, if that soldier

---

[9] *See also Frye,* 10 Cal. Rptr. 2d at 221 n.2 (identifying "homicide done under a valid public authority, such as execution of a death sentence or killing an enemy in a time of war," as examples of justifiable killing that would not be "unlawful" under the California statute describing murder as an "unlawful" killing); Model Penal Code § 3.03(2)(b), at 22 (proposing that criminal statutes expressly recognize a public authority justification for a killing that "occurs in the lawful conduct of war" notwithstanding the Code recommendation that the use of deadly force generally should be justified only if expressly prescribed by law).

intentionally kills a prisoner of war—a violation of the laws of war—
"then he commits murder." 2 LaFave, *Substantive Criminal Law*
§ 10.2(c), at 136; *see also State v. Gut*, 13 Minn. 341, 357 (1868) ("That it
is legal to kill an alien enemy in the heat and exercise of war, is undeniable; but to kill such an enemy after he has laid down his arms, and
especially when he is confined in prison, is murder."); Perkins & Boyce,
Criminal Law at 1093 ("Even in time of war an alien enemy may not be
killed needlessly after he has been disarmed and securely imprisoned. . . ."). Moreover, without invoking the public authority justification by its terms, this Department's OLC has relied on the same notion
in an opinion addressing the intended scope of a federal criminal statute that concerned the use of potentially lethal force. *See United States
Assistance to Countries that Shoot Down Civil Aircraft Involved in Drug*   15
Trafficking, 18 Op. O.L.C. 148, 164 (1994) (concluding that the Aircraft
Sabotage Act of 1984,18 U.S.C. § 32(b)(2) (2006), which prohibits the
willful destruction of a civil aircraft and otherwise applies to U.S. government conduct, should not be construed to have "the surprising and
almost certainly unintended effect of criminalizing actions by military
personnel that are lawful under international law and the laws of armed
conflict").

The fact that an operation may target a U.S. citizen does not alter
this conclusion. As explained above, *see supra* at 3, the Supreme Court
has held that the military may constitutionally use force against a U.S.
citizen who is part of enemy forces. *See Hamdi*, 542 U.S. at 518 (plurality opinion); *id.* at 587, 597 (Thomas, J., dissenting); *Ex parte Quirin*,
317 U.S. at 37–38 ("Citizens who associate themselves with the military
arm of the enemy government, and with its aid, guidance and direction
enter [the United States] bent on hostile acts," may be treated as "enemy
belligerents" under the law of war.). Similarly, under the Constitution
and the inherent right to national self-defense recognized in international law, the President may authorize the use of force against a U.S.
citizen who is a member of al-Qa'ida or its associated forces and who
poses an imminent threat of violent attack against the United States.

In light of these precedents, the Department believes that the use
of lethal force addressed in this white paper would constitute a lawful
killing under the public authority doctrine if conducted in a manner
consistent with the fundamental law of war principles governing the

use of force in a non-international armed conflict. Such an operation would not violate the assassination ban in Executive Order No. 12333. Section 2.11 of Executive Order No. 12333 provides that "[n]o person employed by or acting on behalf of the United States Government shall engage in, or conspire to engage in, assassination." 46 Fed. Reg. 59,941, 59,952 (Dec. 4, 1981). A lawful killing in self-defense is not an assassination. In the Department's view, a lethal operation conducted against a U.S. citizen whose conduct poses an imminent threat of violent attack against the United States would be a legitimate act of national self-defense that would not violate the assassination ban. Similarly, the use of lethal force, consistent with the laws of war, against an individual who is a legitimate military target would be lawful and would not violate the assassination ban.

IV.

The War Crimes Act, 18 U.S.C. § 2441 (2006) makes it a federal crime for a member of the Armed Forces or a national of the United States to "commit[] a war crime." *Id.* § 2441(a). The only potentially applicable provision of section 2441 to operations of the type discussed herein makes it a war crime to commit a "grave breach" of Common Article 3 of the Geneva Conventions when that breach is committed "in the context of and in association with an armed conflict not of an international character."[10] *Id.* § 2441(c)(3). As defined by the statute, a "grave breach" of Common Article 3 includes "[m]urder," described in pertinent part as "[t]he act of a person who intentionally kills, or conspires or attempts to kill . . . one or more persons taking no active part in the hostilities, including those placed out of combat by sickness, wounds, detention, or any other cause." *Id.* § 2441(d)(1)(D).

Whatever might be the outer bounds of this category of covered persons, Common Article 3 does not alter the fundamental law of war principle concerning a belligerent party's right in an armed conflict to

---

[10] The statute also defines "war crime" to include any conduct that is defined as a grave breach in any of the Geneva Conventions (or any Geneva protocol to which the United States is a party); that is prohibited by four specified articles of the Fourth Hague Convention of 1907; or that is a willful killing or infliction of serious injury in violation of the 1996 Protocol on Prohibitions or Restrictions on the Use of Mines, Booby-Traps and Other Devices. 18 U.S.C. § 2441(c).

target individuals who are part of an enemy's armed forces or eliminate a nation's authority to take legitimate action in national self-defense. The language of Common Article 3 "makes clear that members of such armed forces [of both the state and non-state parties to the conflict] . . . are considered as 'taking no active part in the hostilities' only once they have disengaged from their fighting function ('have laid down their arms') or are placed *hors de combat*; mere suspension of combat is insufficient." International Committee of the Red Cross, *Interpretive Guidance on the Notion of Direct Participation in Hostilities Under International Humanitarian Law* 28 (2009). An operation against a senior operational leader of al-Qa'ida or its associated forces who poses an imminent threat of violent attack against the United States would target a person who is taking "an active part in hostilities" and therefore would not constitute a "grave breach" of Common Article 3.

V.

In conclusion, it would be lawful for the United States to conduct a lethal operation outside the United States against a U.S. citizen who is a senior, operational leader of al-Qa'ida or an associated force of al-Qa'ida without violating the Constitution or the federal statutes discussed in this white paper under the following conditions: (1) an informed, high-level official of the U.S. government has determined that the targeted individual poses an imminent threat of violent attack against the United States; (2) capture is infeasible, and the United States continues to monitor whether capture becomes feasible; and (3) the operation is conducted in a manner consistent with the four fundamental principles of the laws of war governing the use of force. As stated earlier, this paper does not attempt to determine the minimum requirements necessary to render such an operation lawful, nor does it assess what might be required to render a lethal operation against a U.S. citizen lawful in other circumstances. It concludes only that the stated conditions would be sufficient to make lawful a lethal operation in a foreign country directed against a U.S. citizen with the characteristics described above.

7

Remarks of Eric Holder, Attorney General of
the United States

Northwestern University School of Law,
Chicago, IL

March 5, 2012

Untitled

Attorney General Eric Holder delivered this speech less than six months
after the U.S. government carried out the killing of Anwar al-Aulaqi. It
is in some respects a summary of the July 2010 OLC memo—though
that memo was not disclosed until the summer of 2014. Holder's speech
was especially controversial because of its provocative assertion that
"the Constitution guarantees due process, not judicial process," but
Holder addresses many other topics here, including the application of
the laws of war to targeted killings, the application of the Gerald Ford–
era assassination ban, and the circumstances in which the government
might use force in foreign nations without those nations' consent.

The document from which this text was transcribed is posted at:
www.ACLU.org/TDM/HolderSpeech.

Thank you, Dean [Daniel] Rodriguez, for your kind words, and for the outstanding leadership that you provide—not only for this academic campus, but also for our nation's legal community. It is a privilege to be with you today—and to be among the distinguished faculty members, staff, alumni, and students who make Northwestern such an extraordinary place.

For more than 150 years, this law school has served as a training ground for future leaders; as a forum for critical, thoughtful debate; and as a meeting place to consider issues of national concern and global consequence. This afternoon, I am honored to be part of this tradition. And I'm grateful for the opportunity to join with you in discussing a defining issue of our time—and a most critical responsibility that we share: how we will stay true to America's founding—and enduring—promises of security, justice and liberty.

Since this country's earliest days, the American people have risen to this challenge—and all that it demands. But, as we have seen—and as President John F. Kennedy may have described best—"In the long history of the world, only a few generations have been granted the role of defending freedom in its hour of maximum danger."

Half a century has passed since those words were spoken, but our nation today confronts grave national security threats that demand our constant attention and steadfast commitment. It is clear that, once again, we have reached an "hour of danger."

We are a nation at war. And, in this war, we face a nimble and determined enemy that cannot be underestimated.

Like President Obama—and my fellow members of his national security team—I begin each day with a briefing on the latest and most urgent threats made against us in the preceding 24 hours. And, like scores of attorneys and agents at the Justice Department, I go to sleep each night thinking of how best to keep our people safe.

I know that—more than a decade after the September 11th attacks; and despite our recent national security successes, including the operation that brought to justice Osama bin Laden last year—there are people currently plotting to murder Americans, who reside in distant countries as well as within our own borders. Disrupting and preventing these plots—and using every available and appropriate tool to keep the American people safe—has been, and will remain, this Administration's top priority.

But just as surely as we are a nation at war, we also are a nation of laws and values. Even when under attack, our actions must always be grounded on the bedrock of the Constitution—and must always be consistent with statutes, court precedent, the rule of law and our founding ideals. Not only is this the right thing to do—history has shown that it is also the most effective approach we can take in combating those who seek to do us harm.

This is not just my view. My judgment is shared by senior national security officials across the government. As the President reminded us in 2009, at the National Archives where our founding documents are housed, "[w]e uphold our most cherished values not only because doing so is right, but because it strengthens our country and it keeps us safe. Time and again, our values have been our best national security asset." Our history proves this. We do not have to choose between security and liberty—and we will not.

Today, I want to tell you about the collaboration across the government that defines and distinguishes this Administration's national security efforts. I also want to discuss some of the legal principles that guide—and strengthen—this work, as well as the special role of the Department of Justice in protecting the American people and upholding the Constitution.

* * *

Now, I realize I have gone into considerable detail about tools we use to identify suspected terrorists and to bring captured terrorists to justice. It is preferable to capture suspected terrorists where feasible—among other reasons, so that we can gather valuable intelligence from them—but we must also recognize that there are instances where our government has the clear authority—and, I would argue, the responsibility—to defend the United States through the appropriate and lawful use of lethal force.

This principle has long been established under both U.S. and international law. In response to the attacks perpetrated—and the continuing threat posed—by al Qaeda, the Taliban, and associated forces, Congress has authorized the President to use all necessary and appropriate force against those groups. Because the United States is in an armed conflict, we are authorized to take action against enemy belligerents under international law. The Constitution empowers the President to protect the nation from any imminent threat of violent attack. And international law recognizes the inherent right of national self-defense. None of this is changed by the fact that we are not in a conventional war.

Our legal authority is not limited to the battlefields in Afghanistan. Indeed, neither Congress nor our federal courts has limited the geographic scope of our ability to use force to the current conflict in Afghanistan. We are at war with a stateless enemy, prone to shifting operations from country to country. Over the last three years alone, al Qaeda and its associates have directed several attacks—fortunately, unsuccessful—against us from countries other than Afghanistan. Our government has both a responsibility and a right to protect this nation and its people from such threats.

This does not mean that we can use military force whenever or wherever we want. International legal principles, including respect for another nation's sovereignty, constrain our ability to act unilaterally. But the use of force in foreign territory would be consistent with these international legal principles if conducted, for example, with the consent of the nation involved—or after a determination that the nation is unable or unwilling to deal effectively with a threat to the United States.

Furthermore, it is entirely lawful—under both United States law and applicable law of war principles—to target specific senior operational leaders of al Qaeda and associated forces. This is not a novel concept. In fact, during World War II, the United States tracked the plane flying Admiral Isoroku Yamamoto—the commander of Japanese forces in the attack on Pearl Harbor and the Battle of Midway—and shot it down specifically because he was on board. As I explained to the Senate Judiciary Committee following the operation that killed Osama bin Laden, the same rules apply today.

Some have called such operations "assassinations." They are not, and the use of that loaded term is misplaced. Assassinations are unlawful killings. Here, for the reasons I have given, the U.S. government's use of lethal force in self defense against a leader of al Qaeda or an associated force who presents an imminent threat of violent attack would not be unlawful—and therefore would not violate the Executive Order banning assassination or criminal statutes.

Now, it is an unfortunate but undeniable fact that some of the threats we face come from a small number of United States citizens who have decided to commit violent attacks against their own country from abroad. Based on generations-old legal principles and Supreme Court decisions handed down during World War II, as well as during this current conflict, it's clear that United States citizenship alone does not make such individuals immune from being targeted. But it does mean that the government must take into account all relevant constitutional considerations with respect to United States citizens—even those who are leading efforts to kill innocent Americans. Of these, the most relevant is the Fifth Amendment's Due Process Clause, which says that the government may not deprive a citizen of his or her life without due process of law.

The Supreme Court has made clear that the Due Process Clause does not impose one-size-fits-all requirements, but instead mandates procedural safeguards that depend on specific circumstances. In cases arising under the Due Process Clause—including in a case involving a U.S. citizen captured in the conflict against al Qaeda—the Court has applied a balancing approach, weighing the private interest that will be affected against the interest the government is trying to protect, and the burdens the government would face in providing additional process. Where national security operations are at stake, due process takes into account the realities of combat.

Here, the interests on both sides of the scale are extraordinarily weighty. An individual's interest in making sure that the government does not target him erroneously could not be more significant. Yet it is imperative for the government to counter threats posed by senior operational leaders of al-Qaeda, and to protect the innocent people whose lives could be lost in their attacks.

Any decision to use lethal force against a United States citizen—even one intent on murdering Americans and who has become an operational leader of al-Qaeda in a foreign land—is among the gravest that government leaders can face. The American people can be—and deserve to be—assured that actions taken in their defense are consistent with their values and their laws. So, although I cannot discuss or confirm any particular program or operation, I believe it is important to explain these legal principles publicly.

Let me be clear: an operation using lethal force in a foreign country, targeted against a U.S. citizen who is a senior operational leader of al Qaeda or associated forces, and who is actively engaged in planning to kill Americans, would be lawful at least in the following circumstances: First, the U.S. government has determined, after a thorough and careful review, that the individual poses an imminent threat of violent attack against the United States; second, capture is not feasible; and third, the operation would be conducted in a manner consistent with applicable law of war principles.

The evaluation of whether an individual presents an "imminent threat" incorporates considerations of the relevant window of opportunity to act, the possible harm that missing the window would cause to civilians, and the likelihood of heading off future disastrous attacks against the United States. As we learned on 9/11, al Qaeda has demonstrated the ability to strike with little or no notice—and to cause devastating casualties. Its leaders are continually planning attacks against the United States, and they do not behave like a traditional military—wearing uniforms, carrying arms openly, or massing forces in preparation for an attack. Given these facts, the Constitution does not require the President to delay action until some theoretical end-stage of planning—when the precise time, place, and manner of an attack become clear. Such a requirement would create an unacceptably high risk that our efforts would fail, and that Americans would be killed.

Whether the capture of a U.S. citizen terrorist is feasible is a fact-specific, and potentially time-sensitive, question. It may depend on, among other things, whether capture can be accomplished in the window of time available to prevent an attack and without undue risk to civilians or to U.S. personnel. Given the nature of how terrorists act and where they tend to hide, it may not always be feasible to capture a United States citizen terrorist who presents an imminent threat of violent attack. In that case, our government has the clear authority to defend the United States with lethal force.

Of course, any such use of lethal force by the United States will comply with the four fundamental law of war principles governing the use of force. The principle of necessity requires that the target have definite military value. The principle of distinction requires that only lawful targets—such as combatants, civilians directly participating in hostilities, and military objectives—may be targeted intentionally. Under the principle of proportionality, the anticipated collateral damage must not be excessive in relation to the anticipated military advantage. Finally, the principle of humanity requires us to use weapons that will not inflict unnecessary suffering.

These principles do not forbid the use of stealth or technologically advanced weapons. In fact, the use of advanced weapons may help to ensure that the best intelligence is available for planning and carrying out operations, and that the risk of civilian casualties can be minimized or avoided altogether.

Some have argued that the President is required to get permission from a federal court before taking action against a United States citizen who is a senior operational leader of al Qaeda or associated forces. This is simply not accurate. "Due process" and "judicial process" are not one and the same, particularly when it comes to national security. The Constitution guarantees due process, not judicial process.

The conduct and management of national security operations are core functions of the Executive Branch, as courts have recognized throughout our history. Military and civilian officials must often make real-time decisions that balance the need to act, the existence of alternative options, the possibility of collateral damage, and other judgments—all of which depend on expertise and immediate access to information that only the Executive Branch may possess in real time. The Constitution's guarantee of due process is ironclad, and it is essential—but, as a recent court decision makes clear, it does not require judicial approval before the President may use force abroad against a senior operational leader of a foreign terrorist organization with which the United States is at war—even if that individual happens to be a U.S. citizen.

That is not to say that the Executive Branch has—or should ever have—the ability to target any such individuals without robust oversight. Which is why, in keeping with the law and our constitutional system of checks and balances, the Executive Branch regularly informs the appropriate members of Congress about our counterterrorism activities, including the legal framework, and would of course follow the same practice where lethal force is used against United States citizens.

Now, these circumstances are sufficient under the Constitution for the United States to use lethal force against a U.S. citizen abroad—but it is important to note that the legal requirements I have described may not apply in every situation—such as operations that take place on traditional battlefields.

The unfortunate reality is that our nation will likely continue to face terrorist threats that—at times—originate with our own citizens. When such individuals take up arms against this country—and join al Qaeda in plotting attacks designed to kill their fellow Americans—there may be only one realistic and appropriate response. We must take steps to stop them—in full accordance with the Constitution. In this hour of danger, we simply cannot afford to wait until deadly plans are carried out—and we will not.

This is an indicator of our times—not a departure from our laws and our values. For this Administration—and for this nation—our values are clear. We must always look to them for answers when we face difficult questions, like the ones I have discussed today. As the President reminded us at the National Archives, "our Constitution has endured through secession and civil rights, through World War and Cold War, because it provides a foundation of principles that can be applied pragmatically; it provides a compass that can help us find our way."

Our most sacred principles and values—of security, justice and liberty for all citizens—must continue to unite us, to guide us forward, and to help us build a future that honors our founding documents and advances our ongoing—uniquely American—pursuit of a safer, more just, and more perfect union. In the continuing effort to keep our people secure, this Administration will remain true to those values that inspired our nation's founding and, over the course of two centuries, have made America an example of strength and a beacon of justice for all the world. This is our pledge.

Thank you for inviting me to discuss these important issues with you today.

8

Remarks of John O. Brennan, Assistant to
the President for Homeland Security and
Counterterrorism

Woodrow Wilson International Center for
Scholars, Washington, D.C.

April 30, 2012

"The Ethics and Efficacy of the President's Counterterrorism Strategy"

In this speech, Brennan acknowledged something that everyone already
knew but that no official had formally acknowledged—that the government had used drones to carry out targeted killings. Brennan argues
here that drone strikes are lawful, ethical, wise, and closely supervised.
He concedes that drone strikes can result in civilian deaths, but he
contends that such deaths are "exceedingly rare," and he defends the
precision of the strikes. "It's this surgical precision—the ability, with
laser-like focus, to eliminate the cancerous tumor called an al-Qa'ida
terrorist while limiting damage to the tissue around it—that makes this
counterterrorism tool so essential."

The document from which this text was transcribed is posted at:
www.ACLU.org/TDM/BrennanSpeech2.

Thank you so much Jane for the very kind introduction, and that very nice and memorable walk down memory lane as our paths did cross so many times over the years, but thank you also for your leadership of the Wilson Center. It is a privilege for me to be here today, and to speak at this group. And you have spent many years in public service, and it continues here at the Wilson Center today, and there are few individuals in this country who can match the range of Jane's expertise from the armed services to intelligence to homeland security, and anyone who has appeared before her committee knew firsthand just how extensive and deep that expertise was. So Jane, I'll just say that I'm finally glad to be sharing the stage with you instead of testifying before you. It's a privilege to be next to you. So to you and everyone here at the Woodrow Wilson Center, thank you for your invaluable contributions, your research, your scholarship, which help further our national security every day.

I very much appreciate the opportunity to discuss President Obama's counterterrorism strategy, in particular its ethics and its efficacy.

It is fitting that we have this discussion here today at the Woodrow Wilson Center. It was here in August of 2007 that then-Senator Obama described how he would bring the war in Iraq to a responsible end and refocus our efforts on "the war that has to be won"—the war against al-Qaeda, particularly in the tribal regions of Afghanistan and Pakistan.

He said that we would carry on this fight while upholding our laws and our values, and that we would work with allies and partners whenever possible. But he also made it clear that he would not hesitate to use military force against terrorists who pose a direct threat to America. And he said that if he had actionable intelligence about high-value terrorist targets, including in Pakistan, he would act to protect the American people.

So it is especially fitting that we have this discussion here today. One year ago today, President Obama was then facing the scenario that he discussed here at the Wilson Center five years ago, and he did not hesitate to act. Soon thereafter, our special operations forces were moving toward the compound in Pakistan where we believed Osama bin Laden might be hiding. By the end of the next day, President Obama could confirm that justice had finally been delivered to the terrorist responsible for the attacks of September 11th, 2001, and for so many other deaths around the world.

The death of bin Laden was our most strategic blow yet against al-Qaeda. Credit for that success belongs to the courageous forces who carried out that mission, at extraordinary risk to their lives; to the many intelligence professionals who pieced together the clues that led to bin Laden's hideout; and to President Obama, who gave the order to go in.

Now one year later, it's appropriate to assess where we stand in this fight. We've always been clear that the end of bin Laden would neither mark the end of al-Qaida, nor our resolve to destroy it. So along with allies and partners, we have been unrelenting. And when we assess the al-Qaida of 2012, I think it is fair to say that, as a result of our efforts, the United States is more secure and the American people are safer. Here's why.

In Pakistan, al-Qaida's leadership ranks have continued to suffer heavy losses. This includes Ilyas Kashmiri, one of al-Qaida's top operational planners, killed a month after bin Laden. It includes Atiyah Abd al-Rahman, killed when he succeeded Ayman al-Zawahiri as al-Qaida's deputy leader. It includes Younis al-Mauritani, a planner of attacks against the United States and Europe, until he was captured by Pakistani forces.

With its most skilled and experienced commanders being lost so quickly, al-Qaida has had trouble replacing them. This is one of the many conclusions we have been able to draw from documents seized at bin Laden's compound, some of which will be published online, for the first time, this week by West Point's Combating Terrorism Center. For example, bin Laden worried about, and I quote, "The rise of lower leaders who are not as experienced and this would lead to the repeat of mistakes."

Al-Qaida leaders continue to struggle to communicate with subordinates and affiliates. Under intense pressure in the tribal regions of Pakistan, they have fewer places to train and groom the next generation of operatives. They're struggling to attract new recruits. Morale is low, with intelligence indicating that some members are giving up and returning home, no doubt aware that this is a fight they will never win. In short, al-Qaida is losing badly. And bin Laden knew it at the time of his death. In documents we seized, he confessed to "disaster after disaster." He even urged his leaders to flee the tribal regions, and go to places, "away from aircraft photography and bombardment."

For all these reasons, it is harder than ever for the al-Qaida core in Pakistan to plan and execute large-scale, potentially catastrophic attacks against our homeland. Today, it is increasingly clear that compared to 9/11, the core al-Qaida leadership is a shadow of its former self. Al-Qaida has been left with just a handful of capable leaders and operatives, and with continued pressure is on the path to its destruction. And for the first time since this fight began, we can look ahead and envision a world in which the al-Qaida core is simply no longer relevant.

Nevertheless, the dangerous threat from al-Qaida has not disappeared. As the al-Qaida core falters, it continues to look to its affiliates and adherents to carry on its murderous cause. Yet these affiliates continue to lose key commanders and capabilities as well. In Somalia, it is indeed worrying to witness al-Qaida's merger with al-Shabaab, whose ranks include foreign fighters, some with U.S. passports. At the same time, al-Shabaab continues to focus primarily on launching regional attacks, and ultimately, this is a merger between two organizations in decline.

In Yemen, al-Qaida in the Arabian Peninsula, or AQAP, continues to feel the effects of the death last year of Anwar al-Awlaki, its leader of external operations who was responsible for planning and directing terrorist attacks against the United States. Nevertheless, AQAP continues to be al-Qaida's most active affiliate, and it continues to seek the opportunity to strike our homeland. We therefore continue to support the government of Yemen in its efforts against AQAP, which is being forced to fight for the territory it needs to plan attacks beyond Yemen. In north and west Africa, another al-Qaida affiliate, al-Qaida in the Islamic Maghreb, or AQIM, continues its efforts to destabilize regional governments and engages in kidnapping of Western citizens for ransom activities designed to fund its terrorist agenda. And in Nigeria, we are monitoring closely the emergence of Boko Haram, a group that appears to be aligning itself with al-Qaida's violent agenda and is increasingly looking to attack Western interests in Nigeria in addition to Nigerian government targets.

More broadly, al-Qaida's killing of innocents, mostly Muslim men, women and children, has badly tarnished its image and appeal in the eyes of Muslims around the world. Even bin Laden and his lieutenants knew this. His propagandist, Adam Gadahn, admitted that they were now seen "as a group that does not hesitate to take people's money by falsehood, detonating mosques, and spilling the blood of scores of people." Bin Laden agreed that "a large portion" of Muslims around the world "have lost their trust" in al-Qaida.

So damaged is al-Qaida's image that bin Laden even considered changing its name. And one of the reasons? As bin Laden said himself, U.S. officials "have largely stopped using the phrase 'the war on terror' in the context of not wanting to provoke Muslims." Simply calling them al-Qaida, bin Laden said, "reduces the feeling of Muslims that we belong to them."

To which I would add, that is because al-Qaida does not belong to Muslims. Al-Qaida is the antithesis of the peace, tolerance, and humanity that is the hallmark of Islam.

Despite the great progress we've made against al-Qaida, it would be a mistake to believe this threat has passed. Al-Qaida and its associated forces still have the intent to attack the United States. And we have seen lone individuals, including American citizens, often inspired by al-Qaida's murderous ideology, kill innocent Americans and seek to do us harm.

Still, the damage that has been inflicted on the leadership core in Pakistan, combined with how al-Qaida has alienated itself from so much of the world, allows us to look forward. Indeed, if the decade before 9/11 was the time of al-Qaida's rise, and the decade after 9/11 was the time of its decline, then I believe this decade will be the one that sees its demise. This progress is no accident.

It is a direct result of intense efforts over more than a decade, across two administrations, across the U.S. government and in concert with allies and partners. This includes the comprehensive counterterrorism strategy being directed by President Obama, a strategy guided by the President's highest responsibility, to protect the safety and security of the American people. In this fight, we are harnessing every element of American power: intelligence, military, diplomatic, development, economic, financial, law enforcement, homeland security, and the power of our values, including our commitment to the rule of law. That's why, for instance, in his first days in office, President

Obama banned the use of enhanced interrogation techniques, which are not needed to keep our country safe. Staying true to our values as a nation also includes upholding the transparency upon which our democracy depends.

A few months after taking office, the President travelled to the National Archives where he discussed how national security requires a delicate balance between secrecy and transparency. He pledged to share as much information as possible with the American people "so that they can make informed judgments and hold us accountable." He has consistently encouraged those of us on his national security team to be as open and candid as possible as well.

Earlier this year, Attorney General Holder discussed how our counterterrorism efforts are rooted in, and are strengthened by, adherence to the law, including the legal authorities that allow us to pursue members of al-Qaida, including U.S. citizens, and to do so using technologically advanced weapons.

In addition, Jeh Johnson, the general counsel at the Department of Defense, has addressed the legal basis for our military efforts against al-Qaida. Stephen Preston, the general counsel at the CIA, has discussed how the agency operates under U.S. law.

These speeches build on a lecture two years ago by Harold Koh, the State Department legal adviser, who noted that "U.S. targeting practices, including lethal operations conducted with the use of unmanned aerial vehicles, comply with all applicable law, including the laws of war."

Given these efforts, I venture to say that the United States government has never been so open regarding its counterterrorism policies and their legal justification. Still, there continues to be considerable public and legal debate surrounding these technologies and how they are sometimes used in our fight against al-Qaida.

Now, I want to be very clear. In the course of the war in Afghanistan and the fight against al-Qaida, I think the American people expect us to use advanced technologies, for example, to prevent attacks on U.S. forces and to remove terrorists from the battlefield. We do, and it has saved the lives of our men and women in uniform. What has clearly captured the attention of many, however, is a different practice, beyond hot battlefields like Afghanistan, identifying specific members of al-Qaida and then targeting them with lethal force, often using aircraft remotely operated by pilots who can be hundreds, if not thousands, of miles away. And this is what I want to focus on today.

Jack Goldsmith, a former assistant attorney general in the administration of George W. Bush and now a professor at Harvard Law School, captured the situation well. He wrote:

"The government needs a way to credibly convey to the public that its decisions about who is being targeted, especially when the target is a U.S. citizen, are sound. First, the government can and should tell us more about the process by which it reaches its high-value targeting decisions. . . . The more the government tells us about the eyeballs on the issue and the robustness of the process, the more credible will be its claims about the accuracy of its factual determinations and the soundness of its legal ones. All of this information can be disclosed in some form without endangering critical intelligence."

Well, President Obama agrees. And that is why I am here today.

I stand here as someone who has been involved with our nation's security for more than 30 years. I have a profound appreciation for the truly remarkable capabilities of our counterterrorism professionals, and our relationships with other nations, and we must never compromise them. I will not discuss the sensitive details of any specific operation today. I will not, nor will I ever, publicly divulge sensitive intelligence sources and methods. For when that happens, our national security is endangered and lives can be lost. At the same time, we reject the notion that any discussion of these matters is to step onto a slippery slope that inevitably endangers our national security. Too often, that fear can become an excuse for saying nothing at all, which creates a void that is then filled with myths and falsehoods. That, in turn, can erode our credibility with the American people and with foreign partners, and it can undermine the public's understanding and support for our efforts. In contrast, President Obama believes that done carefully, deliberately and responsibly we can be more transparent and still ensure our nation's security.

So let me say it as simply as I can. Yes, in full accordance with the law, and in order to prevent terrorist attacks on the United States and to save American lives, the United States Government conducts targeted strikes against specific al-Qaida terrorists, sometimes using remotely piloted aircraft, often referred to publicly as drones. And I'm here today because President Obama has instructed us to be more open with the American people about these efforts.

Broadly speaking, the debate over strikes targeted at individual members of al-Qaida has centered on their legality, their ethics, the wisdom of using them, and the standards by which they are approved. With the remainder of my time today, I would like to address each of these in turn.

First, these targeted strikes are legal. Attorney General Holder, Harold Koh, and Jeh Johnson have all addressed this question at length. To briefly recap, as a matter of domestic law, the Constitution empowers the president to protect the nation from any imminent threat of attack. The Authorization for Use of Military Force, the AUMF, passed by Congress after the September 11th attacks authorizes the president "to use all necessary and appropriate force" against those nations, organizations and individuals responsible for 9/11. There is nothing in the AUMF that restricts the use of military force against al-Qaida to Afghanistan.

As a matter of international law, the United States is in an armed conflict with al-Qaida, the Taliban, and associated forces, in response to the 9/11 attacks, and we may also use force consistent with our inherent right of national self-defense. There is nothing in international law that bans the use of remotely piloted aircraft for this purpose or that prohibits us from using lethal force against our enemies outside of an active battlefield, at least when the country involved consents or is unable or unwilling to take action against the threat.

Second, targeted strikes are ethical. Without question, the ability to target a specific individual, from hundreds or thousands of miles away, raises profound questions. Here, I think it's useful to consider such strikes against the basic principles of the law of war that govern the use of force.

Targeted strikes conform to the principle of necessity, the requirement that the target have definite military value. In this armed conflict, individuals who are part of al-Qaida or its associated forces are legitimate military targets. We have the authority to target them with lethal force just as we targeted enemy leaders in past conflicts, such as German and Japanese commanders during World War II.

Targeted strikes conform to the principle of distinction, the idea that only military objectives may be intentionally targeted and that civilians are protected from being intentionally targeted. With the unprecedented ability of remotely piloted aircraft to precisely target a military objective while minimizing collateral damage, one could argue that never before has there been a weapon that allows us to distinguish more effectively between an al-Qaida terrorist and innocent civilians.

Targeted strikes conform to the principle of proportionality, the notion that the anticipated collateral damage of an action cannot be excessive in relation to the anticipated military advantage. By targeting an individual terrorist or small numbers of terrorists with ordnance that can be adapted to avoid harming others in the immediate vicinity, it is hard to imagine a tool that can better minimize the risk to civilians than remotely piloted aircraft.

For the same reason, targeted strikes conform to the principle of humanity which requires us to use weapons that will not inflict unnecessary suffering. For all these reasons, I suggest to you that these targeted strikes against al-Qaida terrorists are indeed ethical and just.

Of course, even if a tool is legal and ethical, that doesn't necessarily make it appropriate or advisable in a given circumstance. This brings me to my next point.

Targeted strikes are wise. Remotely piloted aircraft in particular can be a wise choice because of geography, with their ability to fly hundreds of miles over the most treacherous terrain, strike their targets with astonishing precision, and then return to base. They can be a wise choice because of time, when windows of opportunity can close quickly and there may be just minutes to act.

They can be a wise choice because they dramatically reduce the danger to U.S. personnel, even eliminating the danger altogether. Yet they are also a wise choice because they dramatically reduce the danger to innocent civilians, especially considered against massive ordnance that can cause injury and death far beyond its intended target.

In addition, compared against other options, a pilot operating this aircraft remotely, with the benefit of technology and with the safety of distance, might actually have a clearer picture of the target and its surroundings, including the presence of innocent civilians. It's this surgical precision, the ability, with laser-like focus, to eliminate the cancerous tumor called an al-Qa'ida terrorist while limiting damage to the tissue around it, that makes this counterterrorism tool so essential.

There's another reason that targeted strikes can be a wise choice, the strategic consequences that inevitably come with the use of force. As we've seen, deploying large armies abroad won't always be our best offense.

Countries typically don't want foreign soldiers in their cities and towns. In fact, large, intrusive military deployments risk playing into al-Qaida's strategy of trying to draw us into long, costly wars that drain us financially, inflame anti-American resentment and inspire the next generation of terrorists. In comparison, there is the precision of targeted strikes.

I acknowledge that we, as a government, along with our foreign partners, can and must do a better job of addressing the mistaken belief among some foreign publics that we engage in these strikes casually, as if we are simply unwilling to expose U.S forces to the dangers faced every day by people in those regions. For, as I'll describe today, there is absolutely nothing casual about the extraordinary care we take in making the decision to pursue an al-Qaida terrorist, and the lengths to which we go to ensure precision and avoid the loss of innocent life.

Still, there is no more consequential a decision than deciding whether to use lethal force against another human being, even a terrorist dedicated to killing American citizens. So in order to ensure that our counterterrorism operations involving the use of lethal force are legal, ethical, and wise, President Obama has demanded that we hold ourselves to the highest possible standards and processes.

This reflects his approach to broader questions regarding the use of force. In his speech in Oslo accepting the Nobel Peace Prize, the president said that "all nations, strong and weak alike, must adhere to standards that govern the use of force." And he added:

"Where force is necessary, we have a moral and strategic interest in binding ourselves to certain rules of conduct. And even as we confront a vicious adversary that abides by no rules, I believe the United States of America must remain a standard bearer in the conduct of war. That is what makes us different from those whom we fight. That is a source of our strength."

The United States is the first nation to regularly conduct strikes using remotely piloted aircraft in an armed conflict. Other nations also possess this technology, and many more nations are seeking it, and more will succeed in acquiring it. President Obama and those of us on his national security team are very mindful that as our nation uses this technology, we are establishing precedents that other nations may follow, and not all of those nations may—not all of them will be nations that share our interests or the premium we put on protecting human life, including innocent civilians.

If we want other nations to use these technologies responsibly, we must use them responsibly. If we want other nations to adhere to high and rigorous standards for their use, then we must do so as well. We cannot expect of others what we will not do ourselves. President Obama has therefore demanded that we hold ourselves to the highest possible standards, that, at every step, we be as thorough and deliberate as possible.

This leads me to the final point I want to discuss today, the rigorous standards and process of review to which we hold ourselves today when considering and authorizing strikes against a specific member of al-Qaida outside the hot battlefield of Afghanistan. What I hope to do is to give you a general sense, in broad terms, of the high bar we require ourselves to meet when making these profound decisions today. That includes not only whether a specific member of al-Qaida can legally be pursued with lethal force, but also whether he should be.

Over time, we've worked to refine, clarify, and strengthen this process and our standards, and we continue to do so. If our counterterrorism professionals assess, for example, that a suspected member of al-Qaida poses such a threat to the United States as to warrant lethal action, they may raise that individual's name for consideration. The proposal will go through a careful review and, as appropriate, will be evaluated by the very most senior officials in our government for decision.

First and foremost, the individual must be a legitimate target under the law. Earlier, I described how the use of force against members of al-Qaida is authorized under both international and U.S. law, including both the inherent right of national self-defense and the 2001 Authorization for Use of Military Force, which courts have held extends to those who are part of al-Qaida, the Taliban, and associated forces. If, after a legal review, we determine that the individual is not a lawful target, end of discussion. We are a nation of laws, and we will always act within the bounds of the law.

Of course, the law only establishes the outer limits of the authority in which counterterrorism professionals can operate. Even if we determine that it is lawful to pursue the terrorist in question with lethal force, it doesn't necessarily mean we should. There are, after all, literally thousands of individuals who are part of al-Qaida, the Taliban, or associated forces, thousands upon thousands. Even if it were possible, going after every single one of these individuals with lethal force would neither be wise nor an effective use of our intelligence and counterterrorism resources.

As a result, we have to be strategic. Even if it is lawful to pursue a specific member of al-Qaida, we ask ourselves whether that individual's activities rise to a certain threshold for action, and whether taking action will, in fact, enhance our security.

For example, when considering lethal force we ask ourselves whether the individual poses a significant threat to U.S. interests. This is absolutely critical, and it goes to the very essence of why we take this kind of exceptional action. We do not engage in legal action—in lethal action in order to eliminate every single member of al-Qaida in the world. Most times, and as we have done for more than a decade, we rely on cooperation with other countries that are also interested in removing these terrorists with their own capabilities and within their own laws. Nor is lethal action about punishing terrorists for past crimes; we are not seeking vengeance. Rather, we conduct targeted strikes because they are necessary to mitigate an actual ongoing threat, to stop plots, prevent future attacks, and save American lives.

And what do we mean by a significant threat? I am not referring to some hypothetical threat, the mere possibility that a member of al-Qaida might try to attack us at some point in the future. A significant threat might be posed by an individual who is an operational leader of al-Qaida or one of its associated forces. Or perhaps the individual is himself an operative, in the midst of actually training for or planning to carry out attacks against U.S. interests. Or perhaps the individual possesses unique operational skills that are being leveraged in a planned attack. The purpose of a strike against a particular individual is to stop him before he can carry out his attack and kill innocents. The purpose is to disrupt his plots and plans before they come to fruition.

In addition, our unqualified preference is to only undertake lethal force when we believe that capturing the individual is not feasible. I have heard it suggested that the Obama Administration somehow prefers killing al-Qaida members rather than capturing them. Nothing could be further from the truth. It is our preference to capture suspected terrorists whenever feasible.

For one reason, this allows us to gather valuable intelligence that we might not be able to obtain any other way. In fact, the members of al-Qaida that we or other nations have captured have been one of our greatest sources of information about al-Qaida, its plans, and its intentions. And once in U.S. custody, we often can prosecute them in our federal courts or reformed military commissions, both of which are used for gathering intelligence and preventing terrorist attacks.

You see our preference for capture in the case of Ahmed Warsame, a member of al-Shabaab who had significant ties to al-Qaida in the Arabian Peninsula. Last year, when we learned that he would be traveling from Yemen to Somalia, U.S. forces captured him in route and we subsequently charged him in federal court.

The reality, however, is that since 2001 such unilateral captures by U.S. forces outside of hot battlefields, like Afghanistan, have been exceedingly rare. This is due in part to the fact that in many parts of the world our counterterrorism partners have been able to capture or kill dangerous individuals themselves.

Moreover, after being subjected to more than a decade of relentless pressure, al-Qaida's ranks have dwindled and scattered. These terrorists are skilled at seeking remote, inhospitable terrain, places where the United States and our partners simply do not have the ability to arrest or capture them. At other times, our forces might have the ability to attempt capture, but only by putting the lives of our personnel at too great a risk. Often times, attempting capture could subject civilians to unacceptable risks. There are many reasons why capture might not be feasible, in which case lethal force might be the only remaining option to address the threat and prevent an attack.

Finally, when considering lethal force we are of course mindful that there are important checks on our ability to act unilaterally in foreign territories. We do not use force whenever we want, wherever we want. International legal principles, including respect for a state's sovereignty and the laws of war, impose constraints. The United States of America respects national sovereignty and international law.

Those are some of the questions we consider; the high standards we strive to meet. And in the end, we make a decision, we decide whether a particular member of al-Qaida warrants being pursued in this manner. Given the stakes involved and the consequence of our decision, we consider all the information available to us, carefully, responsibly.

We review the most up-to-date intelligence, drawing on the full range of our intelligence capabilities. And we do what sound intelligence demands, we challenge it, we question it, including any assumptions on which it might be based. If we want to know more, we may ask the intelligence community to go back and collect additional intelligence or refine its analysis so that a more informed decision can be made.

We listen to departments and agencies across our national security team. We don't just hear out differing views, we ask for them and encourage them. We discuss. We debate. We disagree. We consider the advantages and disadvantages of taking action. We also carefully consider the costs of inaction and whether a decision not to carry out a strike could allow a terrorist attack to proceed and potentially kill scores of innocents.

Nor do we limit ourselves narrowly to counterterrorism considerations. We consider the broader strategic implications of any action, including what effect, if any, an action might have on our relationships with other countries. And we don't simply make a decision and never revisit it again. Quite the opposite. Over time, we refresh the intelligence and continue to consider whether lethal force is still warranted.

In some cases, such as senior al-Qaida leaders who are directing and planning attacks against the United States, the individual clearly meets our standards for taking action. In other cases, individuals have not met our standards. Indeed, there have been numerous occasions where, after careful review, we have, working on a consensus basis, concluded that lethal force was not justified in a given case.

As President Obama's counterterrorism advisor, I feel that it is important for the American people to know that these efforts are overseen with extraordinary care and thoughtfulness. The president expects us to address all of the tough questions I have discussed today. Is capture really not feasible? Is this individual a significant threat to U.S. interests? Is this really the best option? Have we thought through the consequences, especially any unintended ones? Is this really going to help protect our country from further attacks? Is it going to save lives?

Our commitment to upholding the ethics and efficacy of this counterterrorism tool continues even after we decide to pursue a specific terrorist in this way. For example, we only authorize a particular operation against a specific individual if we have a high degree of confidence that the individual being targeted is indeed the terrorist we are pursuing. This is a very high bar. Of course, how we identify an individual naturally involves intelligence sources and methods, which I will not discuss. Suffice it to say, our Intelligence Community has multiple ways to determine, with a high degree of confidence, that the individual being targeted is indeed the al-Qaida terrorist we are seeking.

In addition, we only authorize a strike if we have a high degree of confidence that innocent civilians will not be injured or killed, except in the rarest of circumstances. The unprecedented advances we have made in technology provide us greater proximity to targets for a longer period of time, and as a result allow us to better understand what is happening in real time on the ground in ways that were previously impossible. We can be much more discriminating and we can make more informed judgments about factors that might contribute to collateral damage.

I can tell you today that there have indeed been occasions when we have decided against conducting a strike in order to avoid the injury or death of innocent civilians. This reflects our commitment to doing everything in our power to avoid civilian casualties, even if it means having to come back another day to take out that terrorist, as we have done. And I would note that these standards, for identifying a target and avoiding the loss of innocent—the loss of innocent civilians, exceed what is required as a matter of international law on a typical battlefield. That's another example of the high standards to which we hold ourselves.

Our commitment to ensuring accuracy and effectiveness continues even after a strike. In the wake of a strike, we harness the full range of our intelligence capabilities to assess whether the mission in fact achieved its objective. We try to determine whether there was any collateral damage, including civilian deaths. There is, of course, no such thing as a perfect weapon, and remotely piloted aircraft are no exception.

As the president and others have acknowledged, there have indeed been instances when, despite the extraordinary precautions we take, civilians have been accidentally killed or worse—have been accidentally injured, or worse, killed in these strikes. It is exceedingly rare, but it has happened. When it does, it pains us and we regret it deeply, as we do any time innocents are killed in war. And when this happens we take it seriously. We go back and review our actions. We examine our practices. And we constantly work to improve and refine our efforts so that we are doing everything in our power to prevent the loss of innocent life. This too is a reflection of our values as Americans.

Ensuring the ethics and efficacy of these strikes also includes regularly informing appropriate members of Congress and the committees who have oversight of our counterterrorism programs. Indeed, our counterterrorism programs, including the use of lethal force, have grown more effective over time because of congressional oversight and our ongoing dialogue with members and staff.

This is the seriousness, the extraordinary care, that President Obama and those of us on his national security team bring to this weightiest of questions: Whether to pursue lethal force against a terrorist who is plotting to attack our country.

When that person is a U.S. citizen, we ask ourselves additional questions. Attorney General Holder has already described the legal authorities that clearly allow us to use lethal force against an American citizen who is a senior operational leader of al-Qaida. He has discussed the thorough and careful review, including all relevant constitutional considerations, that is to be undertaken by the U.S. government when determining whether the individual poses an imminent threat of violent attack against the United States.

To recap, the standards and processes I've described today, which we have refined and strengthened over time, reflect our commitment to: ensuring the individual is a legitimate target under the law; determining whether the individual poses a significant threat to U.S. interests; determining that capture is not feasible; being mindful of the important checks on our ability to act unilaterally in foreign territories; having that high degree of confidence, both in the identity of the target and that innocent civilians will not be harmed; and, of course, engaging in additional review if the al-Qaida terrorist is a U.S. citizen.

Going forward, we'll continue to strengthen and refine these standards and processes. As we do, we'll look to institutionalize our approach more formally so that the high standards we set for ourselves endure over time, including as an example for other nations that pursue these capabilities. As the president said in Oslo, in the conduct of war, America must be the standard bearer.

This includes our continuing commitment to greater transparency. With that in mind, I have made a sincere effort today to address some of the main questions that citizens and scholars have raised regarding the use of targeted lethal force against al-Qaida. I suspect there are those, perhaps some in this audience, who feel we have not been transparent enough. I suspect there are those, both inside and outside our government, who feel I have been perhaps too open. If both groups feel a little unsatisfied, then I've probably struck the right balance today.

Again, there are some lines we simply will not and cannot cross because, at times, our national security demands secrecy. But we are a democracy. The people are sovereign. And our counterterrorism tools do not exist in a vacuum. They are stronger and more sustainable when the American people understand and support them. They are weaker and less sustainable when the American people do not. As a result of my remarks today, I hope the American people have a better understanding of this critical tool, why we use it, what we do, how carefully we use it, and why it is absolutely essential to protecting our country and our citizens.

I would just like to close on a personal note. I know that for many people in our government and across the country the issue of targeted strikes raised profound moral questions. It forces us to confront deeply held personal beliefs and our values as a nation. If anyone in government who works in this area tells you they haven't struggled with this, then they haven't spent much time thinking about it. I know I have, and I will continue to struggle with it as long as I remain involved in counterterrorism.

But I am certain about one thing. We are at war. We are at war against a terrorist organization called al-Qaida that has brutally murdered thousands of Americans, men, women and children, as well as thousands of other innocent people around the world. In recent years, with the help of targeted strikes we have turned al-Qaida into a shadow of what it once was. They are on the road to destruction.

Until that finally happens, however, there are still terrorists in hard-to-reach places who are actively planning attacks against us. If given the chance, they will gladly strike again and kill more of our citizens. And the president has a Constitutional and solemn obligation to do everything in his power to protect the safety and security of the American people.

Yes, war is hell. It is awful. It involves human beings killing other human beings, sometimes innocent civilians. That is why we despise war. That is why we want this war against al-Qaida to be over as soon as possible, and not a moment longer. And over time, as al-Qaida fades into history and as our partners grow stronger, I'd hope that the United States would have to rely less on lethal force to keep our country safe.

Until that happens, as President Obama said here five years ago, if another nation cannot or will not take action, we will. And it is an unfortunate fact that to save many innocent lives we are sometimes obliged to take lives, the lives of terrorists who seek to murder our fellow citizens.

On behalf of President Obama and his administration, I am here to say to the American people that we will continue to work to safeguard this nation—this nation and its citizens responsibly, adhering to the laws of this land and staying true to the values that define us as Americans.

Thank you very much.

9

Letter from Attorney General Eric Holder to
Hon. Patrick J. Leahy

May 22, 2013

Untitled

Holder sent this letter to Patrick Leahy, the chairman of the Senate Judiciary Committee, in advance of the speech to be delivered by the president the next day at the National Defense University. Holder's letter
formally acknowledges for the first time that the government had targeted and killed Anwar al-Aulaqi. The letter also acknowledges that the
government had killed three other U.S. citizens—Samir Khan, Abdulrahman al-Aulaqi, and Jude Kenan Mohammed—but it states that these
three individuals had not been "specifically" targeted.

The document from which this text was transcribed is posted at:
www.ACLU.org/TDM/HolderLetter.

May 22, 2013

The Honorable Patrick J. Leahy
Chairman
Committee on the Judiciary
United States Senate
Washington, DC 20530

Dear Mr. Chairman:

Since entering office, the President has made clear his commitment to providing Congress and the American people with as much information as possible about our sensitive counterterrorism operations, consistent with our national security and the proper functioning of the Executive Branch. Doing so is necessary, the President stated in his May 21, 2009, National Archives speech, because it enables the citizens of our democracy to "make informed judgments and hold [their Government] accountable."

In furtherance of this commitment, the Administration has provided an unprecedented level of transparency into how sensitive counterterrorism operations are conducted. Several senior Administration officials, including myself, have taken numerous steps to explain publicly the legal basis for the United States' actions to the American people and the Congress. For example, in March 2012, I delivered an address at Northwestern University Law School discussing certain aspects of the Administration's counterterrorism legal framework. And the Department of Justice and other departments and agencies have continually worked with the appropriate oversight committees in the Congress to ensure that those committees are fully informed of the legal basis for our actions.

The Administration is determined to continue these extensive outreach efforts to communicate with the American people. Indeed, the

President reiterated in his State of the Union address earlier this year that he would continue to engage with the Congress about our counterterrorism efforts to ensure that they remain consistent with our laws and values, and become more transparent to the American people and to the world.

To this end, the President has directed me to disclose certain information that until now has been properly classified. You and other Members of your Committee have on numerous occasions expressed a particular interest in the Administration's use of lethal force against U.S. citizens. In light of this fact, I am writing to disclose to you certain information about the number of U.S. citizens who have been killed by U.S. counterterrorism operations outside of areas of active hostilities. Since 2009, the United States, in the conduct of U.S. counterterrorism operations against al-Qa'ida and its associated forces outside of areas of active hostilities, has specifically targeted and killed one U.S. citizen, Anwar al-Aulaqi. The United States is further aware of three other U.S. citizens who have been killed in such U.S. counterterrorism operations over that same time period: Samir Khan, 'Abd al-Rahman Anwar al-Aulaqi, and Jude Kenan Mohammed. These individuals were not specifically targeted by the United States.

As I noted in my speech at Northwestern, "it is an unfortunate but undeniable fact" that a "small number" of U.S. citizens "have decided to commit violent attacks against their own country from abroad." Based on generations-old legal principles and Supreme Court decisions handed down during World War II, as well as during the current conflict, it is clear and logical that United States citizenship alone does not make such individuals immune from being targeted. Rather, it means that the government must take special care and take into account all relevant constitutional considerations, the laws of war, and other law with respect to U.S. citizens—even those who are leading efforts to kill their fellow, innocent Americans. Such considerations allow for the use of lethal force in a foreign country against a U.S. citizen who is a senior operational leader of al-Qa'ida or its associated forces, and who is actively engaged in planning to kill Americans, in the following circumstances: (1) the U.S. government has determined, after a thorough and careful review, that the individual poses an imminent threat of violent attack against the United States; (2) capture is not feasible;

and (3) the operation would be conducted in a manner consistent with applicable law of war principles.

These conditions should not come as a surprise: the Administration's legal views on this weighty issue have been clear and consistent over time. The analysis in my speech at Northwestern University Law School is entirely consistent with not only the analysis found in the unclassified white paper the Department of Justice provided to your Committee soon after my speech, but also with the classified analysis the Department shared with other congressional committees in May 2011—months before the operation that resulted in the death of Anwar al-Aulaqi. The analysis in my speech is also entirely consistent with the classified legal advice on this issue the Department of Justice has shared with your Committee more recently. In short, the Administration has demonstrated its commitment to discussing with the Congress and the American people the circumstances in which it could lawfully use lethal force in a foreign country against a U.S. citizen who is a senior operational leader of al-Qa'ida or its associated forces, and who is actively engaged in planning to kill Americans.

Anwar al-Aulaqi plainly satisfied all of the conditions I outlined in my speech at Northwestern. Let me be more specific. Al-Aulaqi was a senior operational leader of al- Qa'ida in the Arabian Peninsula (AQAP), the most dangerous regional affiliate of al-Qa'ida and a group that has committed numerous terrorist attacks overseas and attempted multiple times to conduct terrorist attacks against the U.S. homeland. And al-Aulaqi was not just a senior leader of AQAP—he was the group's chief of external operations, intimately involved in detailed planning and putting in place plots against U.S. persons.

In this role, al-Aulaqi repeatedly made clear his intent to attack U.S. persons and his hope that these attacks would take American lives. For example, in a message to Muslims living in the United States, he noted that he had come "to the conclusion that *jihad* against America is binding upon myself just as it is binding upon every other able Muslim." But it was not al-Aulaqi's <u>words</u> that led the United States to act against him: they only served to demonstrate his intentions and state of mind, that he "pray[ed] that Allah [would] destro[y] America and all its allies." Rather, it was al-Aulaqi's <u>actions</u>—and, in particular, his direct personal involvement in the continued planning and execution of terrorist attacks against the U.S. homeland—that made him a lawful target and led the United States to take action.

For example, when Umar Farouk Abdulmutallab—the individual who attempted to blow up an airplane bound for Detroit on Christmas Day 2009—went to Yemen in 2009, al-Aulaqi arranged an introduction via text message. Abdulmutallab told U.S. officials that he stayed at al-Aulaqi's house for three days, and then spent two weeks at an AQAP training camp. Al-Aulaqi planned a suicide operation for Abdulmutallab, helped Abdulmutallab draft a statement for a martyrdom video to be shown after the attack, and directed him to take down a U.S. airliner. Al-Aulaqi's last instructions were to blow up the airplane when it was over American soil. Al-Aulaqi also played a key role in the October 2010 plot to detonate explosive devices on two U.S.-bound cargo planes: he not only helped plan and oversee the plot, but was also directly involved in the details of its execution—to the point that he took part in the development and testing of the explosive devices that were placed on the planes. Moreover, information that remains classified to protect sensitive sources and methods evidences al-Aulaqi's involvement in the planning of numerous other plots against U.S. and Western interests and makes clear he was continuing to plot attacks when he was killed.

Based on this information, high-level U.S. government officials appropriately concluded that al-Aulaqi posed a continuing and imminent threat of violent attack against the United States. Before carrying out the operation that killed al-Aulaqi, senior officials also determined, based on a careful evaluation of the circumstances at the time, that it was not feasible to capture al-Aulaqi. In addition, senior officials determined that the operation would be conducted consistent with applicable law of war principles, including the cardinal principles of (1) necessity—the requirement that the target have definite military value; (2) distinction—the idea that only military objectives may be intentionally targeted and that civilians are protected from being intentionally targeted; (3) proportionality—the notion that the anticipated collateral damage of an action cannot be excessive in relation to the anticipated concrete and direct military advantage; and (4) humanity—a principle that requires us to use weapons that will not inflict unnecessary suffering. The operation was also undertaken consistent with Yemeni sovereignty.

While a substantial amount of information indicated that Anwar al-Aulaqi was a senior AQAP leader actively plotting to kill Americans, the decision that he was a lawful target was not taken lightly. The decision to use lethal force is one of the gravest that our government, at every level, can face. The operation to target Anwar al-Aulaqi was thus subjected to an exceptionally rigorous interagency legal review: not only did I and other Department of Justice lawyers conclude after a thorough and searching review that the operation was lawful, but so too did other departments and agencies within the U.S. government.

The decision to target Anwar al-Aulaqi was additionally subjected to extensive policy review at the highest levels of the U.S. Government, and senior U.S. officials also briefed the appropriate committees of Congress on the possibility of using lethal force against al-Aulaqi. Indeed, the Administration informed the relevant congressional oversight committees that it had approved the use of lethal force against al-Aulaqi in February 2010—well over a year before the operation in question—and the legal justification was subsequently explained in detail to those committees, well before action was taken against Aulaqi. This extensive outreach is consistent with the Administration's strong and continuing commitment to congressional oversight of our counterterrorism operations—oversight which ensures, as the President stated during his State of the Union address, that our actions are "consistent with our laws and system of checks and balances."

The Supreme Court has long "made clear that a state of war is not a blank check for the President when it comes to the rights of the Nation's citizens." *Hamdi v. Rumsfeld*, 542 U.S. 507, 536 (2004); *Youngstown Sheet & Tube Co. v. Sawyer*, 343 U.S. 578, 587 (1952). But the Court's case law and longstanding practice and principle also make clear that the Constitution does not prohibit the Government it establishes from taking action to protect the American people from the threats posed by terrorists who hide in faraway countries and continually plan and launch plots against the U.S. homeland. The decision to target Anwar al-Aulaqi was lawful, it was considered, and it was just.

* * * * *

This letter is only one of a number of steps the Administration will be taking to fulfill the President's State of the Union commitment to engage with Congress and the American people on our counterterrorism efforts. This week the President approved and relevant congressional committees will be notified and briefed on a document that institutionalizes the Administration's exacting standards and processes for reviewing and approving operations to capture or use lethal force against terrorist targets outside the United States and areas of active hostilities; these standards and processes are either already in place or are to be transitioned into place. While that document remains classified, it makes clear that a cornerstone of the Administration's policy is one of the principles I noted in my speech at Northwestern: that lethal force should not be used when it is feasible to capture a terrorist suspect. For circumstances in which capture is feasible, the policy outlines standards and procedures to ensure that operations to take into custody a terrorist suspect are conducted in accordance with all applicable law, including the laws of war. When capture is not feasible, the policy provides that lethal force may be used only when a terrorist target poses a continuing, imminent threat to Americans, and when certain other preconditions, including a requirement that no other reasonable alternatives exist to effectively address the threat, are satisfied. And in all circumstances there must be a legal basis for using force against the target. Significantly, the President will soon be speaking publicly in greater detail about our counterterrorism operations and the legal and policy framework that governs those actions.

5

I recognize that even after the Administration makes unprecedented disclosures like those contained in this letter, some unanswered questions will remain. I assure you that the President and his national security team are mindful of this Administration's pledge to public accountability for our counterterrorism efforts, and we will continue to give careful consideration to whether and how additional information may be declassified and disclosed to the American people without harming our national security.

Sincerely,

Eric H. Holder, Jr.
Attorney General

cc: Ranking Member Charles Grassley
     Chairman Dianne Feinstein
     Vice Chairman Saxby Chambliss
     Chairman Carl Levin
     Ranking Member James Inhofe
     Chairman Bob Goodlatte
     Ranking Member John Conyers, Jr.
     Chairman Mike Rogers
     Ranking Member C.A. Dutch Ruppersberger
     Chairman Howard P. McKeon
     Ranking Member Adam Smith
     Chairman Robert Menendez
     Ranking Member Bob Corker
     Chairman Ed Royce
     Ranking Member Eliot Engel
     Majority Leader Harry Reid
     Minority Leader Mitch McConnell
     Speaker John Boehner
     Majority Leader Eric Cantor
     Minority Leader Nancy Pelosi
     Minority Whip Steny Hoyer

10

Presidential Policy Guidance

May 22, 2013

"Procedures for Approving Direct Action Against Terrorist Targets Located Outside the United States and Areas of Active Hostilities"

President Obama signed this document—the PPG, or the "playbook"— the day before he delivered a major national security speech at the National Defense University. The document throws into stark relief the remarkable bureaucracy behind the drone campaign. It details the process by which executive branch officials adopt "plans for taking direct action" against "terrorist targets." It also details the process by which suspects are "nominated" to government kill lists. The government released a summary of the PPG when President Obama delivered his remarks at the National Defense University, but it did not release the PPG itself until the summer of 2016, when a federal court ordered the government to release it. The government produced the document to the ACLU on August 5, 2016, and the ACLU published it the following day.

The document from which this text was transcribed is posted at: www.ACLU.org/TDM/PPG.

May 22, 2013

PROCEDURES FOR APPROVING DIRECT ACTION AGAINST TERRORIST TARGETS LOCATED OUTSIDE THE UNITED STATES AND AREAS OF ACTIVE HOSTILITIES

This Presidential Policy Guidance (PPG) establishes the standard operating procedures for when the United States takes direct action, which refers to lethal and non-lethal uses of force, including capture operations, against terrorist targets outside the United States and areas of active hostilities.

Any direct action must be conducted lawfully and taken against lawful targets; wherever possible such action will be done pursuant to a ████████████████████ plan. In particular, whether any proposed target would be a lawful target for direct action is a determination that will be made in the first instance by the nominating department's or agency's counsel (with appropriate legal review as provided below) based on the legal authorities of the nominating department or agency and other applicable law. Even if the proposed target is lawful, there remains a separate question whether the proposed target should be targeted for direct action as a matter of policy. That determination will be made pursuant to the interagency review process and policy standards set forth in this PPG. The most important policy objective, particularly informing consideration of lethal action, is to protect American lives.

Capture operations offer the best opportunity for meaningful intelligence gain from counterterrorism (CT) operations and the mitigation and disruption of terrorist threats. Consequently, the United States prioritizes, as a matter of policy, the capture of terrorist suspects as a preferred option over lethal action and will therefore require a feasibility assessment of capture options as a component of any proposal for lethal action. Lethal action should be taken in an effort to prevent terrorist attacks against U.S. persons only when capture of an individual is not feasible and no other reasonable alternatives exist to effectively address the threat. Lethal action should not be proposed or pursued as a punitive step or as a substitute for prosecuting a terrorist suspect in a civilian court or a military commission. Capture is preferred even in circumstances where neither prosecution nor third-country custody are available disposition options at the time.

CT actions, including lethal action against designated terrorist targets, shall be as discriminating and precise as reasonably possible. Absent extraordinary circumstances, direct action against an identified high-value terrorist (HVT) will be taken only when there is near certainty that the individual being targeted is in fact the lawful target and located at the place where the action will occur. Also absent extraordinary circumstances, direct action will be taken only if there is near certainty that the action can be taken without injuring or killing non-combatants. For purposes of this PPG, non-combatants are understood to be individuals who may not be made the object of attack under the law of armed conflict. The term "non-combatant" does not include an individual who is targetable as part of a belligerent party to an armed conflict, an individual who is taking a direct part in hostilities, or an individual who is targetable in the exercise of national self-defense. Moreover, international legal principles, including respect for a state's sovereignty and the laws of war, impose important constraints on the ability of the United States to act unilaterally—and on the way in which the United States can use force—in foreign territories. Direct action should only be undertaken ██

As reflected in the procedures contained in this PPG, whenever possible and appropriate, decisions regarding direct action will be informed by departments and agencies with relevant expertise, knowledge, and equities, ██, as well as by coordinated interagency intelligence analysis. Such interagency coordination and consultation will ensure that decisions on operational matters of such importance are well-informed and will facilitate de-confliction among departments and agencies addressing overlapping threat streams. Such coordination is not intended to interfere with the traditional command and control authority of departments and agencies conducting CT operations.

Lastly, when considering potential direct action against a U.S. person under this PPG, there are additional questions that must be answered. The Department of Justice (DOJ), for example, must conduct a legal analysis to ensure that such action may be conducted against the individual consistent with the laws and Constitution of the United States.

Based on the principles and priorities described above, Section 1 sets forth the procedure for establishing ████████████████ plan for taking direct action against terrorist targets. Section 2 sets forth the approval process for the capture and long-term disposition of suspected terrorists. Section 3 sets forth the policy standard and procedure for designating identified HVTs for lethal action. Section 4 sets forth the policy standard and procedure for approving lethal force against terrorist targets other than identified HVTs[1]. Section 5 sets forth the procedures for approving proposals that vary from the policy guidance otherwise set forth in this PPG. Section 6 sets forth the procedure for after-action reports. Section 7 addresses congressional notification. Section 8 sets forth general provisions.

SECTION 1.   <u>Procedure for Establishing a ████████████████ Plan for taking Direct Action Against Terrorist Targets</u>

1.A Operational Plans for Taking Direct Action Against Terrorist Targets

Each of the operating agencies may propose a detailed operational plan to govern their respective direct action operations ████████ ████████ against: (1) suspected terrorists who may be lawfully detained; (2) identified HVTs who may be lawfully targeted for lethal action; or (3) lawful terrorist targets other than identified HVTs.

1.B Interagency Review of Operational Plans

---

[1] This PPG does not address otherwise lawful and properly authorized activities that may have lethal effects, which are incidental to the primary purpose of the operation.

All operational plans to undertake direct action operations against terrorist targets ██████████████████████ must undergo a legal review by the general counsel(s) of the operating agency executing the ⬚3 plan, and be submitted to the National Security Staff (NSS) for interagency review. All proposed operational plans must conform to the policy standards set forth in this Section. All proposed operational plans to undertake direct action against terrorist targets ████████ ██████████████████ along with the conclusions of the General Counsel, shall be referred to the NSS Legal Adviser. The NSS Legal Adviser and the General Counsel of the proposing operating agency shall consult with other department and agency counsels, as necessary and appropriate. The NSS Legal Adviser shall submit the relevant legal conclusions to the Deputies Committee to inform its consideration of the proposed operational plan. All proposed operational plans to undertake direct action against terrorist targets ████████████ ███ will be reviewed by appropriate members of the Deputies and Principals Committees of the National Security Council (NSC) (defined in Presidential Policy Directive-1 or any successor directive) before presentation to the President for decision.

1.C Guidelines for Operational Plans

Any operational plan for taking direct action against terrorist targets ██████████████████████ shall, among other things, indicate with precision:

1) The U.S. CT objectives to be achieved;
2) The duration of time for which the authority is to remain in force;
3) The international legal basis for taking action ████████████;
4) The strike and surveillance assets that may be employed when taking action against an authorized objective;
5) ████████████████████████████
   ██████████████████████
6) Any proposed stipulation related to the operational plan, including the duration of authority for such stipulation;

7) Any proposed variations from the policies and procedures set forth in this PPG; and

8) The conditions precedent for any operation, which shall include at a minimum the following: (a) near certainty that an identified HVT or other lawful terrorist target other than an identified HVT is present; (b) near certainty that non-combatants will not be injured or killed; (c) ███████████ ██████████████████████████████[2] and (d) if lethal force is being employed: (i) an assessment that capture is not feasible at the time of the operation; (ii) an assessment that the relevant governmental authorities in the country where action is contemplated cannot or will not effectively address the threat to U.S. persons; and (iii) an assessment that no other reasonable alternatives to lethal action exist to effectively address the threat to U.S. persons.

---

[4] **1.D Additional Requirements When Requesting Authority for Directing Lethal Force Against Targets Other Than Identified HVTs**

When requesting authority to direct lethal force against terrorist targets other than identified HVTs, the ████████████████ plan shall also include the following:

1) The types of targets that would qualify as appropriate targets pursuant to Section 4 (Terrorist Targets Other Than Identified HVTs) for purposes of the proposed operational plan; and

2) A description of the operating agency's internal process for nominating and approving the use of lethal force against terrorist targets other than identified HVTs.

1.E Policies and Procedures

---

[2] Operational disagreements ████████████████████████████████ ███████████ shall be elevated to Principals. The President will adjudicate any disagreement among or between Principals.

The operating agencies shall establish harmonized policies and procedures for assessing:

1) Near certainty that a lawful target is present;
2) Near certainty that non-combatants will not be injured or killed; and
3) With respect to a proposal to take direct action against terrorist targets other than identified HVTs, whether the target qualifies pursuant to the policy standard set forth in Section 4.A of this PPG and in the specific operational plan.

1.F   When Using Lethal Action, Employ All Reasonably Available Resources to Ascertain the Identity of the Target

When the use of lethal action is deemed necessary, departments and agencies of the United States Government must employ all reasonably available resources to ascertain the identity of the target so that action can be taken, for example, against identified HVTs in accordance with Section 3 of this PPG. Verifying a target's identity before taking lethal action ensures greater certainty of outcome that lethal action has been taken against identified HVTs who satisfy the policy standard for lethal action in Section 3.A.

1.G   Principals and Deputies Review of Operational Plans for Taking Direct Action Against Terrorists Targets

When considering a proposed operational plan, Principals and Deputies shall evaluate the following issues, along with any others they deem appropriate:

1) The implications for the broader regional and international political interests of the United States; and
2) For an operational plan that includes the option of lethal force against targets other than identified HVTs, an explanation of why authorizing direct action against targets

other than identified HVTs is necessary to achieve U.S. policy objectives.

5 | **1.H Presentation to the President**

1.H.1 If the Principal of the nominating operating agency, after review by Principals and Deputies, continues to support the operational plan, the plan shall be presented to the President for decision, along with the views expressed by departments and agencies during the NSC process.

1.H.2 An appropriate NSS official will communicate, in writing, the President's decision, including any terms or conditions placed on any approval, to appropriate departments and agencies.

1.I   Amendments or Modifications to Operational Plans

Except as described in Section 5, any amendments or modifications to an approved operational plan for direct action ███████████████████ shall undergo the same review and approval process outlined in this Section.

SECTION 2.   <u>Approval Process for Certain Captures and the Long-Term Disposition of Certain Suspects</u>

This Section sets forth the approval process for nominating for capture suspected terrorists or individuals providing operational support to suspected terrorists (in this section, together referred to as "suspects"); proposals to take custody of suspects, including pre- and post-capture screening; ███████████████████████████████ and determining a long-term disposition for suspects.

Unless otherwise approved in an operational plan under Section 1, the NSS shall coordinate for interagency review under this PPG, as described below, the following: (1) operations intended to result ████ ██ (2) operations that result in United States Government personnel taking custody (through a capture or transfer)[3] of a suspect located overseas and outside areas of active hostilities; and (3) long-term disposition decisions with respect to such suspects. The involvement of United States Government personnel in extraditions or transfers initiated for the purpose of prosecution in civilian court or those scenarios to which PPD-14 applies (i.e., circumstances in which an individual is arrested or otherwise taken into custody by the Federal Bureau of Investigation (FBI) or another Federal law enforcement agency)[4] are not covered by this PPG.

Captures and Transfers by Foreign Governments: These procedures do not apply to U.S. law enforcement requests for foreign governments to arrest or otherwise take into custody a suspect or to United States Government provision of training, funds, or equipment to enable a foreign government to capture a suspect. These procedures also do not apply to non-law enforcement United States Government requests to capture a suspect who will remain in the custody of the foreign government or to the provision of actionable intelligence to enable such captures. Every 6 months, departments and agencies shall notify the NSS of any requests made of a foreign government to capture a suspect in the preceding 6 months. Unless covered by the exceptions above or otherwise included in an operational plan under Section 1, if United States Government personnel ████████████████████████████████[5] capture a suspect, or an operation is intended to result in United States Government personnel taking custody of a suspect, the department or agency must submit a proposal

---

[3] "Custody," as referred to here, ████████████████████████████ ██████████ it is anticipated that the United States Government will have temporary or transitory custody of the individual(s) without the presence of officials of the foreign government maintaining custody of the detainee(s).

[4] Consistent with existing policy and practice, DOJ will, as appropriate, continue to notify the NSS, through the Counterterrorism Security Group (CSG), of plans to arrest, or seek the extradition or transfer of, a suspected terrorist, and where appropriate (e.g., to consider other potential disposition options) the NSS, in consultation with DOJ, may arrange for interagency consideration of a request for extradition or transfer.

[5] ██

through the NSS for interagency review. Operational plans ▮▮▮ ▮▮▮▮▮▮▮▮▮▮▮▮▮▮▮▮▮ may include additional conditions requiring interagency review of capture operations involving United States Government personnel, depending on the policy consideration of the particular country or region in which the operations would occur. If United States Government personnel are expected ▮▮▮▮▮▮▮▮▮ ▮▮▮▮▮▮▮▮▮▮▮▮▮▮ to capture or transfer suspects in a particular country or region on an ongoing basis, the department or agency involved should seek to include a proposed plan for such activities in the operational plan approved under Section 1.

2.A Nomination Process

2.A.1 Any department or agency participating in the Deputies Committee review in Section 2.D may identify an individual for consideration, but only an operating agency or DOJ ("nominating agencies" for purposes of Section 2 of this PPG) may formally request that a suspect be considered for capture or custody by U.S. personnel. Additionally, a department or agency that has captured a suspect, or that plans to capture or otherwise take custody of a suspect, shall, whenever practicable, propose a long-term disposition for such individual. Prior to requesting that an individual be considered for capture or custody by the United States, the nominating agency must confirm with its General Counsel that the operation can be conducted lawfully, but it is not necessary to have resolved the long-term disposition plan prior to proposing a capture operation.

2.A.2 Whenever possible, the nominating agency shall notify the Interagency Disposition Planning Group prior to such a request.

2.A.3 A nomination for custody, including capture, or a proposed long-term disposition under Section 2.A.1 shall be referred to the NSS, which shall initiate the screening process described in Section 2.B.

2.A.4 In the event initial screening under Section 2.B has not taken place prior to U.S. personnel taking custody of a suspect, the process for screening after capture described in Section 2.C shall be initiated.

2.B   Screening Prior to a Capture Operation

7

2.B.1 The nominating agency shall prepare a profile for each suspect referred to the NSS for review of a proposal to capture or otherwise take custody of the individual. The profile shall be developed based upon all relevant disseminated information available to the Intelligence Community (IC), as well as any other information needed to present as comprehensive and thorough a profile of the individual as possible. The profile should explain any difference of views among the IC and note, where appropriate, gaps in existing intelligence, as well as inconclusive and contradictory intelligence reports. At a minimum, each individual profile shall include the following information to the extent that such information exists:

2.B.2 Once the profile has been completed, the nominating agency shall provide the profile to the NSS Senior Director for Counterterrorism.

2.B.3 Whenever time permits, the Interagency Disposition Planning Group shall assess the availability, including the strengths and weaknesses, of potential disposition options.

2.B.4 All nominations under this Section for capturing or otherwise taking a suspect into custody must undergo a legal review by the General Counsel of the nominating agency to determine that the suspect may lawfully be captured or taken into custody by the United States and that the operation can be conducted in accordance with applicable law. The General Counsel's conclusions shall be referred to the NSS Legal Adviser. The NSS Legal Adviser and the General Counsel of the nominating agency shall consult with other department and agency counsels, as necessary and appropriate. In addition, in the event that the suspect who has been nominated is a U.S. person, DOJ shall conduct a legal analysis to ensure that the operation may be conducted consistent with the laws and Constitution of the United States. The NSS Legal Adviser shall submit the relevant legal conclusions to the Deputies Committee to inform its consideration of the nomination.

2.B.5 The NSS shall convene a Restricted Counterterrorism Security Group (RCSG)[6] for the purpose of reviewing and organizing material and addressing any issues related to the nomination of an individual for capture, custody, or long-term disposition. Before forwarding to the Deputies the nomination of a suspect for capture or to otherwise be taken into custody, the RCSG shall identify whether any other mate-

---

[6] The RCSG shall be chaired by the NSS Senior Director for Counterterrorism and shall include the following departments and agencies: the Department of State, the Department of the Treasury, DOD, DOJ, the De-

rial is needed for Deputies' consideration of the nomination and issue taskings to departments and agencies, as appropriate. For each nomination, the NSS will request, and the National Counterterrorism Center (NCTC) shall conduct, an assessment of the suspect and provide that assessment to the NSS prior to consideration or the nomination or proposed long-term disposition by the Deputies Committee, and where feasible, prior to RCSG review. The NSS will be responsible for ensuring that all necessary materials, including the profile developed by the nominating agency and the NCTC assessment, are included in the nomination package submitted to Deputies.

2.C Screening After Capture

2.C.1 Whenever feasible, initial screening by the United States of suspects taken into U.S. custody should be conducted before the United States captures or otherwise takes custody of the suspect, as set out in Section 2.B.

2.C.2 In the event initial screening cannot be conducted before the United States takes custody of the individual, immediately after capturing or otherwise taking custody of the suspect, appropriate U.S. personnel shall screen the individual to ensure that the correct individual has been taken into custody and that the individual may be lawfully detained. Such screening shall be conducted consistent with the laws and policies applicable to the authorities pursuant to which the individual is being detained, and

2.C.3

2.C.4 In the event that the suspect is detained pursuant to law of

partment of Homeland Security (DHS), ▮▮, CIA, Joint Chiefs of Staff (JCS), ▮▮▮ and NCTC. Additional departments and agencies may participate in the RCSG meetings, as appropriate.

war authorities by the U.S. military and additional time is needed for purposes of intelligence collection or the development of a long-term disposition option, the Secretary of Defense or his designee, following appropriate interagency consultations coordinated through the NSC process, may approve an extension of the screening period ▮▮▮▮▮▮▮▮▮▮▮▮▮▮▮▮▮▮▮▮▮▮▮▮ subject to the following:

9

1) The suspect's detention must be consistent with U.S. law and policy, as well as all applicable international law;

2)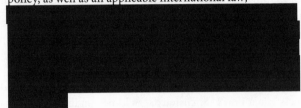

3) The International Committee or the Red Cross must be notified of, and provided timely access to, any suspect held by the U.S. military pursuant to law of war authorities; and

4) When possible and consistent with the primary objective of collecting intelligence, intelligence will be collected in a manner that preserves the availability of long-term disposition options, including prosecution.

2.D Deputies Review

2.D.1 A nomination or disposition package for capture, custody, or long-term disposition forwarded to the Deputies shall include the following:

1) The profile, produced by the nominating agency pursuant to Section 2.B.1, for the suspect or suspects proposed for capture or long-term disposition;

2) Any assessment produced by NCTC pursuant to Section 2.B.5;

3) If appropriate, a description of the planned capture and screening operation and ▮▮▮▮▮▮▮▮▮▮▮▮▮▮▮▮ operational plan under which the capture would be conducted;

4) The department(s) or agency or agencies that would be responsible for carrying out the proposed operation, if not already conducted;

5) A summary of the legal assessment prepared under Section 2.B.4; and

6) An assessment, including the strengths and weaknesses, of potential long-term disposition options.

2.D.2 The Deputies of the Department of State, the Treasury, DOD, DOJ, DHS, the Office of the Director of National Intelligence (DNI), ▮▮, CIA, JCS, ▮▮, NCTC, and any other Deputies or officials a Deputy National Security Advisor (DNSA) may invite to participate, shall promptly consider whether to recommend to the Principal of the nominating agency that a capture operation be conducted in the context of the proposed plan at issue, that the United States Government otherwise take custody of the individual, or that a particular long-term disposition option be pursued.

2.D.3 When considering a proposed nomination, the Deputies shall evaluate the following issues, and any others deemed appropriate by the Deputies:

1) Whether the suspect's capture would further the U.S. CT strategy;

[10]

2) The implications for the broader regional and international political interests of the United States;

3) Whether the proposed action would interfere with any intelligence collection or compromise any intelligence sources or methods;

4) The proposed plan for the detention and interrogation of the suspect;

5) The proposed plan to capture the suspect, including the feasibility of capture and the risk to U.S. personnel;

6) In the event that transfer to a third party or country is anticipated, the proposed plan for obtaining humane treatment assurances from any country;

7) The long-term disposition options for the individual; and

8) ██████████████████████████████████████

2.D.4 When considering the long-term disposition of a suspect who is already in U.S. custody, or whom a department or agency has already been authorized to capture or take into custody, the Deputies' discussion shall be guided by the following principles:

1) Whenever possible, third-country custody options that are consistent with U.S. national security should be explored;

2) Where transfer to a third country is not feasible or consistent with U.S. national security interests, the preferred long-term disposition option for suspects captured or otherwise taken into custody by the United States will be prosecution in a civilian court or, where available, a military commission. Consistent with that preference, wherever possible and consistent with the primary objective of collecting intelligence, intelligence will be collected in a manner that allows it to be used as evidence in a criminal prosecution, and

3) In no event will additional detainees be brought to the detention facilities at the Guantanamo Bay Naval Base.

Following consideration and discussion by the Deputies, departments and agencies shall submit the final positions of their Principals within a timeframe consistent with operational needs.

2.E Presentation to the President and the Principal of the Nominating Agency

2.E.1 If the nominating agency, on behalf of its Principal, continues to support taking action, a DNSA shall inform the President of the views expressed by departments and agencies. As appropriate, the nomination shall be presented to the President for a decision or the nomination will be provided to the Principal of the appropriate operating agency for a decision, along with any views expressed by the President.

11 2.E.2 An appropriate NSS official will communicate in writing the

decision taken, including any terms or conditions placed on such decisions, to the Deputies who participated in the Deputies Committee
review of the nomination.

SECTION 3.   Policy Standard and Procedure for Designating Identified HVTs for Lethal Action

3.A Policy Standard for the Use of Lethal Action Against HVTs

Where the use of lethal action against HVTs has been authorized ███████████████████████, an individual whose identity is known will only be eligible to be targeted, as a policy matter,
consistent with the requirements of the approved operational plan
███████████████████, if the individual's activities pose a continuing, imminent threat to U.S. persons.

3.B Necessary Preconditions for Taking Lethal Action

Lethal action requires that the individual may lawfully be targeted under
existing authorities and that any conditions established in the appropriate operational plan, including those set forth in Section 1.C.8, are met.
The preconditions set forth in Section 1.C.8 for the use of lethal force are
as follows: (a) near certainty that an identified HVT is present; (b) near
certainty that noncombatants will not be injured or killed; (c) ████████
███████████████████████████████;[7] (d) an assessment
that capture is not feasible at the time of the operation;[8] (e) an assessment
that the relevant governmental authorities in the country where action
is contemplated cannot or will not effectively address the threat to U.S.
persons; and (f) an assessment that no other reasonable alternatives to
lethal action exist to effectively address the threat to U.S. persons.

3.C Interagency Review Process

---

[7] Operational disagreements ███████████████████████████
████████ are to be elevated to Principals. The President will adjudicate any disagreement among or between Principals.

[8] This process is designed to review nominations of individuals only where
the capture of any individual at issue is not feasible. If, at any point during or

3.C.1 Any department or agency participating in the Deputies Committee review in Section 3.D may identify an individual for consideration, but only the operating agencies (also known as the "nominating agencies" for purposes of Section 3 of this PPG) may formally propose that an individual be nominated for lethal action following confirmation from the General Counsel of the nominating agency that the individual would be a lawful target.

3.C.2 The nominating agency shall prepare a profile for each individual nominated for lethal action. The profile shall be developed based upon all relevant disseminated information available to the IC, as well as any other information needed to present as comprehensive and thorough a profile of the individual as possible. The profile shall note, where appropriate, gaps in existing intelligence, as well as inconclusive and contradictory intelligence reports. At a minimum, each individual profile shall include a summary of all relevant disseminated intelligence required to determine whether the policy standard set forth in Section 3.A for lethal action against HVTs has been met, and include the following information to the extent that such information is available:

after the approval process capture appears feasible, a capture option in accordance with Section 2 of this PPG (or the relevant operational plan ▓▓▓▓▓▓▓▓▓▓▓ ▓▓▓▓▓▓▓▓▓▓▓▓▓▓▓▓) should be pursued. If the individual has already been approved for lethal action when a capture option becomes feasible, the individual should be referred to the NSS Senior Director for Counterterrorism and undergo an expedited Deputies review focused on identifying disposition options.

3.C.3 The NSS shall convene a meeting of the RCSG for the purpose of reviewing and organizing material, and addressing any issues, related to the nomination of an individual for lethal action.

3.C.4 Before forwarding the nomination of an identified HVT for lethal action to Deputies, the RCSG shall identify other materials needed for Deputies' consideration of the nomination and shall issue such taskings to departments and agencies, as appropriate. For each nomination, the NSS will request, and NCTC shall conduct, an assessment of the nomination and provide that assessment to the NSS prior to consideration of the nomination by the Deputies Committee, and where feasible prior to RCSG review. The NSS will be responsible for ensuring that all necessary materials, including the profile developed by the nominating agency and the NCTC assessment, are included in the nomination package submitted to Deputies.

3.C.5 All nominations for lethal action must undergo a legal review by the General Counsel of the nominating agency to ensure that the action contemplated is lawful and may be conducted in accordance with applicable law. The General Counsel's conclusions shall be referred to the NSS Legal Adviser. In all events, the NSS Legal Adviser and the General Counsel of the nominating agency shall consult with DOJ. The NSS Legal Adviser and the General Counsel of the nominating agency shall also consult with other interagency lawyers depending on the particular nomination. In addition, in the event that the individual proposed for nomination is a U.S. person, DOJ shall conduct a legal analysis to ensure that lethal action may be conducted against that individual consistent with the laws and Constitution of the United States. The NSS Legal Adviser shall submit the relevant legal conclusions to the NSS Senior Director for Counterterrorism for inclusion in the nomination package to be submitted to Deputies.

3.C.6 If the proposal may be conducted lawfully, the nomination shall be referred to a DNSA, or another appropriate NSS official, to facilitate consideration by the Deputies Committee.

3.D Deputies Review

3.D.1 Upon completion of a nomination package, the NSS shall forward the nomination package to the Deputies Committee for consideration. A standard nomination package to be forwarded to the Deputies shall include, at a minimum, the following:

1) The profile, produced by the nominating agency pursuant to Section 3.C.2, for the individual proposed for lethal action;
2) The assessment produced by NCTC pursuant to Section 3.C.4;
3) A description ████████████████ operational plan to

which the nomination would be added, including the timeframe, if any, in which the operation may be executed;

4) The operating agency or agencies that would be responsible
for conducting the proposed lethal action;

5) A summary of the legal assessment; and

6) The determinations made by the nominating agency that
capture is not currently feasible and that the relevant governmental authorities in the country where action is contemplated cannot or will not effectively address the threat
to U.S. persons, as well as the underlying analysis for those
determinations.

3.D.2 The Deputies of the Department of State, DOD, JCS, DOJ, DHS,
DNI, CIA, and NCTC shall promptly consider whether to recommend to
the Principal of the nominating agency that lethal action be taken against
the proposed individual in the context ▮▮▮▮▮▮▮▮▮▮▮▮▮▮▮
operational plan at issue. ▮▮▮▮, ▮▮▮▮▮▮▮▮ shall participate in the review process as observers. A DNSA may invite Deputies
or other officials to participate as appropriate. Following consideration
and discussion by the Deputies, departments and agencies shall submit
to the NSS the final positions of their Principals within a timeframe
consistent with operational needs.

3.D.3 When considering each proposed nomination, the Deputies shall ⬚14
evaluate the following issues, and any others deemed appropriate by the
Deputies:

1) Whether the Deputies can conclude with confidence that the
nominated individual qualifies under the policy standard
in Section 3.A for lethal action, taking into account credible
information that may cast doubt on such a conclusion;

2) Whether the threat posed by the individual to U.S. persons
can be minimized through a response short of lethal action;

3) The implications for the broader regional and international
political interests of the United States;

4) Whether the proposed action would interfere with any

intelligence collection or compromise any intelligence
sources or methods;

5) Whether the individual, if captured, would likely result in
   the collection of valuable intelligence, notwithstanding an
   assessment that capture is not currently feasible; and

6) ████████████████████████████████████

3.E   Presentation to the President and the Principal of the Nominating Agency

3.E.1 The Principal of the nominating agency may approve lethal
action against the proposed individual if: (1) the relevant Principals
unanimously agree that lethal action should be taken against the proposed individual, and (2) the Principal of the nominating agency has
notified the President through a DNSA of his intention to approve lethal
action and has received notice from a DNSA that the President has been
apprised of that intention. The Principal of the nominating agency may
not delegate his authority to approve a nomination.

3.E.2 Nominations shall be presented to the President for decision,
along with the views expressed by departments and agencies during the
process, when: (1) the proposed individual is a U.S. person, or (2) there
is a lack of consensus among Principals regarding the nomination, but
the Principal of the nominating agency continues to support approving
the nomination.

3.E.3 In either case, an appropriate NSS official will communicate in
writing the decision, including any terms or conditions placed on any
approval, to the Deputies who participated in the Deputies Committee
review of the nomination.

3.F   Annual Review; ████████████████████

3.F.1 The NSS, in conjunction with the nominating agency, shall coordinate an annual review of ████████ individuals authorized for possible lethal action to evaluate whether the intelligence continues to sup-

port a determination that the individuals ████████ qualify for lethal action under the standard set forth in Section 3.A. The NSS shall refer the necessary information for the annual review to the Deputies for [15] consideration. Following Deputies review, the information, along with any recommendations from Deputies, shall be forwarded to the Principal of the nominating agency for review. A separate legal review will be conducted, as appropriate. An appropriate official from each nominating agency shall inform a DNSA of what action, if any, the Principal of the nominating agency takes in response to the review.

3.F.2 The Deputy of any department or agency participating in the Deputies Committee review in Section 3.D may propose at any time that an individual be ████████████████ for lethal action. In the event that such a proposal is made, NCTC shall update the IC-coordinated profile for the individual at issue and, as appropriate, the Deputies shall consider whether to propose that the individual be removed by the Principal of the nominating agency.

3.F.3 Following consideration and discussion by the Deputies in accordance with 3.F.1 or 3.F.2, departments and agencies shall submit the final positions of their Principals within an appropriate timeframe determined by the NSS.

SECTION 4. <u>**Policy Standard and Procedure for Approving Lethal Force Against Terrorist Targets Other Than Identified HVTs**</u>

4.A Policy Standard for Directing Lethal Force Against Terrorist Targets Other Than Identified HVTs

This Section applies to the direction of lethal force ████████ ████████ against lawful terrorist targets ████████████ , such as manned or unmanned Vehicle Borne Improvised Explosive Devices or infrastructure, including explosives storage facilities. Where an operating agency has been authorized to take direct action against terrorist targets other than identified HVTs ████████████████ ,

such a terrorist target may be acted against as a policy matter, consistent with the requirements of the approved operational plan
███████████████████, if the target poses a continuing, imminent
threat to U.S. persons.

4.B   Necessary Preconditions for Directing Lethal Force Under This Section

Directing lethal force under this Section requires that: (1) the target
may lawfully be targeted and that any conditions established in the
appropriate operational plan, including those set forth in Section 1.C.8,
are met. The preconditions set forth in Section 1.C.8 for the use of lethal
force are as follows: (a) near certainty that a lawful terrorist target other
than an identified HVT is present; (b) near certainty that non-
combatants will not be injured or killed; (c) ███████████████████
███;[9] (d) ███████████
███████████████████████████████████████;[10] (e) an assessment that
the relevant governmental authorities in the country where action is
contemplated cannot or will not effectively address the threat to U.S.
persons; and (f) an assessment that no other reasonable alternatives to
lethal action exist to effectively address the threat to U.S. persons.

4.C   Nomination and Review of Terrorist Targets Other Than Identified High-Value Individuals

Where an operating agency has been authorized to direct force against
terrorist targets (including ███████████████ property) other than identified HVTs ███████████████████████████ may nominate specific
terrorist targets to target with lethal force consistent with the requirements of the approved operational plan ███████████████████,

---

[9] Operational disagreements ████████████████████████████████████
████████ are to be elevated to Principals. The President will adjudicate any disagreement among or between Principals.

[10] ███
███
███

including the process required by the plan for nominating and approving such targets.

SECTION 5.   <u>Procedures for Approving Proposals that Vary from the Policy Guidance Otherwise Set Forth in this PPG</u>

5.A Already Authorized Targets: Variations from Operational Plan Requirements When Fleeting Opportunities Arise

5.A.1 When direct action has been authorized under this PPG against identified HVTs or against terrorist targets other than identified HVTs ███████████████, the operating agency responsible for conducting approved operations, as a result of unforeseen circumstances and in the event of a fleeting opportunity, may submit an individualized operational plan to the NSS that varies from the requirements of the operational plan ██████████████. In that event, an appropriate NSS official shall consult with other departments and agencies, as appropriate and as time permits, before submitting the proposal to the President for his decision.

5.A.2 All such variations from an operational plan must be reviewed by the General Counsel of the operating agency conducting the operation and the conclusions referred to the NSS Legal Adviser. In all cases, any operational plan must contemplate an operation that is in full compliance with applicable law. Absent extraordinary circumstances, these proposals shall:

1) Identify an international and domestic legal basis for taking action in the relevant country ██████████████████ ████████████████████████████████

2) Mandate that lethal action may only be taken if: (a) there is near certainty that the target is present; (b) there is near certainty that non-combatants will not be injured or killed; (c) it has been determined that capture is not feasible; (d) the relevant governmental authorities in the country where

action is contemplated cannot or will not effectively address the threat to U.S. persons; and (e) no other reasonable alternatives exist to effectively address the threat to U.S. persons.

5.A.3 Any variation from an operational plan shall be presented to the President for decision, and an appropriate NSS official shall communicate the President's decision, including any terms or conditions placed on any approval, to appropriate agencies.

17 5.B   Extraordinary Cases: Variations from the Policy Guidance Otherwise Set Forth in this PPG

Nothing in this PPG shall be construed to prevent the President from exercising his constitutional authority as Commander in Chief and Chief Executive, as well as his statutory authority, to consider a lawful proposal from operating agencies that he authorize direct action that would fall outside of the policy guidance contained herein, including a proposal that he authorize lethal force against an individual who poses a continuing, imminent threat to another country's persons. In extraordinary cases, such a proposal may be brought forward to the President for consideration as follows:

1) A proposal that varies from the policy guidance contained in this PPG may be brought forward by the Principal of one of the operating agencies through the interagency process described in Section 1 of this PPG, after a separate legal review has been undertaken to determine whether action may be taken in accordance with applicable law.

2) Where there is a fleeting opportunity, the Principal of one of the operating agencies may propose to the President that action be taken that would otherwise vary from the guidance contained in this PPG, after a separate legal review has been undertaken to determine whether action may be taken in accordance with applicable law.

3) In all cases, any proposal brought forward pursuant to this subsection must contemplate an operation that is in full compliance with applicable law.

SECTION 6.   Procedures for After Action Reports

6.A   The department or agency that conducted the operation shall provide the following preliminary information in writing to the NSS within 48 hours of taking direct action against any authorized target:

1) A description of the operation;
2) A summary of the basis for determining that the operation satisfied the applicable criteria contained in the approved operational plan;
3) An assessment of whether the operation achieved its objective;
4) An assessment of the number of combatants killed or wounded;
5) A description of any collateral damage that resulted from the operation;
6) A description of all munitions and assets used as part of the operation; and
7) ███████████████████████████████████.

6.B   The department or agency that conducted the operation shall provide subsequent updates to the NSS on the outcome of the operation, as appropriate, including any intelligence collected as a result of the operation. The information provided to the NSS under this Section shall be made available to appropriate officials at the departments and agencies taking part in the review under Sections 1 and 3 of this PPG. `18`

SECTION 7.   Congressional Notification

A congressional notification shall be prepared and promptly provided to the appropriate Members of the Congress by the department or agency approved to carry out such actions when:

1) A new operational plan for taking direct action ███████████████████████ is approved;
2) Authority is expanded under an operational plan for

directing lethal force against lawfully targeted individuals
███████████████ and against lawful terrorist targets
other than individuals; or

3) An operation has been conducted pursuant to such
approval(s).

In addition, appropriate Members of the Congress will be provided, no
less than every 3 months, updates on identified HVTs who have been
approved for lethal action under Section 3. Each department or agency
required to submit congressional notifications under this Section shall
inform the NSS of how it intends to comply with this Section prior to
providing any such notifications to Congress.

SECTION 8.   <u>General Provisions</u>

8.A   This PPG is not intended to, and does not, create any right or
benefit, substantive or procedural, enforceable at law or in equity by any
party against the United States, its departments, agencies, or entities, its
officers, employees, or agents, or any other person.

8.C   Twelve months after entry into force of this PPG, Principals shall
review the implementation and operation of the PPG, including any lessons learned from evaluating the information provided under Section
6, and consider whether any adjustments are warranted.

11

Fact Sheet

May 23, 2013

"U.S. Policy Standards and Procedures for the Use of Force in Counterterrorism Operations Outside the United States and Areas of Active Hostilities"

The Obama administration published this document in connection with the president's remarks at the National Defense University on May 23, 2013. The document is a summary of the classified Presidential Policy Guidance that was issued by President Obama the day before.

The document from which this text was transcribed is posted at: www.ACLU.org/TDM/FactSheet.

Since his first day in office, President Obama has been clear that the United States will use all available tools of national power to protect the American people from the terrorist threat posed by al-Qa'ida and its associated forces. The President has also made clear that, in carrying on this fight, we will uphold our laws and values and will share as much information as possible with the American people and the Congress, consistent with our national security needs and the proper functioning of the Executive Branch. To these ends, the President has approved, and senior members of the Executive Branch have briefed to the Congress, written policy standards and procedures that formalize and strengthen the Administration's rigorous process for reviewing and approving operations to capture or employ lethal force against terrorist targets outside the United States and outside areas of active hostilities. Additionally, the President has decided to share, in this document, certain key elements of these standards and procedures with the American people so that they can make informed judgments and hold the Executive Branch accountable.

This document provides information regarding counterterrorism policy standards and procedures that are either already in place or will be transitioned into place over time. As Administration officials have stated publicly on numerous occasions, we are continually working to refine, clarify, and strengthen our standards and processes for using force to keep the nation safe from the terrorist threat. One constant is our commitment to conducting counterterrorism operations lawfully. In addition, we consider the separate question of whether force should be used as a matter of policy. The most important policy consideration, particularly when the United States contemplates using lethal force, is whether our actions protect American lives.

Preference for Capture
The policy of the United States is not to use lethal force when it is feasible to capture a terrorist suspect, because capturing a terrorist offers the best opportunity to gather meaningful intelligence and to mitigate and disrupt terrorist plots. Capture operations are conducted only against suspects who may lawfully be captured or otherwise taken into custody by the United States and only when the operation can be conducted in accordance with all applicable law and consistent with our obligations to other sovereign states.

Standards for the Use of Lethal Force

Any decision to use force abroad—even when our adversaries are terrorists dedicated to killing American citizens—is a significant one. Lethal force will not be proposed or pursued as punishment or as a substitute for prosecuting a terrorist suspect in a civilian court or a military commission. Lethal force will be used only to prevent or stop attacks against U.S. persons, and even then, only when capture is not feasible and no other reasonable alternatives exist to address the threat effectively. In particular, lethal force will be used outside areas of active hostilities only when the following preconditions are met:

First, there must be a legal basis for using lethal force, whether it is against a senior operational leader of a terrorist organization or the forces that organization is using or intends to use to conduct terrorist attacks.

Second, the United States will use lethal force only against a target that poses a continuing, imminent threat to U.S. persons. It is simply not the case that all terrorists pose a continuing, imminent threat to U.S. persons; if a terrorist does not pose such a threat, the United States will not use lethal force.

Third, the following criteria must be met before lethal action may be taken:

1. Near certainty that the terrorist target is present;
2. Near certainty that non-combatants[1] will not be injured or killed;
3. An assessment that capture is not feasible at the time of the operation;
4. An assessment that the relevant governmental authorities in the country where action is contemplated cannot or will not effectively address the threat to U.S. persons; and

---

[1] Non-combatants are individuals who may not be made the object of attack under applicable international law. The term "non-combatant" does not include an individual who is part of a belligerent party to an armed conflict, an individual who is taking a direct part in hostilities, or an individual who is targetable in the exercise of national self-defense. Males of military age may be non-combatants; it is not the case that all military-aged males in the vicinity of a target are deemed to be combatants.

5.   An assessment that no other reasonable alternatives exist to effectively address the threat to U.S. persons.

Finally, whenever the United States uses force in foreign territories, international legal principles, including respect for sovereignty and the law of armed conflict, impose important constraints on the ability of the United States to act unilaterally—and on the way in which the United States can use force. The United States respects national sovereignty and international law.

U.S. Government Coordination and Review
Decisions to capture or otherwise use force against individual terrorists outside the United States and areas of active hostilities are made at the most senior levels of the U.S. Government, informed by departments and agencies with relevant expertise and institutional roles. Senior national security officials—including the deputies and heads of key departments and agencies—will consider proposals to make sure that our policy standards are met, and attorneys—including the senior lawyers of key departments and agencies—will review and determine the legality of proposals.

These decisions will be informed by a broad analysis of an intended target's current and past role in plots threatening U.S. persons; relevant intelligence information the individual could provide; and the potential impact of the operation on ongoing terrorism plotting, on the capabilities of terrorist organizations, on U.S. foreign relations, and on U.S. intelligence collection. Such analysis will inform consideration of whether the individual meets both the legal and policy standards for the operation.

Other Key Elements
U.S. Persons. If the United States considers an operation against a terrorist identified as a U.S. person, the Department of Justice will conduct an additional legal analysis to ensure that such action may be conducted against the individual consistent with the Constitution and laws of the United States.

Reservation of Authority. These new standards and procedures do not limit the President's authority to take action in extraordinary circumstances when doing so is both lawful and necessary to protect the United States or its allies.

Congressional Notification. Since entering office, the President has made certain that the appropriate Members of Congress have been kept fully informed about our counterterrorism operations. Consistent with this strong and continuing commitment to congressional oversight, appropriate Members of the Congress will be regularly provided with updates identifying any individuals against whom lethal force has been approved. In addition, the appropriate committees of Congress will be notified whenever a counterterrorism operation covered by these standards and procedures has been conducted.

12

Remarks of President Barack Obama

National Defense University, Fort McNair,
Washington, D.C.

May 23, 2013

Untitled

Before he delivered this speech, President Obama had said very little
about the drone campaign in public. In his speech at the National
Defense University, Obama sought to reassure the public that his
administration's targeted-killing policies were legal, effective, and
properly supervised within the executive branch and by Congress. The
president also announced that his administration had established a
framework to govern the use of force against suspected terrorists, and
that the framework—which came to be called the "playbook"—had
been codified in Presidential Policy Guidance issued the previous day.

The document from which this text was transcribed is posted at:
www.ACLU.org/TDM/ObamaSpeech.

Good afternoon, everybody. Please be seated.

It is a great honor to return to the National Defense University. Here, at Fort McNair, Americans have served in uniform since 1791—standing guard in the earliest days of the Republic, and contemplating the future of warfare here in the 21st century.

For over two centuries, the United States has been bound together by founding documents that defined who we are as Americans, and served as our compass through every type of change. Matters of war and peace are no different. Americans are deeply ambivalent about war, but having fought for our independence, we know a price must be paid for freedom. From the Civil War to our struggle against fascism, on through the long twilight struggle of the Cold War, battlefields have changed and technology has evolved. But our commitment to consti-tutional principles has weathered every war, and every war has come to an end.

With the collapse of the Berlin Wall, a new dawn of democracy took hold abroad, and a decade of peace and prosperity arrived here at home. And for a moment, it seemed the 21st century would be a tranquil time. And then, on September 11, 2001, we were shaken out of complacen-cy. Thousands were taken from us, as clouds of fire and metal and ash descended upon a sun-filled morning. This was a different kind of war. No armies came to our shores, and our military was not the principal target. Instead, a group of terrorists came to kill as many civilians as they could.

And so our nation went to war. We have now been at war for well over a decade. I won't review the full history. What is clear is that we quickly drove al Qaeda out of Afghanistan, but then shifted our focus and began a new war in Iraq. And this carried significant consequences for our fight against al Qaeda, our standing in the world, and—to this day—our interests in a vital region.

Meanwhile, we strengthened our defenses—hardening targets, tightening transportation security, giving law enforcement new tools to prevent terror. Most of these changes were sound. Some caused inconvenience. But some, like expanded surveillance, raised difficult questions about the balance that we strike between our interests in security and our values of privacy. And in some cases, I believe we compromised our basic values—by using torture to interrogate our enemies, and detaining individuals in a way that ran counter to the rule of law.

So after I took office, we stepped up the war against al Qaeda but we also sought to change its course. We relentlessly targeted al Qaeda's leadership. We ended the war in Iraq, and brought nearly 150,000 troops home. We pursued a new strategy in Afghanistan, and increased our training of Afghan forces. We unequivocally banned torture, affirmed our commitment to civilian courts, worked to align our policies with the rule of law, and expanded our consultations with Congress.

Today, Osama bin Laden is dead, and so are most of his top lieutenants. There have been no large-scale attacks on the United States, and our homeland is more secure. Fewer of our troops are in harm's way, and over the next 19 months they will continue to come home. Our alliances are strong, and so is our standing in the world. In sum, we are safer because of our efforts.

Now, make no mistake, our nation is still threatened by terrorists. From Benghazi to Boston, we have been tragically reminded of that truth. But we have to recognize that the threat has shifted and evolved from the one that came to our shores on 9/11. With a decade of experience now to draw from, this is the moment to ask ourselves hard questions—about the nature of today's threats and how we should confront them.

And these questions matter to every American.

For over the last decade, our nation has spent well over a trillion dollars on war, helping to explode our deficits and constraining our ability to nation-build here at home. Our service members and their families have sacrificed far more on our behalf. Nearly 7,000 Americans have made the ultimate sacrifice. Many more have left a part of themselves on the battlefield, or brought the shadows of battle back home. From our use of drones to the detention of terrorist suspects, the decisions that we are making now will define the type of nation—and world—that we leave to our children.

So America is at a crossroads. We must define the nature and scope of this struggle, or else it will define us. We have to be mindful of James Madison's warning that "No nation could preserve its freedom in the midst of continual warfare." Neither I, nor any President, can promise the total defeat of terror. We will never erase the evil that lies in the hearts of some human beings, nor stamp out every danger to our open society. But what we can do—what we must do—is dismantle networks that pose a direct danger to us, and make it less likely for new groups to gain a foothold, all the while maintaining the freedoms and ideals that we defend. And to define that strategy, we have to make decisions based not on fear, but on hard-earned wisdom. That begins with understanding the current threat that we face.

Today, the core of al Qaeda in Afghanistan and Pakistan is on the path to defeat. Their remaining operatives spend more time thinking about their own safety than plotting against us. They did not direct the attacks in Benghazi or Boston. They've not carried out a successful attack on our homeland since 9/11.

Instead, what we've seen is the emergence of various al Qaeda affiliates. From Yemen to Iraq, from Somalia to North Africa, the threat today is more diffuse, with Al Qaeda's affiliates in the Arabian Peninsula—AQAP—the most active in plotting against our homeland. And while none of AQAP's efforts approach the scale of 9/11, they have continued to plot acts of terror, like the attempt to blow up an airplane on Christmas Day in 2009.

Unrest in the Arab world has also allowed extremists to gain a foothold in countries like Libya and Syria. But here, too, there are differences from 9/11. In some cases, we continue to confront state-sponsored networks like Hezbollah that engage in acts of terror to achieve political goals. Other of these groups are simply collections of local militias or extremists interested in seizing territory. And while we are vigilant for signs that these groups may pose a transnational threat, most are focused on operating in the countries and regions where they are based. And that means we'll face more localized threats like what we saw in Benghazi, or the BP oil facility in Algeria, in which local operatives—perhaps in loose affiliation with regional networks—launch periodic attacks against Western diplomats, companies, and other soft targets, or resort to kidnapping and other criminal enterprises to fund their operations.

And finally, we face a real threat from radicalized individuals here in the United States. Whether it's a shooter at a Sikh Temple in Wisconsin, a plane flying into a building in Texas, or the extremists who killed 168 people at the Federal Building in Oklahoma City, America has confronted many forms of violent extremism in our history. Deranged or alienated individuals—often U.S. citizens or legal residents—can do enormous damage, particularly when inspired by larger notions of violent jihad. And that pull towards extremism appears to have led to the shooting at Fort Hood and the bombing of the Boston Marathon.

So that's the current threat—lethal yet less capable al Qaeda affiliates; threats to diplomatic facilities and businesses abroad; homegrown extremists. This is the future of terrorism. We have to take these threats seriously, and do all that we can to confront them. But as we shape our response, we have to recognize that the scale of this threat closely resembles the types of attacks we faced before 9/11.

In the 1980s, we lost Americans to terrorism at our Embassy in Beirut; at our Marine Barracks in Lebanon; on a cruise ship at sea; at a disco in Berlin; and on a Pan Am flight—Flight 103—over Lockerbie. In the 1990s, we lost Americans to terrorism at the World Trade Center; at our military facilities in Saudi Arabia; and at our Embassy in Kenya. These attacks were all brutal; they were all deadly; and we learned that left unchecked, these threats can grow. But if dealt with smartly and proportionally, these threats need not rise to the level that we saw on the eve of 9/11.

Moreover, we have to recognize that these threats don't arise in a vacuum. Most, though not all, of the terrorism we faced is fueled by a common ideology—a belief by some extremists that Islam is in conflict with the United States and the West, and that violence against Western targets, including civilians, is justified in pursuit of a larger cause. Of course, this ideology is based on a lie, for the United States is not at war with Islam. And this ideology is rejected by the vast majority of Muslims, who are the most frequent victims of terrorist attacks.

Nevertheless, this ideology persists, and in an age when ideas and images can travel the globe in an instant, our response to terrorism can't depend on military or law enforcement alone. We need all elements of national power to win a battle of wills, a battle of ideas. So what I want to discuss here today is the components of such a comprehensive counterterrorism strategy.

First, we must finish the work of defeating al Qaeda and its associated forces.

In Afghanistan, we will complete our transition to Afghan responsibility for that country's security. Our troops will come home. Our combat mission will come to an end. And we will work with the Afghan government to train security forces, and sustain a counterterrorism force, which ensures that al-Qaeda can never again establish a safe haven to launch attacks against us or our allies.

Beyond Afghanistan, we must define our effort not as a boundless "global war on terror," but rather as a series of persistent, targeted efforts to dismantle specific networks of violent extremists that threaten America. In many cases, this will involve partnerships with other countries. Already, thousands of Pakistani soldiers have lost their lives fighting extremists. In Yemen, we are supporting security forces that have reclaimed territory from AQAP. In Somalia, we helped a coalition of African nations push al-Shabaab out of its strongholds. In Mali, we're providing military aid to French-led intervention to push back al Qaeda in the Maghreb, and help the people of Mali reclaim their future.

Much of our best counterterrorism cooperation results in the gathering and sharing of intelligence, the arrest and prosecution of terrorists. And that's how a Somali terrorist apprehended off the coast of Yemen is now in a prison in New York. That's how we worked with European allies to disrupt plots from Denmark to Germany to the United Kingdom. That's how intelligence collected with Saudi Arabia helped us stop a cargo plane from being blown up over the Atlantic. These partnerships work.

But despite our strong preference for the detention and prosecution of terrorists, sometimes this approach is foreclosed. Al Qaeda and its affiliates try to gain foothold in some of the most distant and unforgiving places on Earth. They take refuge in remote tribal regions. They hide in caves and walled compounds. They train in empty deserts and rugged mountains.

In some of these places—such as parts of Somalia and Yemen—the state only has the most tenuous reach into the territory. In other cases, the state lacks the capacity or will to take action. And it's also not possible for America to simply deploy a team of Special Forces to capture every terrorist. Even when such an approach may be possible, there are places where it would pose profound risks to our troops and local civilians—where a terrorist compound cannot be breached without triggering a firefight with surrounding tribal communities, for example, that pose no threat to us; times when putting U.S. boots on the ground may trigger a major international crisis.

To put it another way, our operation in Pakistan against Osama bin Laden cannot be the norm. The risks in that case were immense. The likelihood of capture, although that was our preference, was remote given the certainty that our folks would confront resistance. The fact that we did not find ourselves confronted with civilian casualties, or embroiled in an extended firefight, was a testament to the meticulous planning and professionalism of our Special Forces, but it also depended on some luck. And it was supported by massive infrastructure in Afghanistan.

And even then, the cost to our relationship with Pakistan—and the backlash among the Pakistani public over encroachment on their territory—was so severe that we are just now beginning to rebuild this important partnership.

So it is in this context that the United States has taken lethal, targeted action against al Qaeda and its associated forces, including with remotely piloted aircraft commonly referred to as drones.

As was true in previous armed conflicts, this new technology raises profound questions—about who is targeted, and why; about civilian casualties, and the risk of creating new enemies; about the legality of such strikes under U.S. and international law; about accountability and morality. So let me address these questions.

To begin with, our actions are effective. Don't take my word for it. In the intelligence gathered at bin Laden's compound, we found that he wrote, "We could lose the reserves to enemy's air strikes. We cannot fight air strikes with explosives." Other communications from al Qaeda operatives confirm this as well. Dozens of highly skilled al Qaeda commanders, trainers, bomb makers and operatives have been taken off the battlefield. Plots have been disrupted that would have targeted international aviation, U.S. transit systems, European cities and our troops in Afghanistan. Simply put, these strikes have saved lives.

Moreover, America's actions are legal. We were attacked on 9/11. Within a week, Congress overwhelmingly authorized the use of force. Under domestic law, and international law, the United States is at war with al Qaeda, the Taliban, and their associated forces. We are at war with an organization that right now would kill as many Americans as they could if we did not stop them first. So this is a just war—a war waged proportionally, in last resort, and in self-defense.

And yet, as our fight enters a new phase, America's legitimate claim of self-defense cannot be the end of the discussion. To say a military tactic is legal, or even effective, is not to say it is wise or moral in every instance. For the same human progress that gives us the technology to strike half a world away also demands the discipline to constrain that power—or risk abusing it. And that's why, over the last four years, my administration has worked vigorously to establish a framework that governs our use of force against terrorists—insisting upon clear guidelines, oversight and accountability that is now codified in Presidential Policy Guidance that I signed yesterday.

In the Afghan war theater, we must—and will—continue to support our troops until the transition is complete at the end of 2014. And that means we will continue to take strikes against high value al Qaeda targets, but also against forces that are massing to support attacks on coalition forces. But by the end of 2014, we will no longer have the same need for force protection, and the progress we've made against core al-Qaeda will reduce the need for unmanned strikes.

Beyond the Afghan theater, we only target al Qaeda and its associated forces. And even then, the use of drones is heavily constrained. America does not take strikes when we have the ability to capture individual terrorists; our preference is always to detain, interrogate, and prosecute. America cannot take strikes wherever we choose; our actions are bound by consultations with partners, and respect for state sovereignty.

America does not take strikes to punish individuals; we act against terrorists who pose a continuing and imminent threat to the American people, and when there are no other governments capable of effectively addressing the threat. And before any strike is taken, there must be near-certainty that no civilians will be killed or injured—the highest standard we can set.

Now, this last point is critical, because much of the criticism about drone strikes—both here at home and abroad—understandably centers on reports of civilian casualties. There's a wide gap between U.S. assessments of such casualties and nongovernmental reports. Nevertheless, it is a hard fact that U.S. strikes have resulted in civilian casualties, a risk that exists in every war. And for the families of those civilians, no words or legal construct can justify their loss. For me, and those in my chain of command, those deaths will haunt us as long as we live, just as we are haunted by the civilian casualties that have occurred throughout conventional fighting in Afghanistan and Iraq.

But as Commander-in-Chief, I must weigh these heartbreaking tragedies against the alternatives. To do nothing in the face of terrorist networks would invite far more civilian casualties—not just in our cities at home and our facilities abroad, but also in the very places like Sana'a and Kabul and Mogadishu where terrorists seek a foothold. Remember that the terrorists we are after target civilians, and the death toll from their acts of terrorism against Muslims dwarfs any estimate of civilian casualties from drone strikes. So doing nothing is not an option.

Where foreign governments cannot or will not effectively stop terrorism in their territory, the primary alternative to targeted lethal action would be the use of conventional military options. As I've already said, even small special operations carry enormous risks. Conventional airpower or missiles are far less precise than drones, and are likely to cause more civilian casualties and more local outrage. And invasions of these territories lead us to be viewed as occupying armies, unleash a torrent of unintended consequences, are difficult to contain, result in large numbers of civilian casualties and ultimately empower those who thrive on violent conflict.

So it is false to assert that putting boots on the ground is less likely to result in civilian deaths or less likely to create enemies in the Muslim world. The results would be more U.S. deaths, more Black Hawks down, more confrontations with local populations, and an inevitable mission creep in support of such raids that could easily escalate into new wars.

Yes, the conflict with al Qaeda, like all armed conflict, invites tragedy. But by narrowly targeting our action against those who want to kill us and not the people they hide among, we are choosing the course of action least likely to result in the loss of innocent life.

Our efforts must be measured against the history of putting American troops in distant lands among hostile populations. In Vietnam, hundreds of thousands of civilians died in a war where the boundaries of battle were blurred. In Iraq and Afghanistan, despite the extraordinary courage and discipline of our troops, thousands of civilians have been killed. So neither conventional military action nor waiting for attacks to occur offers moral safe harbor, and neither does a sole reliance on law enforcement in territories that have no functioning police or security services—and indeed, have no functioning law.

Now, this is not to say that the risks are not real. Any U.S. military action in foreign lands risks creating more enemies and impacts public opinion overseas. Moreover, our laws constrain the power of the President even during wartime, and I have taken an oath to defend the Constitution of the United States. The very precision of drone strikes and the necessary secrecy often involved in such actions can end up shielding our government from the public scrutiny that a troop deployment invites. It can also lead a President and his team to view drone strikes as a cure-all for terrorism.

And for this reason, I've insisted on strong oversight of all lethal action. After I took office, my administration began briefing all strikes outside of Iraq and Afghanistan to the appropriate committees of Congress. Let me repeat that: Not only did Congress authorize the use of force, it is briefed on every strike that America takes. Every strike. That includes the one instance when we targeted an American citizen—Anwar Awlaki, the chief of external operations for AQAP.

This week, I authorized the declassification of this action, and the deaths of three other Americans in drone strikes, to facilitate transparency and debate on this issue and to dismiss some of the more outlandish claims that have been made. For the record, I do not believe it would be constitutional for the government to target and kill any U.S. citizen—with a drone, or with a shotgun—without due process, nor should any President deploy armed drones over U.S. soil.

But when a U.S. citizen goes abroad to wage war against America and is actively plotting to kill U.S. citizens, and when neither the United States, nor our partners are in a position to capture him before he carries out a plot, his citizenship should no more serve as a shield than a sniper shooting down on an innocent crowd should be protected from a SWAT team.

That's who Anwar Awlaki was—he was continuously trying to kill people. He helped oversee the 2010 plot to detonate explosive devices on two U.S.-bound cargo planes. He was involved in planning to blow up an airliner in 2009. When Farouk Abdulmutallab—the Christmas Day bomber—went to Yemen in 2009, Awlaki hosted him, approved his suicide operation, helped him tape a martyrdom video to be shown after the attack, and his last instructions were to blow up the airplane when it was over American soil. I would have detained and prosecuted Awlaki if we captured him before he carried out a plot, but we couldn't. And as President, I would have been derelict in my duty had I not authorized the strike that took him out.

Of course, the targeting of any American raises constitutional issues that are not present in other strikes—which is why my administration submitted information about Awlaki to the Department of Justice months before Awlaki was killed, and briefed the Congress before this strike as well. But the high threshold that we've set for taking lethal action applies to all potential terrorist targets, regardless of whether or not they are American citizens. This threshold respects the inherent dignity of every human life. Alongside the decision to put our men and women in uniform in harm's way, the decision to use force against individuals or groups—even against a sworn enemy of the United States—is the hardest thing I do as President. But these decisions must be made, given my responsibility to protect the American people.

Going forward, I've asked my administration to review proposals to extend oversight of lethal actions outside of warzones that go beyond our reporting to Congress. Each option has virtues in theory, but poses difficulties in practice. For example, the establishment of a special court to evaluate and authorize lethal action has the benefit of bringing a third branch of government into the process, but raises serious constitutional issues about presidential and judicial authority. Another idea that's been suggested—the establishment of an independent oversight board in the executive branch—avoids those problems, but may introduce a layer of bureaucracy into national security decision-making, without inspiring additional public confidence in the process. But despite these challenges, I look forward to actively engaging Congress to explore these and other options for increased oversight.

* * *

Our victory against terrorism won't be measured in a surrender ceremony at a battleship, or a statue being pulled to the ground. Victory will be measured in parents taking their kids to school; immigrants coming to our shores; fans taking in a ballgame; a veteran starting a business; a bustling city street; a citizen shouting her concerns at a President.

The quiet determination; that strength of character and bond of fellowship; that refutation of fear—that is both our sword and our shield. And long after the current messengers of hate have faded from the world's memory, alongside the brutal despots, and deranged madmen, and ruthless demagogues who litter history—the flag of the United States will still wave from small-town cemeteries to national monuments, to distant outposts abroad. And that flag will still stand for freedom.

Thank you very, everybody. God bless you. May God bless the United States of America.

13

Remarks of Brian J. Egan, Legal Adviser, U.S.
Department of State

Annual Meeting of the American Society of
International Law, Washington, D.C.

April 1, 2016

"International Law, Legal Diplomacy, and the Counter-ISIL Campaign"

Toward the end of President Obama's second term, administration officials began to grapple with the fact that the powers they had claimed would soon be in the hands of a new president. In March 2016, Lisa Monaco, the president's chief counterterrorism adviser, stated in remarks at the Council on Foreign Relations that the administration would soon release "an assessment of combatant and non-combatant casualties resulting from strikes taken outside areas of active hostilities since 2009." In the same speech, she stated—in what appeared to be an attempt to commit the next administration to transparency that the Obama administration had eschewed—that, "going forward," casualty assessments would be provided annually. State Department Legal Adviser Brian Egan's remarks to the American Society of International Law a few weeks later were an additional effort on the part of the Obama administration to explain its policies as well as to influence the policies of the next administration.

The document from which this text was transcribed is posted at: www.ACLU.org/TDM/EganSpeech.

Thank you to Lori, Mark, and ASIL for inviting me. I am truly honored and humbled to be here today.

I am here today to talk about some key international law aspects of the United States' ongoing armed conflict against ISIL. In so doing, I am following in the footsteps of others who have gone to some lengths in recent years to explain our government's positions on key aspects of the law of armed conflict. This includes, most prominently, President Obama in his 2013 speech at the National Defense University and his 2014 remarks at West Point. A number of Administration lawyers have also spoken on these topics, including my predecessor, Harold Hongju Koh; former Attorney General Holder; and former Defense Department General Counsels Jeh Johnson and Stephen Preston. The Defense Department's promulgation of its Law of War Manual last year has also made a significant contribution to the public discourse on these issues.

Some have said, however, that our legal approach to the counter-ISIL conflict has been one of the "most discussed and least understood" topics of U.S. practice in recent years.

Thus, at the risk of disappointing you at the outset of this talk, I suspect and hope that much of what I will say today will not be surprising. I also hope, however, that these remarks will provide clarity and help you understand better the U.S. international law approach to these important and consequential operations.

International law matters a great deal in how we as a country approach counterterrorism operations. Prior to my confirmation, I served as a Deputy White House Counsel and Legal Adviser to the National Security Council for nearly three years. Based on my experience in that position, I can tell you that the President, a lawyer himself, and his national security team have been guided by international law in setting the strategy for counterterrorism operations against ISIL. I can attest personally that the President cares deeply about these issues, and that he goes to great lengths to be sure that he understands them.

To start from first principles—the United States complies with the international law of armed conflict in our military campaign against ISIL, as we do in all armed conflicts. We comply with the law of armed conflict because it is the international legal obligation of the United

States; because we have a proud history of standing for the rule of law; because it is essential to building and maintaining our international coalition; because it enhances rather than compromises our military effectiveness; and because it is the right thing to do.

I do not mean to suggest that identifying and applying key international law principles to this fight is easy or without controversy. The United States is engaged in an armed conflict with a non-State actor that controls significant territory, in circumstances in which multiple States and non-State actors also have been engaging in military operations against this enemy, other groups, and each other for several years. These conflicts raise novel and difficult questions of international law that the United States is called to address literally on a daily basis in conducting operations.

Of course, international law is also vitally important to other States. And as the President's counterterrorism strategy has prioritized the development of partnerships with those who share our interests, I submit that it is increasingly important for the United States to engage in what I will call legal diplomacy with those countries with which we partner, as well as those with which we may not see eye to eye. Our ability to engage and work with partners can and often does turn on international legal considerations. We want to work with partners who will comply with international law, and our partners expect the same from us. In this way, international law serves as a critical enabler of international cooperation and joint action on a full range of matters, from the mundane to those that hit the front pages, such as the Iran nuclear deal, efforts to promote peace in Syria, maritime claims in the South China Sea, data privacy, and surveillance.

I will address three topics in my remarks. First, I will attempt to explain in greater detail the United States' international legal basis for using force against ISIL, and some of the key rules of the law of armed conflict that apply to our fight against ISIL. Second, I will address how law of armed conflict–related considerations arise in the context of "partnered" operations—an area in which legal diplomacy is particularly critical. Third, I will address the interplay between law and policy in the conduct of hostilities by the United States—specifically those undertaken under the Presidential Policy Guidance that the President signed on May 22, 2013, known as the "PPG."

Jus ad bellum

I will begin with the United States' international law justification for resorting to the use of force, or the *jus ad bellum.*

As I mentioned a few minutes ago, the United States' armed conflict with ISIL is taking place in a complicated environment—one in which a non-State actor, ISIL, controls significant territory and where multiple States and non-State actors have been engaging in military operations against ISIL, other groups, and each other for several years. Unfortunately, this scenario is not unprecedented in today's world. Iraq and Syria resemble other countries where multiple armed conflicts may be going on simultaneously—countries like Yemen and Libya.

In such complex circumstances, States can potentially find themselves in more than one armed conflict or with multiple legal bases for using force. This complexity is why it is all the more important that we are clear and systematic in our thinking through how *jus ad bellum* principles for resorting to force apply to our actions and what uses of force those principles permit.

The U.N. Charter identifies the key international law principles that must guide State behavior when considering whether to resort to the use of force. Article 2(4) of the U.N. Charter provides in relevant part that "[a]ll Members shall refrain in their international relations from the threat or use of force against the territorial integrity or political independence of any state." Article 51 of the U.N. Charter, on the other hand, specifies that "[n]othing in the present Charter shall impair the inherent right of individual or collective self-defense if an armed attack occurs." Thus, the U.N. Charter recognizes the inherent right to resort to force in individual or collective self-defense. Similarly, the Charter does not prohibit an otherwise lawful use of force when undertaken with the consent of the State upon whose territory the force is to be used.

As a matter of international law, the United States has relied on both consent and self-defense in its use of force against ISIL. Let's start with ISIL's ground offensive and capture of Iraqi territory in June 2014 and the resulting decision by the United States and other States to assist with a military response. Beginning in the summer of 2014, the United

States' actions in Iraq against ISIL have been premised on Iraq's request for, and consent to, U.S. and coalition military action against ISIL on Iraq's territory in order to help Iraq prosecute the armed conflict against the terrorist group.

Upon commencing air strikes against ISIL in Syria in September 2014, the United States submitted a letter to the U.N. Security Council explaining the international legal basis for our use of force in Syria in accordance with Article 51 of the U.N. Charter. As the letter explained, Iraq had made clear it was facing a serious threat of continuing attacks from ISIL coming out of safe havens in Syria and had requested that the United States lead international efforts to strike ISIL in Syria. Consistent with the inherent right of individual and collective self-defense, the United States initiated necessary and proportionate actions in Syria against ISIL. The letter also articulated the United States' position that Syria was unable or unwilling to effectively confront the threat that ISIL posed to Iraq, the United States, and our partners and allies.

Thus, although the United States maintains an individual right of self-defense against ISIL, it has not relied solely on that international law basis in taking action against ISIL. In Iraq, U.S. operations against ISIL are conducted with Iraqi consent and in furtherance of Iraq's own armed conflict against the group. And in Syria, U.S. operations against ISIL are conducted in individual self-defense and the collective self-defense of Iraq and other States.

To say a few more words about self-defense: First, the inherent right of individual and collective self-defense recognized in the U.N. Charter is not restricted to threats posed by States. Nor is the right of self-defense on the territory of another State against non-State actors, such as ISIL, something that developed after 9/11. To the contrary, for at least the past two hundred years, States have invoked the right of self-defense to justify taking action on the territory of another State against non-State actors. As but one example, the oft-cited *Caroline* incident involved the use of force by the United Kingdom in self-defense against a non-State actor located in the United States. Although the precise wording of the justification for the exercise of self-defense against non-State actors may have varied, the acceptance of this right has remained the same.

Under the *jus ad bellum*, a State may use force in the exercise of its inherent right of self-defense not only in response to armed attacks that have occurred, but also in response to *imminent* ones before they occur.

When considering whether an armed attack is imminent under the *jus ad bellum* for purposes of the initial use of force against a particular non-State actor, the United States analyzes a variety of factors, including those identified by Sir Daniel Bethlehem in the enumeration he set forth in the American Journal of International Law—the ASIL's own in-house publication—in 2012. These factors include the nature and immediacy of the threat; the probability of an attack; whether the anticipated attack is part of a concerted pattern of continuing armed activity; the likely scale of the attack and the injury, loss, or damage likely to result therefrom in the absence of mitigating action; and the likelihood that there will be other opportunities to undertake effective action in self-defense that may be expected to cause less serious collateral injury, loss, or damage. The absence of specific evidence of where an attack will take place or of the precise nature of an attack does not preclude a conclusion that an armed attack is imminent for purposes of the exercise of the right of self-defense, provided that there is a reasonable and objective basis for concluding that an armed attack is imminent.

In the view of the United States, once a State has lawfully resorted to force in self-defense against a particular armed group following an actual or imminent armed attack by that group, it is not necessary as a matter of international law to reassess whether an armed attack is imminent prior to every subsequent action taken against that group, provided that hostilities have not ended. Under the PPG, however, the concept of imminence plays an important role as a matter of policy in certain U.S. counterterrorism operations, even when it is not legally required.

I'd also like to say a few words on how State sovereignty and consent factor into the international legal analysis when considering the use of force. President Obama has made clear that "America cannot take strikes wherever we choose; our actions are bound by consultations with partners, and respect for state sovereignty." This is true of our operations against ISIL as it has been true in our non-international armed conflict against al-Qa'ida and associated forces.

Indeed, under the *jus ad bellum*, the international legal basis for the resort to force in self-defense on another State's territory takes into account State sovereignty. The international law of self-defense requires that such uses of force be necessary to address the threat giving rise to the right to use force in the first place. States therefore must consider whether unilateral actions in self-defense that would impinge on a territorial State's sovereignty are *necessary* or whether it might be possible to secure the territorial State's consent before using force on its territory against a non-State actor. In other words, international law not only requires a State to analyze whether it has a legal basis for the use of force against a particular non-State actor—which I'll call the "against whom" question—but also requires a State to analyze whether it has a legal basis to use force against that non-State actor in a particular location—which I'll call the "where" question.

It is with respect to this "where" question that international law requires that States must either determine that they have the relevant government's consent or, if they must rely on self-defense to use force against a non-State actor on another State's territory, determine that the territorial State is "unable or unwilling" to address the threat posed by the non-State actor on its territory. In practice, States generally rely on the consent of the relevant government in conducting operations against ISIL or other non-State actors even when they may also have a self-defense basis to use force against those non-State actors, and this consent often takes the form of a request for assistance from a government that is itself engaged in an armed conflict against the relevant group. This is the case with respect to ISIL in Iraq.

Of course, the concept of consent can pose challenges in a world in which governments are rapidly changing, or have lost control of significant parts of their territory, or have shown no desire to address the threat. Thus, it sometimes can be a complex matter to identify the appropriate person or entity from whom consent should be sought. The U.S. Government carefully considers these issues when considering the question of consent.

In some cases, international law does not require a State to obtain the consent of the State on whose territory force will be used. In particular, there will be cases in which there is a reasonable and objective basis for concluding that the territorial State is unwilling or unable to effectively confront the non-State actor in its territory so that it is necessary to act in self-defense against the non-State actor in that State's territory without the territorial State's consent. For example, in the case of ISIL in Syria, as indicated in our Article 51 letter, we could act in self-defense without Syrian consent because we had determined that the Syrian regime was unable or unwilling to prevent the use of its territory for armed attacks by ISIL. This "unable or unwilling" standard is, in our view, an important application of the requirement that a State, when relying on self-defense for its use of force in another State's territory, may resort to force only if it is necessary to do so—that is, if measures short of force have been exhausted or are inadequate to address the threat posed by the non-State actor emanating from the territory of another State.

The unable or unwilling standard is not a license to wage war globally or to disregard the borders and territorial integrity of other States. Indeed, this legal standard does not dispense with the importance of respecting the sovereignty of other States. To the contrary, applying the standard ensures that the sovereignty of other States is respected. Specifically, applying the standard ensures that force is used on foreign territory without consent only in those exceptional circumstances in which a State cannot or will not take effective measures to confront a non-State actor that is using its territory as a base for attacks and related operations against other States.

With respect to the "unable" prong of the standard, inability perhaps can be demonstrated most plainly, for example, where a State has lost or abandoned effective control over the portion of its territory from which the non-State actor is operating. This is the case with respect to the situation in Syria. By September 2014, the Syrian government had lost effective control of much of eastern and northeastern Syria, with much of that territory under ISIL's control.

Jus in bello

In the next few minutes I'd like to shed some light on the *jus in bello*—the legal rules we follow in carrying out the fight against ISIL. As a threshold matter, some of our foreign partners have asked us how we classify the conflict with ISIL and thus what set of rules applies. Because we are engaged in an armed conflict against a non-State actor, our war against ISIL is a non-international armed conflict, or NIAC. Therefore, the applicable international legal regime governing our military operations is the law of armed conflict covering NIACs, most importantly, Common Article 3 of the 1949 Geneva Conventions and other treaty and customary international law rules governing the conduct of hostilities in non-international armed conflicts.

The rules applicable in NIACs have received close scrutiny since the September 11 attacks within the U.S. Government, in our courts in the context of ongoing litigation concerning detention and military commission prosecutions, and in the expanding and ever more sophisticated treatment that these issues receive in academia.

I would like to clarify briefly some of the rules that the United States is bound to comply with as a matter of international law in the conduct of hostilities during NIACs. In particular, I'd like to spend a few minutes walking through some of the targeting rules that the United States regards as customary international law applicable to all parties in a NIAC:

- First, parties must distinguish between military objectives, including combatants, on the one hand, and civilians and civilian objects on the other. Only military objectives, including combatants, may be made the object of attack.

- Insofar as objects are concerned, military objectives are those objects which by their nature, location, purpose or use make an effective contribution to military action and whose total or partial destruction, capture or neutralization, in the circumstances ruling at the time, offers a definite military advantage. The United States has interpreted this definition to include objects that make an effective contribution to the enemy's war-fighting or war-sustaining capabilities.

- Feasible precautions must be taken in conducting an attack to reduce the risk of harm to civilians, such as, in certain circumstances, warnings to civilians before bombardments.

- Customary international law also specifically prohibits a number of targeting measures in NIACs. First, attacks directed against civilians or civilian objects as such are prohibited. Additionally, indiscriminate attacks, including but not limited to attacks using inherently indiscriminate weapons, are prohibited.

- Attacks directed against specifically protected objects such as cultural property and hospitals are also prohibited unless their protection has been forfeited.

- Also prohibited are attacks that violate the principle of proportionality—that is, attacks against combatants or other military objectives that are expected to cause incidental harm to civilians that would be excessive in relation to the concrete and direct military advantage anticipated.

- Moreover, acts or threats of violence the primary purpose of which is to spread terror among the civilian population are prohibited.

To elaborate further and correct some possible misunderstandings regarding who the United States targets as an enemy in its ongoing armed conflicts, I'd like to explain how the United States assesses whether a specific individual may be made the object of attack.

In many cases we are dealing with an enemy who does not wear uniforms or otherwise seek to distinguish itself from the civilian population. In these circumstances, we look to all available real-time and historical information to determine whether a potential target would be a lawful object of attack. To emphasize a point that we have made previously, it is not the case that all adult males in the vicinity of a target are deemed combatants. Among other things, the United States may consider certain operational activities, characteristics, and identifiers when determining whether an individual is taking a direct part in hostilities or whether the individual may formally or functionally be considered a member of an organized armed group with which we are engaged in an armed conflict. For example, with respect to membership in an organized armed group, we may examine the extent to which the individual performs functions for the benefit of the group that are analogous to those traditionally performed by members of State militaries that are liable to attack; is carrying out or giving orders to others within the group to perform such functions; or has undertaken certain acts that reliably indicate meaningful integration into the group.

Partnerships and legal diplomacy

I'd like to turn next to discussing the international coalitions and other partnerships that are critical to the fight against ISIL and the legal diplomacy that helps facilitate and sustain those partnerships. Sixty-six partners are engaged as part of the coalition that is steadily degrading ISIL. In the course of building and maintaining that strong coalition, we have also sought to navigate legal differences and find common legal ground. Some of our allies and partners have different international legal obligations because of the different treaties to which they are party, and others may hold different legal interpretations of our common obligations. Legal diplomacy plays a key role in building and maintaining the counter-ISIL military coalition and fostering interoperability between its members. Legal diplomacy builds on common understandings of international law, while also seeking to bridge or manage the specific differences in any particular State's international obligations or interpretations.

Public explanations of legal positions are an important part of legal diplomacy. The United States is not alone in providing such public explanations. Over the last 18 months, for example, nine of our coalition partners have submitted public Article 51 notifications to the U.N. Security Council explaining and justifying their military actions in Syria against ISIL. Though the exact formulations vary from letter to letter, the consistent theme throughout these reports to the Security Council is that the right of self-defense extends to using force to respond to actual or imminent armed attacks by non-State armed groups like ISIL. Those States' military actions against ISIL in Syria and their public notifications are perhaps the clearest evidence of this understanding of the international law of self-defense.

More frequently, however, it is through private consultations that governments seek to understand each other's legal rationale for military operations. These private discussions help frame the public conversation on some of the central legal issues, and they are crucial to securing the vital cooperation of partners who want to understand our legal basis for acting. For example, there are times when the United States has sought the assistance of key allies in taking direct action against terrorist targets, but before these allies would aid us, the lawyers in their foreign ministries have sought a better understanding of the legal basis for our operations. The prompt, compelling, and—at times—very early morning explanations provided by our attorneys can be crucial to enabling such operations.

These conversations also go the other way. The U.S. commitment to upholding the law of armed conflict also extends to promoting law of armed conflict compliance by our partners. In the campaign against ISIL and beyond, coalitions and partnerships with other States and non-State actors are increasingly prominent features of current U.S. military operations. When others seek our assistance with military operations, we ensure that we understand their legal basis for acting. We also take a variety of measures to help our partners comply with the law of armed conflict and to avoid facilitating violations through our assistance. Examples of such measures include vetting and training recipients of our assistance and monitoring how our assistance is used.

Some have argued that the obligation in Common Article 1 of the Geneva Conventions to "ensure respect" for the Conventions legally requires us to undertake such steps and more vis-à-vis not only our partners, but all States and non-State actors engaged in armed conflict. Although we do not share this expansive interpretation of Common Article 1, as a matter of policy, we always seek to promote adherence to the law of armed conflict generally and encourage other States to do the same. As a matter of international law, we would look to the law of State responsibility and our partners' compliance with the law of armed conflict in assessing the lawfulness of our assistance to, and joint operations with, those military partners.

Law and Policy
Finally, I'd like to touch on the interplay between law and policy when the United States takes lethal action in armed conflicts and how the United States often applies policy standards that exceed what the law of armed conflict requires.

As a matter of international law, the United States is bound to adhere to the law of armed conflict. In many cases, the United States imposes standards on its direct action operations that go beyond the requirements of the law of armed conflict. For example, the U.S. military may impose an upper limit as a matter of policy on the anticipated number of non-combatant casualties that is much lower than that which would be lawful under the rule that prohibits attacks that are expected to cause excessive incidental harm.

Additionally, although the United States is not a party to the 1977 Additional Protocol II to the 1949 Geneva Conventions and therefore not bound to comply with its provisions as a matter of treaty law, current U.S. practice is already consistent with the Protocol's provisions, which provide rules applicable to States parties in non-international armed conflict. This is a treaty that the Reagan Administration submitted to the Senate for its advice and consent to ratification, and every subsequent Administration has continued that support.

I'd like to focus my comments over the next few minutes on U.S. operations to capture or employ lethal force against terrorist targets outside areas of active hostilities. In addition to the law of armed conflict, these operations are governed by policy guidance issued by the President in 2013. This policy guidance, known as the PPG, reflects this Administration's efforts to strengthen and refine the process for reviewing and approving counterterrorism operations outside of the United States and "areas of active hostilities."

The phrase "areas of active hostilities" is not a legal term of art—it is a term specific to the PPG. For the purpose of the PPG, the determination that a region is an "area of active hostilities" takes into account, among other things, the scope and intensity of the fighting. The Administration currently considers Afghanistan, Iraq, and Syria to be "areas of active hostilities," which means that the PPG does not apply to operations in those States.

Substantively, the PPG imposes certain heightened policy standards that exceed the requirements of the law of armed conflict for lethal targeting. The President has done so out of a belief that implementing such heightened standards outside of hot battlefields is the right approach to using force to meet U.S. counterterrorism objectives and protect American lives consistent with our values.

Of course, the President always retains authority to take lethal action consistent with the law of armed conflict, even if the PPG's heightened policy standards may not be met. But in every case in which the United States takes military action, whether in or outside an area of active hostilities, we are bound to adhere as a matter of international law to the law of armed conflict. This includes, among other things, adherence to the fundamental law of armed conflict principles of distinction, proportionality, necessity, and humanity.

The Administration has already identified a number of the aspects in which the PPG imposes policy standards for the use of lethal force in counterterrorism operations that go beyond the requirements of the law of armed conflict. I'd like to focus on one key aspect here. The PPG establishes measures that go beyond the law of armed conflict in order to minimize risks to civilians to the greatest extent possible. In particular, the PPG establishes a threshold of "near certainty" that non-combatants will not be injured or killed. This standard is also higher than that imposed by the law of armed conflict, which contemplates that civilians will inevitably and tragically be killed in armed conflict.

In addition, with respect to lethal action, the PPG generally requires an assessment that capture of the targeted individual is not feasible at the time of the operation. The law of armed conflict does not itself impose any such "least restrictive means" obligation; instead, combatants may be targeted with lethal force at any time, provided that they are not "out of the fight" due to capture, surrender, illness, or injury.

I hope that this discussion of the PPG and other distinctions between law and policy has given you an understanding not only of the difference between the legal and policy constraints on U.S. lethal targeting, but also better appreciation of the lengths this government goes to in order to minimize harm to civilians outside of hot battlefields while also taking the direct action necessary to protect the United States, our partners, and allies.

Conclusion

In closing, I'll speak to a final aspect of legal diplomacy, one which my predecessors have emphasized in their public remarks as well. As Legal Adviser, one of my roles is to serve as a spokesperson for the U.S. Government on the importance and relevance of international law, and how the U.S. Government interprets, applies, and complies with international law. Part of our legal diplomacy is carried out with our foreign counterparts behind closed doors. But public legal diplomacy is a critical aspect of our work as well, as my predecessors—several of whom are in the audience today—have ably demonstrated.

It is not enough that we act lawfully or regard ourselves as being in the right. It is important that our actions be understood as lawful by others both at home and abroad in order to show respect for the rule of law and promote it more broadly, while also cultivating partnerships and building coalitions. Even if other governments or populations do not agree with our precise legal theories or conclusions, we must be able to demonstrate to others that our most consequential national security and foreign policy decisions are guided by a principled understanding and application of international law.

I hope that I have succeeded in providing some clarity today on the United States' approach to international law in the counter-ISIL campaign. I am confident, however, that I have not answered all of your questions. We will seek opportunities to provide additional clarity on these issues in the months ahead. In the meantime, I have reserved the remainder of my time for questions. Thank you.

14

Fact Sheet

July 1, 2016

"Executive Order on the U.S. Policy on Pre & Post-Strike Measures to Address Civilian Casualties in the U.S. Operations Involving the Use of Force & the DNI Release of Aggregate Data on Strikes Outside Areas of Active Hostilities"

This fact sheet summarizes the Executive Order and casualty statistics released by the administration the same day.

The document from which this text was transcribed is posted at: www.ACLU.org/TDM/FactSheet2.

Since President Obama took office, he has been clear that, when necessary, the United States will use force abroad to protect the American
people consistent with our values and all applicable law, including
the law of armed conflict. He has also emphasized the need to be as
transparent as possible with the American people about the basis for
our counterterrorism operations and the manner in which they are
conducted in order to enhance the public's confidence in these activities, set standards for other nations to follow, and counter terrorist
propaganda and false accusations about U.S. operations. Additionally, the President has underscored that we will continue to develop
a sustainable legal and policy architecture to guide our counterterrorism activities going forward. To these ends, in 2013 the President
approved and publicly described policy guidance formalizing and
strengthening the rigorous standards and procedures governing our
use of lethal force against terrorist targets outside areas of active hostilities. Today, the Administration is taking additional steps to institutionalize and enhance best practices regarding U.S. counterterrorism
operations and other U.S. operations involving the use of force, as well
as to provide greater transparency and accountability regarding these
operations.

These steps include promulgating an Executive Order on *United
States Policy on Pre- and Post-Strike Measures to Address Civilian
Casualties in U.S. Operations Involving the Use of Force*, as well as
releasing aggregate data regarding both the number of strikes undertaken during this Administration by the U.S. Government against terrorist targets located outside areas of active hostilities and the range of
assessed combatant and non-combatant deaths resulting from those
strikes. The Executive Order provides additional information on best
practices and procedures that are already in place for current operations and that will be applied in future operations, regardless of the
location. Collectively, these measures demonstrate the professionalism and high standards employed by U.S. Government personnel who
help keep Americans safe from terrorist threats overseas, while also
underscoring our commitment to constantly refine and strengthen
our counterterrorism framework and enhance accountability for our
actions.

Executive Order to Address Civilian Casualties

As President Obama has said, "All armed conflict invites tragedy. But by narrowly targeting our action against those who want to kill us and not the people they hide among, we are choosing the course of action least likely to result in the loss of innocent life." In that spirit, this Executive Order applies to all of our operations, regardless of where they are conducted, and underscores that our legal and policy commitments regarding the protection of civilians are fundamentally consistent with the effective, efficient, and decisive use of force in pursuit of our Nation's interests.

First, this Executive Order catalogues the best practices the U.S. Government currently implements to protect civilians in the context of operations involving the use of force inside and outside areas of active hostilities, and it directs relevant departments and agencies to sustain such measures in present and future operations. These measures include conducting training on implementation of best practices that help reduce the likelihood of civilian casualties and dedicating operational resources to mitigate that risk. It also includes, as appropriate, maintaining channels for engagement with the International Committee of the Red Cross and non-governmental organizations that can assist in efforts to distinguish between military objectives and civilians; acknowledging U.S. Government responsibility for civilian casualties and offering condolences, including *ex gratia* payments, to civilians who are injured, or to the families of civilians who are killed; and, when civilian casualties have occurred, taking steps to minimize the likelihood of future such incidents.

Second, to help address challenges associated with assessing the credibility of reports of civilian casualties in non-permissive environments, the Executive Order emphasizes the U.S. Government's consideration of credible reporting provided by non-governmental organizations in its post-strike reviews, including drawing on existing information-sharing arrangements to ensure the availability of such reporting to those conducting post-strike analyses.

Third, it directs the Director of National Intelligence (DNI), or such other officials as the President may designate, to release publicly an annual summary of information obtained from relevant departments and agencies about the number of strikes undertaken by the U.S. Government against terrorist targets outside areas of active hostilities and the assessed range of combatant and non-combatant deaths resulting from those strikes, based on relevant and credible post-strike reporting and consistent with the need to protect sources and methods. The annual report will also include information regarding the general sources of information and methodology used to conduct these assessments and address general reasons for discrepancies between post-strike assessments by the U.S. Government and credible reporting from nongovernmental organizations.

Finally, the Executive Order establishes a mechanism for experts from relevant U.S. Government departments and agencies to convene to consult on civilian casualty trends and consider potential improvements to the U.S. Government's civilian casualty mitigation efforts.

Background on Processes and Procedures Taken by the U.S. Government to Mitigate Civilian Casualties

In May 2013, President Obama issued Presidential Policy Guidance (PPG) that, among other things, set forth policy standards for U.S. direct action outside the United States and outside areas of active hostilities. These policy standards generally include that the United States will use lethal force only against a target that poses a "continuing, imminent threat to U.S. persons," and that direct action will be taken only if there is "near certainty" that the terrorist target is present and "near certainty" that non-combatants will not be killed or injured. As the President has said, the "near certainty" standard is the "highest standard we can set."

Thus, unlike terrorist organizations, which deliberately target civilians and violate the law of armed conflict, the United States takes great care to adhere to the law of armed conflict and, in many circumstances, applies policy standards that offer protections for civilians that exceed the requirements of the law of armed conflict. Moreover, even when the United States is not operating under the PPG—for example, when the United States is taking action in "areas of active hostilities," such as it is today in Afghanistan, Iraq, and Syria, or when the United States is acting quickly to defend U.S. or partner forces from attack—the United

States goes to extraordinary lengths to minimize the risk of civilian casualties.

In particular, in dealing with enemy forces that do not wear uniforms or carry their arms openly, the United States goes to great lengths to apply the fundamental law of armed conflict principle of distinction, which, among other things, requires that attacks be directed only against military objectives and not against civilians and civilian objects. The United States considers all available information about a potential target's current and historical activities to inform an assessment of whether the individual is a lawful target. For example, an individual may be targetable if the individual is formally or functionally a member of an armed group against which we are engaged in an armed conflict. As Administration officials have stated publicly, to determine if an individual is a member of an armed group, we may look to, among other things: the extent to which the individual performs functions for the benefit of the group that are analogous to those traditionally performed by members of a country's armed forces; whether that person is carrying out or giving orders to others within the group; or whether that person has undertaken certain acts that reliably connote meaningful integration into the group.

Before a strike against a terrorist target is considered in any theater, U.S. Government personnel review all available information to determine whether any of the individuals at the location of the potential strike is a non-combatant. A body of standards, methods, techniques, and computer modeling, supported by weapons testing data and combat observations, informs the analysis as to whether those not specifically targeted would likely be injured or killed in a strike.

Releasing Aggregate Data on Strikes Undertaken by the U.S. Government Against Terrorist Targets Outside Areas of Active Hostilities

Demonstrating the legitimacy of our counterterrorism efforts requires not only complying with the law of armed conflict and setting policy standards that offer protection that exceeds the law's requirements, but also providing information to the American people about our counterterrorism efforts. As President Obama has said, when we cannot explain our efforts clearly and publicly, we face terrorist propaganda and international suspicion, we erode the legitimacy of our actions in the eyes of our partners and our people, and we undermine accountability in our own government. That is why the President believes it is important to provide the public with as much information as possible regarding the basis for and results of U.S. counterterrorism operations. In keeping with this commitment, today the DNI is releasing a summary of information obtained from relevant departments and agencies about both the number of strikes undertaken by the U.S. Government against terrorist targets outside areas of active hostilities between January 20, 2009, and December 31, 2015, and the best assessed range of combatant and non-combatant deaths resulting from those strikes. Going forward, figures for the preceding year will be released annually on May 1, consistent with the need to protect sources and methods.

We recognize that U.S. counterterrorism strikes have killed non-combatants, a reality that exists in all conflicts. As the statement today from the DNI notes, in releasing these figures, the U.S. Government also acknowledges that there are differences between U.S. Government assessments and reporting from non-governmental organizations on non-combatant deaths resulting from U.S. operations. Although the U.S. Government has access to a wide range of information, the figures we are releasing today should be considered in light of the inherent limitations on the ability to determine the precise number of combatant and non-combatant deaths outside areas of active hostilities, including the non-permissive environments in which these strikes often occur. But as the information we are releasing also shows, the rigorous standards and procedures we apply to such strikes have resulted in extraordinarily precise targeting. The U.S. Government remains committed to continually refining, clarifying, and strengthening the standards and procedures that govern our use of force abroad to keep the Nation safe from terrorist threats.

15

Report of the Director of National Intelligence

July 1, 2016

"Summary of Information Regarding U.S. Counterterrorism Strikes Outside Areas of Active Hostilities"

The Director of National Intelligence published this document approximately three months after Lisa Monaco, the president's chief counterterrorism adviser, announced that the administration would publicly release casualty statistics. While the release of the information was welcome, the government's casualty estimates were much lower than those of independent research groups, and the government's refusal to release more granular data—for example, data by year, or by country, or by strike—made the data difficult to interpret and assess.

The document from which this text was transcribed is posted at: www.ACLU.org/TDM/DNIReport.

Summary of Information Regarding U.S. Counterterrorism Strikes Outside Areas of Active Hostilities

In accordance with the President's direction and consistent with the President's commitment to providing as much information as possible to the American people about U.S. counterterrorism activities, the Director of National Intelligence (DNI) is releasing today a summary of information provided to the DNI about both the number of strikes taken by the U.S. Government against terrorist targets outside areas of active hostilities and the assessed number of combatant and non-combatant[a] deaths resulting from those strikes. "Areas of active hostilities" currently include Afghanistan, Iraq, and Syria.

Summary of U.S. Counterterrorism Strikes Outside Areas of Active Hostilities between January 20, 2009 and December 31, 2015	
Total Number of Strikes Against Terrorist Targets Outside Areas of Active Hostilities	473
Combatant Deaths	2372–2581
Non-Combatant Deaths	64–116

The assessed range of non-combatant deaths provided to the DNI reflects consideration of credible reports of non-combatant deaths drawn from all-source information, including reports from the media and non-governmental organizations. The assessed range of non-combatant deaths includes deaths for which there is an insufficient basis for assessing that the deceased is a combatant.

---

[a] Non-combatants are individuals who may not be made the object of attack under applicable international law. The term "non-combatant" does not include an individual who is part of a belligerent party to an armed conflict, an individual who is taking a direct part in hostilities, or an individual who is targetable in the exercise of U.S. national self-defense. Males of military age may be non-combatants; it is not the case that all military-aged males in the vicinity of a target are deemed to be combatants.

U.S. Government Post-Strike Review Processes and Procedures

The information that was provided to the DNI regarding combatant and non-combatant deaths is the result of processes that include careful reviews of all strikes after they are conducted to assess the effectiveness of operations. These review processes have evolved over time to ensure that they incorporate the best available all-source intelligence, media reporting, and other information and may result in reassessments of strikes if new information becomes available that alters the original judgment. The large volume of pre- and post-strike data available to the U.S. Government can enable analysts to distinguish combatants from non-combatants, conduct detailed battle damage assessments, and separate reliable reporting from terrorist propaganda or from media reports that may be based on inaccurate information.

Discrepancies Between U.S. Government and Non-Governmental Assessments

In releasing these figures, the U.S. Government acknowledges that there [2] are differences between U.S. Government assessments and reporting from non-governmental organizations. Reports from non-governmental organizations can include both aggregate data regarding non-combatant deaths as well as case studies addressing particular strikes, and generally rely on a combination of media reporting and, in some instances, field research conducted in areas of reported strikes. Although these organizations' reports of non-combatant deaths resulting from U.S strikes against terrorist targets outside areas of active hostilities vary widely, such reporting generally estimates significantly higher figures for non-combatant deaths than is indicated by U.S. Government information. For instance, for the period between January 20, 2009 and December 31, 2015, non-governmental organizations' estimates range from more than 200 to slightly more than 900 possible non-combatant deaths outside areas of active hostilities.

Consistent with the requirements applicable to future reporting under Section 3(b) of the Executive Order "United States Policy on Pre- and Post-Strike Measures to Address Civilian Casualties in U.S. Operations Involving the Use of Force," the information we are releasing today addresses general reasons for discrepancies between post-strike assessments from the United States Government and credible reporting from non-governmental organizations regarding non-combatant deaths and does not address specific incidents. There are a number of possible reasons that these non-governmental organizations' reports of the number of non-combatants killed may differ from the U.S. Government assessments, based on the information provided to the DNI.

First, although there are inherent limitations on determining the precise number of combatant and non-combatant deaths, particularly when operating in non-permissive environments, the U.S. Government uses post-strike methodologies that have been refined and honed over the years and that use information that is generally unavailable to non-governmental organizations. The U.S. Government draws on all available information (including sensitive intelligence) to determine whether an individual is part of a belligerent party fighting against the United States in an armed conflict; taking a direct part in hostilities against the United States; or otherwise targetable in the exercise of national self-defense. Thus, the U.S. Government may have reliable information that certain individuals are combatants, but are being counted as non-combatants by non-governmental organizations. For example, further analysis of an individual's possible membership in an organized armed group may include, among other things: the extent to which an individual performs functions for the benefit of the group that are analogous to those traditionally performed by members of a country's armed forces; whether that person is carrying out or giving orders to others within the group; or whether that person has undertaken certain acts that reliably connote meaningful integration into the group.

Second, according to information provided to the DNI, U.S. Government post-strike reviews involve the collection and analysis of multiple sources of intelligence before, during, and after a strike, including video observations, human sources and assets, signals intelligence, geospatial intelligence, accounts from local officials on the ground, and open source reporting. Information collected before a strike is intended to provide clarity regarding the number of individuals at a strike location as well as whether the individuals are engaged in terrorist activity. Post-strike collection frequently enables U.S. Government analysts to confirm, among other things, the number of individuals killed as well

3

as their combatant status. The information is then analyzed along with other all-source intelligence reporting. This combination of sources is unique and can provide insights that are likely unavailable to non-governmental organizations.

Finally, non-governmental organizations' reports of counterterrorism strikes attributed to the U.S. Government—particularly their identification of non-combatant deaths—may be further complicated by the deliberate spread of misinformation by some actors, including terrorist organizations, in local media reports on which some non-governmental estimates rely.

Although the U.S. Government has access to a wide range of information, the figures released today should be considered in light of the inherent limitations on the ability to determine the precise number of combatant and non-combatant deaths given the non-permissive environments in which these strikes often occur. The U.S. Government remains committed to considering new, credible information regarding non-combatant deaths that may emerge and revising previous assessments, as appropriate.

16

Executive Order

July 1, 2016

"United States Policy on Pre- and Post-Strike Measures to Address Civilian Casualties in U.S. Operations Involving the Use of Force"

President Obama signed this Executive Order on the same day his administration released official casualty statistics for the first time. The order requires relevant federal agencies to train their personnel on compliance with legal obligations relating to the protection of civilians, as well as to "review or investigate" incidents involving civilian casualties. The order also provides for the annual release of "information about the number of strikes undertaken by the U.S. Government against terrorist targets outside areas of active hostilities . . . as well as assessments of combatant and non-combatant deaths resulting from those strikes."

The document from which this text was transcribed is posted at: www.ACLU.org/TDM/ExecutiveOrder.

EXECUTIVE ORDER

- - - - - - -

UNITED STATES POLICY ON PRE- AND POST-STRIKE MEASURES TO ADDRESS CIVILIAN CASUALTIES IN U.S. OPERATIONS INVOLVING THE USE OF FORCE

By the authority vested in me as President by the Constitution and the laws of the United States of America, I hereby direct as follows:

Section 1. Purpose. United States policy on civilian casualties resulting from U.S. operations involving the use of force in armed conflict or in the exercise of the Nation's inherent right of self-defense is based on our national interests, our values, and our legal obligations. As a Nation, we are steadfastly committed to complying with our obligations under the law of armed conflict, including those that address the protection of civilians, such as the fundamental principles of necessity, humanity, distinction, and proportionality.

The protection of civilians is fundamentally consistent with the effective, efficient, and decisive use of force in pursuit of U.S. national interests. Minimizing civilian casualties can further mission objectives; help maintain the support of partner governments and vulnerable populations, especially in the conduct of counterterrorism and counterinsurgency operations; and enhance the legitimacy and sustainability of U.S. operations critical to our national security. As a matter of policy, the United States therefore routinely imposes certain heightened policy standards that are more protective than the requirements of the law of armed conflict that relate to the protection of civilians.

Civilian casualties are a tragic and at times unavoidable consequence of the use of force in situations of armed conflict or in the exercise of a state's inherent right of self-defense. The U.S. Government shall maintain and promote best practices that reduce the likelihood of civilian casualties, take appropriate steps when such casualties occur, and draw lessons from our operations to further enhance the protection of civilians.

Sec. 2. Policy. In furtherance of U.S. Government efforts to protect civilians in U.S. operations involving the use of force in armed conflict or in the exercise of the Nation's inherent right of self-defense, and with a view toward enhancing such efforts, relevant departments and agencies (agencies) shall continue to take certain measures in present and future operations.

(a) In particular, relevant agencies shall, consistent with mission objectives and applicable law, including the law of armed conflict:

(i) train personnel, commensurate with their responsibilities, on compliance with legal obligations and policy guidance that address the protection of civilians and on implementation of best practices that reduce the likelihood of civilian casualties, including through exercises, predeployment training, and simulations of complex operational environments that include civilians;

(ii) develop, acquire, and field intelligence, surveillance, and reconnaissance systems that, by enabling more accurate battlespace awareness, contribute to the protection of civilians;

(iii) develop, acquire, and field weapon systems and other technological capabilities that further enable the discriminate use of force in different operational contexts;

(iv) take feasible precautions in conducting attacks to reduce the likelihood of civilian casualties, such as providing warnings to the civilian population (unless the circumstances do not permit), adjusting the timing of attacks, taking steps to ensure military objectives and civilians are clearly distinguished, and taking other measures appropriate to the circumstances; and

(v) conduct assessments that assist in the reduction of civilian casualties by identifying risks to civilians and evaluating efforts to reduce risks to civilians.

(b) In addition to the responsibilities above, relevant agencies shall also, as appropriate and consistent with mission objectives and applicable law, including the law of armed conflict:

(i) review or investigate incidents involving civilian casualties, including by considering relevant and credible information from all available sources, such as other agencies, partner governments, and nongovernmental organizations, and take measures to mitigate the likelihood of future incidents of civilian casualties;

(ii) acknowledge U.S. Government responsibility for civilian casualties and offer condolences, including ex gratia payments, to civilians who are injured or to the families of civilians who are killed;

(iii) engage with foreign partners to share and learn best practices for reducing the likelihood of and responding to civilian casualties, including through appropriate training and assistance; and

(iv) maintain channels for engagement with the International Committee of the Red Cross and other nongovernmental organizations that operate in conflict zones and encourage such organizations to assist in efforts to distinguish between military objectives and civilians, including by appropriately marking protected facilities, vehicles, and personnel, and by providing updated information on the locations of such facilities and personnel.

Sec. 3. Report on Strikes Undertaken by the U.S. Government Against Terrorist Targets Outside Areas of Active Hostilities. (a) The Director of National Intelligence (DNI), or such other official as the President may designate, shall obtain from relevant agencies information about the number of strikes undertaken by the U.S. Government against terrorist targets outside areas of active hostilities from January 1, 2016, through December 31, 2016, as well as assessments of combatant and non-combatant deaths resulting from those strikes, and publicly release an unclassified summary of such information no later than May 1, 2017. By May 1 of each subsequent year, as consistent with the need to protect sources and methods, the DNI shall publicly release a report with the same information for the preceding calendar year.

(b) The annual report shall also include information obtained from relevant agencies regarding the general sources of information and methodology used to conduct these assessments and, as feasible and appropriate, shall address the general reasons for discrepancies between post-strike assessments from the U.S. Government and credible reporting from nongovernmental organizations regarding non-combatant deaths resulting from strikes undertaken by the U.S. Government against terrorist targets outside areas of active hostilities.

(c) In preparing a report under this section, the DNI shall review relevant and credible post-strike all-source reporting, including such information from nongovernmental sources, for the purpose of ensuring that this reporting is available to and considered by relevant agencies in their assessment of deaths.

(d) The Assistant to the President for National Security Affairs may, as appropriate, request that the head of any relevant agency conduct additional reviews related to the intelligence assessments of deaths from strikes against terrorist targets outside areas of active hostilities.

Sec. 4. Periodic Consultation. In furtherance of the policies and practices set forth in this order, the Assistant to the President for National Security Affairs, through the National Security Council staff, will convene agencies with relevant defense, counterterrorism, intelligence, legal, civilian protection, and technology expertise to consult on civilian casualty trends, consider potential improvements to U.S. Government civilian casualty mitigation efforts, and, as appropriate, report to the Deputies and Principals Committees, consistent with Presidential Policy Directive 1 or its successor. Specific incidents will not be considered in this context, and will continue to be examined within relevant chains of command.

Sec. 5. General Provisions. (a) The policies and practices set forth above are not intended to alter, and shall be implemented consistent with, the authority and responsibility of commanders and other U.S. personnel to execute their mission as directed by the President or other appropriate authorities, which necessarily includes the inherent right of self-defense and the maintenance of good order and discipline among U.S. personnel. No part of this order modifies the chain of command of the U.S. Armed Forces or the authority of U.S. commanders.

(b) No part of this order modifies priorities in the collection of intelligence or the development, acquisition, or fielding of weapon systems and other technological capabilities.

(c) No part of this order shall prejudice or supplant established procedures pertaining to administrative or criminal investigative or judicial processes in the context of the military justice system or other applicable law and regulation.

(d) The policies set forth in this order are consistent with existing U.S. obligations under international law and are not intended to create new international legal obligations; nor shall anything in this order be construed to derogate from obligations under applicable law, including the law of armed conflict.

(e) This order is not intended to, and does not, create any right or benefit, substantive or procedural, enforceable at law or in equity by any party against the United States, its departments, agencies, or entities, its officers, employees, or agents, or any other person.

BARACK OBAMA
THE WHITE HOUSE,
July 1, 2016.

ACKNOWLEDGMENTS

Many people contributed to this book in one way or another. I would like to thank, first, my family, and especially Alice, for having encouraged this project, tolerated my preoccupation with it, and given me the time to complete it.

I would also like to thank the lawyers and journalists who won the release of some of the documents presented here. At the ACLU, I was fortunate to work with Hina Shamsi, Arthur Spitzer, Brett Max Kaufman, Matthew Spurlock, and Nathan Freed Wessler—all talented and dedicated advocates who spent many hours drafting and editing legal briefs and devising new ways to escape the reach of old precedents. Because one of our Freedom of Information Act suits overlapped with a suit filed by Charlie Savage and Scott Shane of the *New York Times*, we had the opportunity to work with David McCraw, the *Times*'s assistant general counsel, and some of the *Times*'s First Amendment fellows, including Victoria Baranetsky, Stephen Gikow, Jeremy Kutner, and Nabiha Syed. Working with them was a privilege, as well as a reminder of the often invisible but always crucial role that lawyers for news organizations play in making investigative journalism possible.

I would also like to thank some of the people who read and commented on drafts of this book, particularly Kade Ellis, Ryan Goodman, Megan Graham, Jonathan Hafetz, Matthew Harwood, Lisa Magarrell, Amrit Singh, Hina Shamsi, Steven R. Shapiro, Matthew Spurlock, and Ben Wizner, as well as my editors at The New Press, Diane Wachtell, Jed

Bickman, and Emily Albarillo. Going well beyond the call of duty, Brett Max Kaufman and Larry Siems read multiple drafts. Dorothy Samuels deserves special mention for her generosity and patience as a reader and reviewer, which extended to interrupting her improbable visit to the Ronald Reagan Presidential Library to call me with yet another round of inspired edits. I was fortunate to have the help of many legal assistants, paralegals, and interns at the ACLU, but I am particularly grateful for the assistance provided by Molly Buckley, Mary Byrne, Dinesh McCoy, Erica Mildner, Sameera Rahman, and Eliza Relman.

I owe an especially significant debt to Steven R. Shapiro and Anthony D. Romero for having made it possible for me and my colleagues to do the work reflected in this book.

Finally, I would like to thank the Open Society Foundation (and particularly Leonard Benardo, Stephen Hubbell, and Bipasha Ray of the Open Society Fellowship Program), as well as the Carnegie Foundation (and particularly Geri Mannion of the U.S. Democracy Program), for financial support during my leave from the ACLU in 2013.

NOTES

v **Power must never be trusted without a Check** Letter from John Adams to Thomas Jefferson, Feb. 2, 1816, available at Founders Online, *National Archives*, http://founders.archives.gov/documents/Jefferson/03-09-02-0285.

v **it shouldn't be hanging there** Valentine Tschebotarioff Bill, *Chekhov: The Silent Voice of Freedom* (New York: Philosophical Library, 1987).

v **putting a bullet in your head** Tara McKelvey, "Inside the Killing Machine," *Newsweek*, Feb. 13, 2011.

1 **killing three or four people and injuring another** "Obama 2016 Pakistan Drone Strikes," *Bureau of Investigative Journalism*, Jan. 11, 2016 (as updated), https://www.thebureauinvestigates.com/2016/01/11/obama-2016-pakistan-drone-strikes.

1 **strikes against targets in Libya** Oriana Pawlyk, "As Libya Mission Intensifies, Italy OKs U.S. to Fly Armed Drone Missions," *Military Times*, Feb. 22, 2016.

1 **in the governorate of Abyan** "Yemen: Reported Covert Actions 2016," *Bureau of Investigative Journalism*, Jan. 18, 2016 (as updated), https://www.thebureauinvestigates.com/2016/01/18/yemen-reported-us-covert-actions-2016/#YEM217.

1 **suspected Islamic State fighter in northern Iraq** Stephen Kalin, "US Says It Killed IS Militant Who Killed Marine in Iraq," *Reuters*, Apr. 4, 2016; K.V. Aditya Bharadwaj, "Islamic State Recruiter from Bhatkal Killed in US Airstrike in Syria," *The Hindu*, Apr. 25, 2016.

1 **training camp for terrorists** Helene Cooper, "U.S. Strikes in Somalia Kill 150 Shabab Fighters," *New York Times*, Mar. 7, 2016.

1 became worried about the others Farooq Jan Mangal and Mujib Mashal, "At Least 17 Civilians Killed in U.S. Airstrikes, Afghan Officials Say," *New York Times*, Apr. 7, 2016.

2 the drone strikes they authorized were lawful See, e.g., Remarks of Director of Central Intelligence Agency, Leon E. Panetta, at the Pacific Council on International Policy, May 18, 2009, https://www.cia.gov/news -information/speeches-testimony/directors-remarks-at-pacific-council .html.

3 tribal areas of Pakistan Spencer Ackerman, "Victim of Obama's First Drone Strike: 'I Am the Living Example of What Drones Are,'" *The Guardian*, Jan. 23, 2016.

3 "bombs that subsequently killed more innocents" Jo Becker and Scott Shane, "Secret 'Kill List' Proves a Test of Obama's Principles and Will," *New York Times*, May 29, 2012. See also Mark Mazzetti, *The Way of the Knife: The CIA, a Secret Army, and a War at the Ends of the Earth* at 230–32 (New York: The Penguin Press, 2013); Greg Miller, "Obama's New Drone Policy Leaves Room for CIA Role," *Washington Post*, May 25, 2013.

3 many hundreds of civilian bystanders "Get the Data: Drone Wars," *Bureau of Investigative Journalism*, https://www.thebureauinvestigates.com/ category/projects/drones/drones-graphs.

3 Joint Special Operations Command Dana Priest, "U.S. Military Teams, Intelligence Deeply Involved in Aiding Yemen on Strikes," *Washington Post*, Jan. 27, 2010; Greg Miller, "Muslim Cleric Aulaqi Is 1st U.S. Citizen on List of Those CIA Is Allowed to Kill," *Washington Post*, Apr. 7, 2010.

3 invited to dine at the Pentagon My account of Anwar al-Aulaqi's background, and of the strikes that killed Anwar al-Aulaqi, Samir Khan, and Abdulrahman al-Aulaqi, is derived principally from Scott Shane, *Objective Troy: A Terrorist, A President, and the Rise of the Drone* (New York: Tim Duggan Books, 2015), Jeremy Scahill, *Dirty Wars: The World Is a Battlefield* (New York: Nation Books, 2013), and Mark Mazzetti, *The Way of the Knife: The CIA, A Secret Army, and a War at the Ends of the Earth* (New York: The Penguin Press, 2013), as well as from my own conversations with Nasser al-Aulaqi in May 2010 (Sana'a) and January 2012 (Cairo).

4 where most of his family still lived Massimo Calabresi, Timothy J. Burger, and Elaine Shannon, "Why Did the Imam Befriend Hijackers?," *Time*, Aug. 4, 2003.

4 had marked him for death Aamer Madhani, "Cleric al-Awlaki Dubbed 'Bin Laden of the Internet,'" *USA Today*, Aug. 24, 2010; Matthew Cole and Aaron Katersky, "Awlaki: 'The Most Dangerous Man in the World,'" *ABC News*, Nov. 10, 2010.

5 justifying its actions to a court Warren Richey, "US Says It Has Legal Authority to Kill American-Born Anwar Al-Awlaki," *Christian Science Mon-*

itor, Nov. 8, 2010; Transcript of Oral Argument, *Al-Aulaqi v. Obama* (D.D.C., Nov. 8, 2010), http://ccrjustice.org/sites/default/files/attach/2015/05/2010 .11.08%20Al-Aulaqi%20Motions%20Hearing%20Transcript.pdf.

5 procedural and jurisdictional grounds *Al-Aulaqi v. Obama,* 727 F. Supp. 2d 1 (D.D.C. 2010).

5 published and edited *Inspire* "Islamist Cleric Anwar al-Awlaki Killed in Yemen," *BBC,* Sept. 30, 2011.

5 "a tribute to the intelligence community" David Jackson, "Obama: Terrorists Will Find 'No Safe Haven Anywhere,'" *USA Today,* Sept. 30, 2011.

6 not available in this one *Al-Aulaqi v. Panetta,* 35 F. Supp. 3d 56 (D.D.C. 2014).

7 narrowing the powers they had asserted Charlie Savage, *Power Wars: Inside Obama's Post-9/11 Presidency* at 283 (New York: Little, Brown, 2015); Scott Shane, "Election Spurred a Move to Codify U.S. Drone Policy," *New York Times,* Nov. 24, 2012.

8 they would leave to their successors Jameel Jaffer and Brett Max Kaufman, "Limit the Next President's Power to Wage Drones Warfare," *New York Times,* Mar. 8, 2016.

8 144,000 were deployed in Iraq Amy Belasco, "Troop Levels in the Afghan and Iraq Wars FY2001-FY2012: Cost and Other Potential Issues," *Congressional Research Service,* July 2, 2009 (as updated), https://www.fas .org/sgp/crs/natsec/R40682.pdf; "Facts and Figures on Drawdown in Iraq," Office of the Press Secretary, The White House, Aug. 2, 2010, https://www .whitehouse.gov/the-press-office/facts-and-figures-drawdown-iraq.

8 domestic surveillance for eight years James Risen and Eric Lichtblau, "Bush Lets U.S. Spy on Callers Without Courts," *New York Times,* Dec. 16, 2005.

8 Bagram Air Base in Afghanistan "Guantánamo by the Numbers," *Human Rights First,* May 2016, https://www.humanrightsfirst.org/sites/ default/files/gtmo-by-the-numbers.pdf; "ACLU Obtains List of Bagram Detainees," *American Civil Liberties Union,* Jan. 15, 2010, https://www.aclu .org/news/aclu-obtains-list-bagram-detainees.

8 procedurally defective military commissions Andy Worthington, "The Full List of Prisoners Charged in the Military Commissions at Guantánamo," *andyworthington.co.uk,* Mar. 2014, http://www.andyworthington.co.uk/the -full-list-of-prisoners-charged-in-the-military-commissions-at-guantanamo.

9 without charge or trial "Establishing a New Normal: National Security, Civil Liberties, and Human Rights Under the Obama Administration," *American Civil Liberties Union,* July 2010, https://www.aclu.org/report/esta blishing-new-normal.

9 United States was mired Daniel Klaidman, *Kill or Capture: The War* *on Terror and the Soul of the Obama Presidency* at 50 (Boston: Houghton Mifflin Harcourt, 2012).

9 last year of his second term Jack Serle, "Monthly Updates on the Covert War," *Bureau of Investigative Journalism*, Feb. 2, 2015, https://www.thebureauinvestigates.com/2015/02/02/almost-2500-killed-covert-us-drone-strikes-obama-inauguration. In 2002, the CIA carried out a single drone strike in Yemen that killed six men, including an American citizen, For an account of that strike, see Mark Mazzetti, *The Way of the Knife: The CIA, a Secret Army, and a War at the Ends of the Earth* at 85–87 (New York: The Penguin Press, 2013).

9 drone deaths had quadrupled Peter Bergen, "Drone Is Obama's Weapon of Choice," *CNN*, Sept. 19, 2012.

9 "the most heavily drone-bombed country in the world" Alice K. Ross, "Who Is Dying in Afghanistan's 1,000-Plus Drone Strikes?" *Bureau of Investigative Journalism*, July 24, 2014, https://www.thebureauinvestigates.com/2014/07/24/who-is-dying-in-afghanistans-1000-plus-drone-strikes.

9 killing more than 700 people "Obama 2010 Pakistan Strikes," *Bureau of Investigative Journalism*, Aug. 10, 2011, https://www.thebureauinvestigates.com/2011/08/10/obama-2010-strikes.

9 killed more than 200 "US Strikes in Yemen, 2002 to Present," *Bureau of Investigative Journalism*, https://docs.google.com/spreadsheets/d/1lb1hEYJ_omI8lSe33izwS2a2lbiygs0hTp2Al_Kz5KQ/edit#gid=323032473.

9 Libyan government's attacks against civilians "Security Council Approves 'No-Fly Zone' over Libya, Authorizing 'All Necessary Measures' to Protect Civilians, by Vote of 10 in Favour with 5 Abstentions," *United Nations Security Council*, Mar. 17, 2011, http://www.un.org/press/en/2011/sc10200.doc.htm; Chris Woods and Alice K. Ross, "Revealed: US and Britain Launched 1,200 Drone Strikes in Recent Wars," *Bureau of Investigative Journalism*, Dec. 4, 2012, https://www.thebureauinvestigates.com/2012/12/04/revealed-us-and-britain-launched-1200-drone-strikes-in-recent-wars.

10 attempting to broker a truce Scott Shane, *Objective Troy: A Terrorist, a President, and the Rise of the Drone* at 277 (New York: Tim Duggan Books, 2015); Mark Mazzetti, Charlie Savage, and Scott Shane, "How a U.S. Citizen Came to Be in America's Cross Hairs," *New York Times*, Mar. 9, 2013. JSOC also suspended strikes in Yemen in 2013 after a strike killed at least a dozen people in a wedding convoy. Greg Miller, "CIA Didn't Know Strike Would Hit Al-Qaeda Leader," *Washington Post*, June 17, 2015.

10 killed twenty-four Pakistani soldiers Ken Dilanian, "CIA Has Suspended Drone Attacks in Pakistan, U.S. Officials Say," *Los Angeles Times*, Dec. 23, 2011; Eric Schmitt, "3 Killed as Drone Strikes Resume in Pakistan," *New York Times*, Jan. 10, 2012. Three years later, the CIA would suspend drone strikes in Pakistan again to avoid derailing peace talks between the Pakistani government and the Pakistani Taliban. Alice K. Ross, "CIA Drone Strikes Resume in Pakistan After Five-Month Pause," *Bureau of Investigative Journalism*, June 12, 2014, https://www.thebureauinvestigates.com/2014 /06/12/drone-strikes-resume-in-pakistan-after-five-month-pause.

10 whom the drone operators should kill next Jo Becker and Scott Shane, "Secret 'Kill List' Proves a Test of Obama's Principles and Will," *New York Times*, May 29, 2012.

10 "track them down" Greg Miller, "Plan for Hunting Terrorists Signals U.S. Intends to Keep Adding Names to Kill Lists," *Washington Post*, Oct. 23, 2012.

10 consider the center's nominations Greg Miller, "Plan for Hunting Terrorists Signals U.S. Intends to Keep Adding Names to Kill Lists," *Washington Post*, Oct. 23, 2012; Daniel Klaidman, "John Brennan, Obama's CIA Chief Nominee Could Restrain the Agency," *Newsweek*, Feb. 5, 2013.

10 as well as the kill lists Greg Miller, "Plan for Hunting Terrorists Signals U.S. Intends to Keep Adding Names to Kill Lists," *Washington Post*, Oct. 23, 2012; Cora Currier, "The Kill Chain: The Lethal Bureaucracy Behind Obama's Drone War," *The Intercept*, Oct. 15, 2015.

10 to recruit, imprison, or kill Greg Miller and Julie Tate, "CIA Shifts Focus to Killing Targets," *Washington Post*, Sept. 1, 2011.

10 "sustaining a seemingly permanent war" Greg Miller, "Plan for Hunting Terrorists Signals U.S. Intends to Keep Adding Names to Kill Lists," *Washington Post*, Oct. 23, 2012.

10 new administration took a broader approach Greg Miller and Bob Woodward, "Secret Memos Reveal Explicit Nature of U.S., Pakistan Agreement on Drones," *Washington Post*, Oct. 24, 2013.

11 as opposed to foot soldiers Peter Bergen, "Drone Is Obama's Weapon of Choice," *CNN*, Sept. 19, 2012. See also David Rohde, "The Obama Doctrine," *Foreign Policy*, Feb. 27, 2012.

11 direct threat to the United States Peter Bergen, "Drone Is Obama's Weapon of Choice," *CNN*, Sept. 19, 2012; Greg Miller and Bob Woodward, "Secret Memos Reveal Explicit Nature of U.S., Pakistan Agreement on Drones," *Washington Post*, Oct. 24, 2013.

11 "lighting these people up all over the place" Mark Mazzetti, *The Way of the Knife: The CIA, a Secret Army, and a War at the Ends of the Earth* at 319 (New York: The Penguin Press, 2013).

11 the CIA did not know David S. Cloud, "CIA Drones Have Broader List of Targets," *Los Angeles Times*, May 5, 2010.

11 lawful targets and those who were not Kevin Jon Heller, "'One Hell of a Killing Machine': Signature Strikes and International Law," *Journal of*

International Criminal Justice 11, no. 1 (2013): 89 (identifying 14 distinct signatures used by the United States, and concluding that 5 were "legally adequate"; 4 were "never legally adequate"; and 5 were "possibly legally adequate").

11 something more sinister Salman Masood and Pir Zubair Shah, "CIA Drone Kill Civilians in Pakistan," *New York Times*, Mar. 17, 2011.

11 There were other mistakes Scott Shane, "Drone Strikes Reveal Uncomfortable Truth: U.S. Is Often Unsure About Who Will Die," *New York Times*, Apr. 23, 2015; Dan De Luce and Paul McLeary, "Obama's Most Dangerous Drone Tactic Is Here to Stay," *Foreign Policy*, Apr. 5, 2016.

11 reportedly based on such assumptions David Rohde, "The Obama Doctrine," *Foreign Policy*, Feb. 27, 2012.

11 "when arriving at a suspect site" Greg Miller and Bob Woodward, "Secret Memos Reveal Explicit Nature of U.S., Pakistan Agreement on Drones," *Washington Post*, Oct. 24, 2013.

12 in fact a terrorist training cell Jo Becker and Scott Shane, "Secret 'Kill List' Proves a Test of Obama's Principles and Will," *New York Times*, May 29, 2012.

12 "a chump who went to a meeting" Tara McKelvey, "A Former Ambassador to Pakistan Speaks Out," *Daily Beast*, Nov. 20, 2012.

12 associates of those initially targeted Chris Woods and Christina Lamb, "CIA Tactics in Pakistan Include Targeting Rescuers and Funerals," *Bureau of Investigative Journalism*, Feb. 4, 2012, https://www.thebureauinvestigates.com/2012/02/04/obama-terror-drones-cia-tactics-in-pakistan-include-targeting-rescuers-and-funerals.

12 extract bodies from the rubble Ibid.; Farooq Jan Mangal and Mujib Mashal, "At Least 17 Civilians Killed in U.S. Airstrikes, Afghan Officials Say," *New York Times*, Apr. 7, 2016.

12 New York University identified others Chris Woods and Christina Lamb, "CIA Tactics in Pakistan Include Targeting Rescuers and Funerals," *Bureau of Investigative Journalism*, Feb. 4, 2012, https://www.thebureauinvestigates.com/2012/02/04/obama-terror-drones-cia-tactics-in-pakistan-include-targeting-rescuers-and-funerals; "Living Under Drones: Death, Injury, and Trauma to Civilians from US Drone Practices in Pakistan," *International Human Rights and Conflict Resolution Clinic (Stanford Law School) and Global Justice Clinic (NYU School of Law)*, Sept. 2012, 74–76, http://chrgj.org/wp-content/uploads/2012/10/Living-Under-Drones.pdf.

13 carry out such strikes in Yemen Daniel Klaidman, "John Brennan, Obama's CIA Chief Nominee Could Restrain the Agency," *Newsweek*, Feb. 5, 2013.

13 "terrorist attack disruption strikes" Greg Miller, "CIA Didn't Know Strike Would Hit Al-Qaeda Leader," *Washington Post*, June 17, 2015.

13 "broaden the aperture slightly" Eric Schmitt, "U.S. to Step Up Drone Strikes Inside Yemen," *New York Times*, Apr. 25, 2012.

13 more than two hundred deaths "U.S. Strikes in Yemen, 2002 to Present," *Bureau of Investigative Journalism*, https://docs.google.com/spreadsheets/d/1lb1hEYJ_omI8lSe33izwS2a2lbiygs0hTp2Al_Kz5KQ/edit#gid=977256262.

13 "precision" of the government's weapons Remarks of John Brennan concerning "Obama Administration Counterterrorism Strategy," *C-SPAN*, June 29, 2011, http://www.c-span.org/video/?300266-1/obama-administration-counterterrorism-strategy.

13 "in the single digits" each year Lee Ferran, "Intel Chair: Civilian Drone Casualties in 'Single Digits' Year-to-Year," *ABC News*, Feb. 7, 2013.

13 "on a very tight leash" Mark Landler, "Civilian Deaths Due to Drones Are Not Many, Obama Says," *New York Times*, Jan. 30, 2012.

14 citing national security considerations Jameel Jaffer, "A Less-Secret Drone Campaign," *Just Security*, June 27, 2016, https://www.justsecurity.org/31687/secret-drone-campaign.

14 "posthumously proved them innocent" Jo Becker and Scott Shane, "Secret 'Kill List' Proves a Test of Obama's Principles and Will," *New York Times*, May 29, 2012.

14 they were innocent bystanders Ryan Devereaux, "Manhunting in the Hindu Kush," *The Intercept*, Oct. 15, 2015. In a document released in 2013, the government declared that "it is not the case that all military-aged males in the vicinity of a target are deemed to be combatants" (255), but it did not squarely address the contention that military-aged males were *presumed* to be combatants.

14 had adopted exactly that presumption Marty Lederman, "Troubling Proportionality and Rule-of-Distinction Provisions in the Law of War Manual," *Just Security*, June 27, 2016, https://www.justsecurity.org/31661/law-war-manual-distinction-proportionality/.

14 whose information was often unreliable Scott Shane, *Objective Troy: A Terrorist, a President, and the Rise of the Drone* at 204 (New York: Tim Duggan Books, 2015); Cora Currier, "The Kill Chain: The Lethal Bureaucracy Behind Obama's Drone War," *The Intercept*, Oct. 15, 2015.

15 intelligence used to justify strikes Cora Currier and Peter Maass, "Firing Blind: Flawed Intelligence and the Limits of Drone Technology," *The Intercept*, Oct. 15, 2015.

15 had died a year earlier Matthew Rosenberg and Ihsanullah Tipu Mehsud, "Founder of Haqqani Network Is Long Dead, Aide Says," *New York Times*, July 31, 2015.

15 died two years earlier in a Pakistani hospital Rod Nordland and Joseph Goldstein, "Taliban Leader Mullah Omar Died in 2013, Afghans Declare," *New York Times,* July 29, 2015.

15 al-Banna was someone else In 2014, the State Department offered $5 million for information about al-Banna's location—presumably with the hope that such information would allow the CIA or JSOC to make another attempt on his life. Office of the Spokesperson, "Rewards for Justice—Reward Offers for Information on Al-Qaida in the Arabian Peninsula (AQAP) Leaders," *Media Note, U.S. Department of State,* Oct. 14, 2014, http://www.state.gov/r/pa/prs/ps/2014/10/232932.htm.

15 consistent with the U.S. government's policies Tom Finn and Noah Browning, "An American Teenager in Yemen: Paying for the Sins of His Father?," *Time,* Oct. 27, 2011.

16 from local concerns to international ones David Rohde, "The Obama Doctrine," *Foreign Policy,* Feb. 27, 2012; Declaration of Bernard Haykel, *al-Aulaqi v. Obama,* No. 10-cv-01469 (D.D.C., Oct. 2010), https://www.aclu.org/sites/default/files/field_document/Haykel_Declaration.100810.PDF.

16 one southern Yemeni city alone Yara Bayoumy, Noah Browning, and Mohammed Ghobari, "How Saudi Arabia's War in Yemen Has Made Al Qaeda Stronger—and Richer," *Reuters,* Apr. 8, 2016.

16 the ones the United States had weakened Mark Tran, "Who Are Isis? A Terror Group Too Extreme Even for Al-Qaida," *The Guardian,* June 11, 2014.

16 "I came back to Yemen as an ambassador of the U.S." Farea al-Muslimi, "In Senate Testimony, Yemeni Activist Describes Human Costs of Targeted Killing Program," *ACLU Speak Freely Blog,* Apr. 24, 2013, https://www.aclu.org/blog/senate-testimony-yemeni-activist-describes-human-costs-targeted-killing-program.

16 "one drone strike accomplished in an instant" Ibid.

17 driving young men into the group's arms Spencer Ackerman, "Victim of Obama's First Drone Strike: 'I Am the Living Example of What Drones Are,'" *The Guardian,* Jan. 23, 2016.

17 killing "too many" innocent people "Pakistani Public Opinion Ever More Critical of U.S.," *Pew Research Center,* June 27, 2012, http://www.pewglobal.org/2012/06/27/chapter-1-views-of-the-u-s-and-american-foreign-policy-5/.

17 "unchecked American power" David Rohde, "The Obama Doctrine," *Foreign Policy,* Feb. 27, 2012.

17 "We always have this fear in our head" "Living Under Drones: Death, Injury, and Trauma to Civilians from US Drone Practices in Pakistan," at 74–76, *International Human Rights and Conflict Resolution Clinic (Stanford*

Law School) and Global Justice Clinic (NYU School of Law), Sept. 2012, http: //chrgj.org/wp-content/uploads/2012/10/Living-Under-Drones.pdf.

18 "broader strategy against radicalization" Jo Becker and Scott Shane, "Secret 'Kill List' Proves a Test of Obama's Principles and Will," *New York Times*, May 29, 2012.

18 "win some battles but lose the war?" Tara McKelvey, "A Former Ambassador to Pakistan Speaks Out," *Daily Beast*, Nov. 11, 2012.

18 as many as thirty-nine civilians David Rohde, "The Obama Doctrine," *Foreign Policy*, Feb. 27, 2012. McKelvey reports that the strike killed ten militants and nineteen civilians. Tara McKelvey, "A Former Ambassador to Pakistan Speaks Out," *Daily Beast*, Nov. 20, 2012.

18 strikes would be counterproductive David Rohde, "The Obama Doctrine," *Foreign Policy*, Feb. 27, 2012.

18 whether drone strikes were backfiring Ibid.

18 "never seen one or seen the effects of one" David Alexander, "Retired General Cautions Against Overuse of 'Hated' Drones," *Reuters*, Jan. 7, 2013; see also Ryan Goodman, "General Stanley McChrystal Discusses the Downsides of Drones," *Just Security*, Jan. 22, 2014, https://www.justsecurity .org/6054/general-stanley-mcchrystals-statement-drone-warfare.

18 "shoes of their departed colleagues" Jeffrey Gettleman, "Despite Several Blows to Shabab, Worries Persist About Their Resilience," *New York Times*, Apr. 5, 2016.

18 "over the long term" Jo Becker and Scott Shane, "Secret 'Kill List' Proves a Test of Obama's Principles and Will," *New York Times*, May 29, 2012.

18 "advance America's long-term interests" Dennis Blair, "Drones Alone Are Not the Answer," *New York Times*, Aug. 14, 2011.

19 "that's what they are doing" Jo Becker and Scott Shane, "Secret 'Kill List' Proves a Test of Obama's Principles and Will," *New York Times*, May 29, 2012.

19 conference in the spring of 2013 Dan Roberts, "US Drone Strikes Being Used as Alternative to Guantánamo, Lawyer Says," *The Guardian*, May 2, 2013.

19 justify the use of lethal force? Micah Zenko, "Kill > Capture," *Foreign Policy*, Apr. 14, 2015.

20 arraigned in New York in April 2015 Mark Mazzetti and Eric Schmitt, "Terrorism Case Renews Debate Over Drone Hits," *New York Times*, Apr. 12, 2015.

20 told the *Washington Post* Greg Miller, "Plan for Hunting Terrorists Signals U.S. Intends to Keep Adding Names to Kill Lists," *Washington Post*, Oct. 23, 2012.

20 **"alienating wide segments of the globe"** Phil Klay, "What Defines a Modern Warrior," *New York Times*, Dec. 9, 2015.

20 **"answered that question yet"** David Rohde, "The Obama Doctrine," *Foreign Policy*, Feb. 27, 2012.

22 **more information about individual strikes** Charlie Savage, *Power Wars: Inside Obama's Post-9/11 Presidency* at 284–85 (New York: Little, Brown, 2015); Dan De Luce and Paul McLeary, "Obama's Most Dangerous Drone Tactic Is Here to Stay," *Foreign Policy*, Apr. 5, 2016.

22 **CIA's drone campaign in Pakistan** Greg Miller, Ellen Nakashima, and Karen DeYoung, "CIA Drone Strikes Will Get Pass in Counterterrorism 'Playbook,' Officials Say," *Washington Post*, Jan. 19, 2013.

22 **identified four such strikes** Amrit Singh, "Death by Drone: Civilian Harm Caused by U.S. Targeted Killings in Yemen," *Open Society Justice Initiative*, Apr. 2015, https://www.opensocietyfoundations.org/sites/default/files/death-drones-report-eng-20150413.pdf.

22 **eight of whom were civilians** "Yemen: Reported US Covert Actions 2014," *Bureau of Investigative Journalism*, Jan. 6, 2014 (as updated), https://www.thebureauinvestigates.com/2014/01/06/yemen-reported-us-covert-actions-2014.

23 **complied with the laws of war** "A Wedding That Became a Funeral," *Human Rights Watch*, Feb. 19, 2014, https://www.hrw.org/report/2014/02/19/wedding-became-funeral/us-drone-attack-marriage-procession-yemen.

23 **carried out by JSOC** Greg Miller, "U.S. Launches Secret Drone Campaign to Hunt Islamic State Leaders in Syria," *Washington Post*, Sept. 1, 2015.

23 **continued to conduct signature strikes** Charlie Savage, *Power Wars: Inside Obama's Post-9/11 Presidency* at 285 (New York: Little, Brown, 2015); Greg Miller, "CIA Didn't Know Strike Would Hit Al-Qaeda Leader," *Washington Post*, June 17, 2015. Miller suggests that rules of engagement may have been tightened in Yemen after the president's speech but loosened again after the collapse of the U.S.-backed government in Sana'a in early 2015.

23 **taken hostage several years earlier** Greg Miller, "CIA Didn't Know Strike Would Hit Al-Qaeda Leader," *Washington Post*, June 17, 2015; Editorial, "Regret over a Drone's Deadly Damage," *New York Times*, Apr. 24, 2015.

23 **killed several dozen people** Jack Serle, "Drone War Report, January—June 2015," *The Bureau of Investigative Journalism*, July 1, 2015, https://www.thebureauinvestigates.com/2015/07/01/drone-war-report-january-june-2015-controversial-signature-strikes-hit-yemen-and-pakistan.

23 **carrying out targeted strikes** Ken Dilanian, "Debate Grows over Proposal for CIA to Turn Over Drones to Pentagon," *Los Angeles Times*, May 11, 2014.

23 the military could do the same Greg Miller, "Obama's New Drone Policy Leaves Room for CIA Role," *Washington Post*, May 25, 2013.

23 any narrowing of the CIA's role Greg Miller, "U.S. Launches Secret Drone Campaign to Hunt Islamic State Leaders in Syria," *Washington Post*, Sept. 1, 2015.

23 identifying targets for elimination Greg Miller, "Why CIA Drone Strikes Have Plummeted," *Washington Post*, June 16, 2016.

23 some new legal line Kathy Gilsinan, "The Drone War Crosses Another Line," *The Atlantic*, May 23, 2016.

25 "discuss the circumstances of his death" Press Briefing by Press Secretary Jay Carney, Sept. 30, 2011, http://www.presidency.ucsb.edu/ws/index.php?pid=96831.

26 Brennan's confirmation as CIA director Michael D. Shear and Scott Shane, "Congress to See Memo Backing Drone Attacks on Americans," *New York Times*, Feb. 6, 2013.

26 for another fifteen months Greg Miller, "White House to Provide Lawmakers Access to Drone Memo Authorizing Killing of American," *Washington Post*, May 6, 2014.

26 the more there needed to be Transcript of Oral Argument at 4, *New York Times v. Department of Justice*, No. 14-4432 (2d Cir., June 23, 2015), https://www.aclu.org/sites/default/files/field_document/transcript-_expartehearing-2ndcircuit20150706.pdf.

27 infrequency of bystander casualties Lena Groeger and Cora Currier, "Stacking Up the Administration's Drone Claims," *ProPublica*, Sept. 13, 2012.

27 "who [was] speaking to the reporter" Jack Goldsmith, "Drone Stories, the Secrecy System, and Public Accountability," *Lawfare*, May 31, 2012, http://www.lawfareblog.com/drone-stories-secrecy-system-and-public-accountability.

27 the sphere of national security See, e.g., Affidavit of Max Frankel, Washington Bureau Chief for the *New York Times*, *United States of America v. New York Times, Co.*, No. 71-cv-2662 (S.D.N.Y., June 17, 1971), http://www.pbs.org/wgbh/pages/frontline/newswar/part1/frankel.html.

27 information would be leaked to the media Jameel Jaffer and Nate Freed Wessler, "First the Targeted-Killing Campaign, Then the Targeted-Propaganda Campaign," *The Guardian*, June 6, 2012.

27 CIA's role was still a classified fact "Senator Dianne Feinstein on Drones, Assault Weapons Ban," *Takeaway* (Mar. 20, 2013), at 2:00.

27 the government wrote in its legal briefs Brief for Defendants-Appellees at 37, *New York Times v. Department of Justice*, No. 13-422 (2d

Cir., June 14, 2013), https://www.aclu.org/sites/default/files/field_document /95._govt_reply_brief_2013.06.14.pdf.

27 legal memos relating to targeted killings *New York Times v. Department of Justice*, 756 F.3d 100 (2d Cir. 2014).

27 memo's contents to be secret Brief for Defendants-Appellees at 58 n.12, *New York Times v. Department of Justice*, No. 13-422 (2d Cir., June 14, 2013), https://www.aclu.org/sites/default/files/field_document/95._govt_reply _brief_2013.06.14.pdf. See also Jameel Jaffer, "The Unreal Secrecy About Drone Killings," *Just Security*, Apr. 9, 2015, https://www.justsecurity.org /21881/unreal-secrecy-drone-killings/.

27 "information that must not be disclosed" Declaration and Formal Claim of State Secrets Privilege and Statutory Privileges by Leon E. Panetta at 8 n.5, *Al Aulaqi v. Obama*, No. 10-1469 (D.D.C. Sept. 23, 2010), https://www .aclu.org/sites/default/files/field_document/107-3._panetta_declaration_6 .10.2015.pdf.

28 "hardly [be] competent to evaluate it" Defendants' Motion to Dismiss at 14, *Al Aulaqi v. Panetta*, No. 12-1192 (D.D.C., Dec. 14, 2012), https://www .aclu.org/sites/default/files/field_document/tk_govt_motion_to_dismiss.pdf.

28 to compromise national security *ACLU v. Department of Justice*, 808 F. Supp. 2d 280, 292 (D.D.C. 2011).

29 "unilateral action of the Executive," she wrote *New York Times v. Department of Justice*, 915 F. Supp. 2d 508 (S.D.N.Y 2013).

29 "keeping the reasons for its conclusion a secret" Ibid.

29 corrupted the democratic process Some commentators have argued that overbroad secrecy had the additional effect of making it difficult for the government to correct misunderstandings and inaccuracies. See, e.g., David E. Sanger, *Confront and Conceal: Obama's Secret Wars and Surprising Use of American Power* at 245 (New York: Broadway Books, 2012); Scott Shane, *Objective Troy: A Terrorist, a President, and the Rise of the Drone* at 298 (New York: Tim Duggan Books, 2015). There is certainly some truth to this. It is also true, though, that in most instances the purported need for secrecy did not prevent the administration from disclosing the information it wanted to disclose, or making the claims it wanted to make. See, e.g., Jameel Jaffer, "Selective Disclosure About Targeted Killing," *Just Security*, Oct. 7, 2013, https://www.justsecurity.org/1704/selective-disclosure-targeted-killing.

30 "suddenly charged with leading a war" Jo Becker and Scott Shane, "Secret 'Kill List' Proves a Test of Obama's Principles and Will," *New York Times*, May 29, 2012.

30 beyond conventional battlefields Daniel Klaidman, *Kill or Capture: The War on Terror and the Soul of the Obama Presidency* at 140, 219 (Boston: Houghton Mifflin Harcourt, 2012); David Cole, *Engines of Liberty: The*

Power of Citizen Activists to Make Constitutional Law at 212 (New York: Basic Books, 2016); Charlie Savage, *Power Wars: Inside Obama's Post-9/11 Presidency* at 274–282 (New York: Little, Brown, 2015); Ryan Goodman, "The Strange Case of Harold Koh at NYU," *Just Security*, Apr. 21, 2015, https://www.justsecurity.org/21912/harold-koh-nyu-asil-2010-speech-adva ncing-human-rights/.

30 it was Koh who delivered it Charlie Savage, *Power Wars: Inside Obama's Post-9/11 Presidency* at 244 (New York: Little, Brown, 2015).

30 "they're good enough for me" Daniel Klaidman, *Kill or Capture: The War on Terror and the Soul of the Obama Presidency* at 214 (Boston: Houghton Mifflin Harcourt, 2012).

31 not based on any intimate knowledge A February 2012 poll indicated that 83 percent of Americans approved of the government's use of armed drones to kill terrorism suspects, and 65 percent approved the use of armed drones to kill American terrorism suspects in particular. Greg Sargent, "Liberals, Dems Approve of Drone Strikes on American Citizens Abroad," *Washington Post*, Feb. 8, 2012.

31 "in defense of the Lethal Presidency" Tom Junod, "The Lethal Presidency of Barack Obama," *Esquire*, Aug. 2012. See also Quinta Jurecic, "Obama's Moral Muse," *Lawfare*, Oct. 6, 2015, https://www.lawfareblog .com/obamas-moral-muse.

31 "locked in a D.O.J. safe" Jo Becker and Scott Shane, "Secret 'Kill List' Proves a Test of Obama's Principles and Will," *New York Times*, May 29, 2012.

32 "the subject [had] become ludicrous" David E. Sanger, *Confront and Conceal: Obama's Secret Wars and Surprising Use of American Power* at 249 (New York: Broadway Books, 2012).

32 "cause damage to national security" *ACLU v. Department of Justice*, 808 F. Supp. 2d 280, 287 (D.D.C. 2011).

32 "aware of *any* case that's like this?" Transcript of Oral Argument at 19, *ACLU v. Central Intelligence Agency*, No. 11-5320 (D.C. Cir., Sept. 20, 2012), https://www.emptywheel.net/wp-content/uploads/2013/03/Transcript-of -Oral-Argument-2012.09.20.pdf.

33 "documents regarding the subject of drone strikes" *ACLU v. Central Intelligence Agency*, 710 F.3d 422, 431 (D.C. Cir. 2013).

33 without compromising national security Transcript of Oral Argument, *New York Times v. Department of Justice*, Nos. 13-422(L) & 13-445(Con) (2d. Cir., Oct. 1, 2013), https://www.emptywheel.net/wp -content/uploads/2013/10/131001-Second-Circuit-Argument.pdf.

34 "analysis in the Memorandum is a secret" *New York Times v. Department of Justice*, 756 F.3d 100, 116 (2d. Cir. 2014).

34 his performance on the bench Jeremy W. Peters, "Judicial Nominee's

Memos on Drones Stirring Bipartisan Concern in the Senate," *New York Times*, May 5, 2014.

34 Barron took his seat on the federal bench "The Barron Nomination and the Second Circuit Drone Case," *Open Government*, May 20, 2014, http://www.openthegovernment.org/Barron-Nomination-Second-Circuit -Drone-Case.

34 factual basis for the al-Aulaqi strike—were redacted *New York Times v. Department of Justice*, 752 F.3d 123, 138 (2d Cir. 2014); Charlie Savage, *Power Wars: Inside Obama's Post-9/11 Presidency* at 468 (New York: Little, Brown, 2015).

35 government had not acknowledged Opinion, *New York Times v. Department of Justice*, No. 14-4432, No. 14-4764 (S.D.N.Y., Oct. 22, 2015), https://www.aclu.org/legal-document/aclu-v-doj-opinion.

35 as well as its targeted-killing campaign Brett Max Kaufman, "Still Secret: Second Circuit Keeps More Drone Memos from the Public," *Just Security*, Nov. 24, 2015, https://www.justsecurity.org/27854/secret-circuit -drone-memos-public.

35 adopted by the Defense Department or CIA Opinion, *New York Times v. Department of Justice*, No. 14-4432, No. 14-4764 (S.D.N.Y., Oct. 22, 2015); Order Denying Petition for Rehearing, *New York Times v. Department of Justice*, No. 14-4432, No. 14-4764 (Mar. 31, 2016).

35 make a redacted version of the PPG public Jameel Jaffer, "A Less-Secret Drone Campaign," *Just Security*, June 27, 2016, https://www.justsecurity.org /31687/secret-drone-campaign.

35 in the summer of 2016 Charlie Savage, "U.S. Releases Rules for Air-strike Killings of Terror Suspects," *New York Times*, Aug. 6, 2016.

36 *Time* magazine called it Amanda Ripley, "The Case of the Dirty Bomber," *Time*, June 16, 2002.

36 denied access to counsel Complaint, *Padilla v. Rumsfeld*, No, 07-civ.-410 (D.S.C., July 23, 2008), https://www.aclu.org/sites/default/files/ pdfs/natsec/padilla/2008_07_23(dkt91)PlsThirdAmendedComplaint.pdf. For a comprehensive account of the Padilla case, see Larry Siems, *The Torture Report: What the Documents Say About America's Post-9/11 Torture Program* (New York: OR Books, 2012).

37 whom the CIA had brutally tortured See, e.g., "Committee Study of the Central Intelligence Agency's Detention and Interrogation Program," *Senate Select Committee on Intelligence* at 85, 90, 214, Dec. 13, 2012, http:// fas.org/irp/congress/2014_rpt/ssci-rdi.pdf.

37 an extortive tit for tat "'Dirty Bomb' Plotter Jose Padilla Resentenced to 21 Years on Terrorism Charges," *Chicago Tribune*, Sept. 9, 2014.

37 the geographic scope of the battlefield For a good account of the al-

Marri case and its significance, see Jane Mayer, "The Hard Cases," *New Yorker*, Feb. 23, 2009, (quoting al-Marri's ACLU lawyer, Jonathan Hafetz: "How far does the battlefield extend? In the past, they treated Peoria as a battlefield. Can an American be arrested in his own home and jailed indefinitely, on the say-so of the President?"). See also Jane Mayer, "Al-Marri Indictment Today," *New Yorker*, Feb. 26, 2009.

37 "validate al-Qaida's twisted world-view" See Toby Harnden, "Barack Obama Adviser Rejects 'Global War on Terror,'" *The Telegraph*, Aug. 7, 2009; see also "Obama Scraps 'Global War on Terror' for 'Overseas Contingency Operation,'" *Fox News*, Mar. 25, 2009.

38 specific threats that were truly imminent Memorandum in Support of Motion for Preliminary Injunction, *Al-Aulaqi v. Obama*, No. 10-civ.-469 (D.D.C., Aug. 30, 2010), https://www.aclu.org/sites/default/files/field_document/alaulaqi_v_obma_pibrief_0.pdf.

38 obviously and inarguably unlawful See, e.g., United Nations, General Assembly, *Report of the Special Rapporteur on Extrajudicial, Summary or Arbitrary Executions*, A/HRC/14/24/Add.6 (May 28, 2010) ¶ 33, http://www2.ohchr.org/english/bodies/hrcouncil/docs/14session/A.HRC.14.24.Add6.pdf ("under human rights law, a targeted killing in the sense of an intentional, premeditated and deliberate killing by law enforcement officials cannot be legal"); Danielle C. Jefferis, "Battlefield Borders, Threat Rhetoric, and the Militarization of State and Local Law Enforcement," *American University National Security Law Brief* 3, no. 1 (2012), 45.

39 rested on dubious foundations See generally Nathalie Weizmann, "A Drone Strike and the Debate on the Geography of the War Against Al-Qaeda and Its Associates," *Just Security*, July 14, 2015, https://www.justsecurity.org/24646/drone-strike-debate-geography-war-al-qaeda-associates.

39 Senator Dick Durbin told *Politico* Gregory D. Johnsen, "60 Words and a War Without End: The Untold Story of the Most Dangerous Sentence in U.S. History," *BuzzFeed News*, Jan. 16, 2014.

39 the United States was indisputably at war *Hamdan v. Rumsfeld*, 548 U.S. 557 (2006). See also *Hussain v. Obama*, 134 S. Ct. 1621, 1622 (2014) (Breyer, J., respecting the denial of certiorari).

40 the application of the laws of war *Report of the Special Rapporteur*, at para 53; Mary Ellen O'Connell, "Combatants and the Combat Zone," *University of Richmond Law Review* 43 (2009): 845, 858 ("In addition to exchange, intensity, and duration, armed conflicts have a spatial dimension. It is not the case that if there is an armed conflict in one state—for example, Afghanistan—that all the world is at war, or even that Afghanis and Americans are at war with each other all over the planet."); *Prosecutor v. Tadić*, Case No. IT-94-1-T, Judgment, ¶ 562 (Int'l Crim. Trib. for the Former Yugoslavia May 7, 1997) (distinguishing non-international armed conflicts from "banditry, unorganized and short-lived insurrections, or terrorist activities, which are not subject to international humanitarian law."); cf. *Ex Parte Milligan*, 71 U.S. (4 Wall.) 2, 127 (1866) ("Martial rule . . . is . . . confined to the locality of actual war.").

40 behind the September 2001 terrorist attacks *Report of the Special Rapporteur* at ¶ 55 ("al-Qaeda and other alleged 'associated' groups are often only loosely linked, if at all. Sometimes they appear to be not even groups, but a few individuals who take 'inspiration' from al Qaeda."). Kevin Jon Heller, "The DoJ White Paper's Fatal International Law Flaw—Organization," *Opinio Juris*, Feb. 5, 2013, http://opiniojuris.org/2013/02/05/the-doj-white-papers-fatal-international-law-flaw; Gabor Rona, "Killing a Cleric: Many More Questions Than Answers," *Just Security*, Apr. 16, 2015, https://www.justsecurity.org/22133/killing-cleric-questions-answers.

40 the one the administration articulated Nathalie Weizmann, "Associated Forces and Co-belligerency," *Just Security*, Feb. 24, 2015, https://www.justsecurity.org/20344/isil-aumf-forces-co-belligerency.

40 Hayden acknowledged in 2012 Doyle McManus, "Who Reviews the U.S. Kill List?," *Los Angeles Times*, Feb. 5, 2012.

40 "a conflict of global dimensions is or has been taking place" *International Humanitarian Law and the Challenges of Contemporary Armed Conflicts—ICRC Report*, ICRC Resource Centre report (2011), https://www.icrc.org/eng/assets/files/red-cross-crescent-movement/31st-international-conference/31-int-conference-ihl-challenges-report-11-5-1-2-en.pdf.

40 "concept of a 'global battlefield'" Nathalie Weizmann, "A Drone Strike and the Debate on the Geography of the War Against Al-Qaeda and Its Associates," *Just Security*, July 14, 2015, https://www.justsecurity.org/24646/drone-strike-debate-geography-war-al-qaeda-associates.

41 conjuring an aura of legal constraint Shirin Sinnar, *Rule of Law Tropes in National Security*, 129 Harv. L. Rev. 1566 (Apr. 2016). See also David Pozen, "The Rhetorical Presidency Meets the Drone Presidency," *New Rambler*, 2015 ("The executive branch's substantive standards on targeting, in short, remain shrouded in mystery, while its decision-making procedures remain shrouded in secrecy.").

41 "due process to protect that right" *Xuncax v. Gramajo*, 886 F. Supp. 162, 185 (D. Ma. 1995).

42 a "continuing, imminent threat" It was not always clear what body of law the administration meant the "continuing, imminent threat" standard to invoke. See Marty Lederman, "The Egan Speech and the Bush Doctrine: Imminence, Necessity, and 'First Use' in Jus ad Bellum," *Just Security*, Apr. 11, 2016, https://www.justsecurity.org/30522/egan-speech-bush-doctrine-imminence-necessity-first-use-jus-ad-bellum ("The term 'imminent' or 'imminence' is, of course, used in many diverse legal contexts, and it can have subtly different meanings or applications across various doctrines."). In some contexts—for example, in Brian Egan's remarks to the American Society of International Law (271–286)—the administration plainly meant to address the international law of self-defense, which delineates the circumstances in which states may use force without U.N. Security Council authorization in the territory of non-consenting states. See, e.g., Jack Goldsmith, "Obama's Embrace of Bush's Preemption Doctrine," *Lawfare*, Apr. 6, 2016, https://lawfareblog .com/obamas-embrace-bushs-preemption-doctrine. In other contexts, the phrase "continuing, imminent threat" may have reflected a construction of the Executive Order that bans "assassination." See, e.g., Charlie Savage, *Power Wars: Inside Obama's Post-9/11 Presidency* at 237 (New York: Little, Brown, 2015); Ben Wittes, "Why Imminence? The Assassinations Ban and That OLC Al-Aulaqi Memo," *Lawfare*, June 26, 2014, https://www.lawfareblog.com/why -imminence-assassinations-ban-and-olc-al-aulaqi-memo. In his speech at Northwestern University Law School (191–198), Attorney General Eric Holder seems to have been using the phrase to describe the requirements of the U.S. Constitution in relation to the targeting of a U.S. citizen.

43 responding—as it often is Jeremy Scahill, "The Assassination Complex," *The Intercept*, Oct. 15, 2015 (noting that, according to one Defense Department document, "it took the U.S. six years to develop a target in Somalia" and "8.3 months to kill the target once the president had approved his addition to the kill list").

43 the government's proposed targets were legitimate ones Editorial, "A Court for Targeted Killings," *New York Times*, Feb. 13, 2013; Editorial, "Lethal Force Under Law," *New York Times*, Oct. 9, 2010; Jeffrey S. Brand and Amos N. Guiora, "Judicial Review of Planned Drone Attacks Would Save Lives," *New York Times Room for Debate*, Apr. 24, 2015; Steven J. Barela, "The Imperative of a 'Drone Court,'" *Just Security*, Oct. 28, 2015,   https://www.justsecurity.org/27155/imperative-drone-court/.   See also David Medine and Eliza Sweren-Becker, "The United States Needs a Drone Board," *Defense One*, Apr. 23, 2015, http://cdn.defenseone.com/ defenseone/interstitial.html?v=2.1.1&rf=http%3A%2F%2Fwww.defenseone .com%2Fideas%2F2015%2F04%2Foversight-targeted-killing-americans -overseas-new-model%2F110926%2F.

43 Angus King of Maine observed Scott Shane, "Debating a Court to Vet Drone Strikes," *New York Times*, Feb. 8, 2013.

43 some kind of drone court Carlo Muñoz, "Sens. Feinstein, Leahy Push for Court Oversight of Armed Drone Strikes," *The Hill*, Feb. 20, 2013; Mark Hosenball, "Support Grows for U.S. 'Drone Court' to Review Lethal Strikes," *Reuters*, Feb. 8, 2013.

43 the idea was "worth considering" Kimberly Dozier, "CIA Nominee Brennan Says a Special Drone Court Overseeing Deadly Strikes Is Worth Considering," *Associated Press*, Feb. 15, 2013.

44 encroachment on the president's war powers Lyle Denniston, "Constitutional Check: Would a 'Drone Court' Be Unconstitutional?," *ConstitutionCenter.org*, Feb. 26, 2013, http://blog.constitutioncenter.org/2013/02/constitution-check-would-a-drone-court-be-unconstitutional.

44 far removed from actual battlefields Monica Hakimi, "A Drone Court Wouldn't Rein in a President or Set Standards," *New York Times Room for Debate*, Apr. 24, 2015; Stephen I. Vladeck, "Judicial Review, but Not Secretive Drone Courts," *New York Times Room for Debate*, Feb. 1, 2016; Jeffrey Rosen, "Courting Disaster," *New Republic*, Feb. 11, 2013; Jameel Jaffer, "Judicial Review of Targeted Killings," 126 Harv. L. Rev. F. 185 (Apr. 9, 2013), http://harvardlawreview.org/2013/04/judicial-review-of-targeted-killings/.

44 "what the Constitution and international law permit" Complaint for Declaratory and Injunctive Relief, *Al-Aulaqi. v. Obama*, No. 10-1469 (D.D.C., Aug. 30, 2010), https://www.aclu.org/sites/default/files/field_document/alaulaqi_v_obama_complaint_0.pdf.

45 "expertise to assume these tasks" Opposition to Plaintiff's Motion for Preliminary Injunction and Memorandum in Support of Defendants' Motion to Dismiss at 19, *Al-Aulaqi. v. Obama*, No. 10-1469 (D.D.C., Sept. 24, 2010), https://www.aclu.org/sites/default/files/field_document/Al-Aulaqi_USG_PI_Opp__MTD_Brief_FILED.pdf.

45 "'imminent threat to the security of U.S. nationals'" Transcript of Oral Argument at 35, *Al-Aulaqi v. Obama* (D.D.C., Nov. 8, 2010), http://ccrjustice.org/sites/default/files/attach/2015/05/2010.11.08%20Al-Aulaqi%20Motions%20Hearing%20Transcript.pdf.

45 to say what the law was See also Owen Fiss, *A War Like No Other: The Constitution in a Time of Terror* at 264 (New York: The New Press, 2015) (noting that Dr. al-Aulaqi's suit "was not seeking judicial review of an executive decision to target Anwar al-Aulaqi but—much as Aharon Barak and the Israeli Supreme Court had done in 2005—to have the court formulate and announce the legal standards that should govern the practice of targeting alleged terrorists such as al-Aulaqi.").

45 use lethal force against its own citizens? I tried to press this point at oral argument. Transcript of Oral Argument, *Al-Aulaqi v. Obama*, 51–52 ("[W]e haven't proposed that the Court oversee the President's real-time targeting decisions. We are not asking for something akin to a prior warrant requirement where the government goes to the court with evidence of an imminent threat, evidence that there are no means short of lethal force that can be used to address the threat. We are not asking for the Court to get involved at that point at all with those kinds of targeting decisions. What we are asking for, though, is that the Court be involved in setting the general limits under which lethal force can be used.").

45 How does that all make sense? Transcript of Oral Argument at 34–35,

Al-Aulaqi v. Obama (D.D.C., Nov. 8, 2010), http://ccrjustice.org/sites/default
/files/attach/2015/05/2010.11.08%20Al-Aulaqi%20Motions%20Hearing%20
Transcript.pdf.

46 "committed to the political branches and judicially unreviewable"
Al-Aulaqi v. Obama, 727 F. Supp. 2d 1, 51 (D.D.C. 2010).

46 Congress and the executive branch, not to the courts Judge Bates
found it unnecessary to decide whether the "state secrets" privilege precluded the litigation. The Obama administration had invoked the privilege but
asked Judge Bates to address the application of the privilege only if he could
find no other way to dispose of the case. For an account of how the administration decided to invoke the privilege, see Charlie Savage, *Power Wars:
Inside Obama's Post-9/11 Presidency* at 415–18 (New York: Little, Brown,
2015).

46 "I believe we would, your honor," Letter conceded Transcript of Oral
Argument at 34, *Al-Aulaqi v. Obama* (D.D.C., Nov. 8, 2010), http://ccrjustice
.org/sites/default/files/attach/2015/05/2010.11.08%20Al-Aulaqi%20
Motions%20Hearing%20Transcript.pdf.

**46 "multifarious pronouncements by various departments on one ques-
tion"** *Al-Aulaqi v. Obama*, 727 F. Supp. 2d 1, 48 (D.D.C. 2010).

46 no right of redress in any event Defendants' Motion to Dismiss, *Al-
Aulaqi v. Panetta*, No. 12-civ.1192 (D.D.C., Dec. 14, 2012), https://www.aclu
.org/sites/default/files/field_document/tk_govt_motion_to_dismiss.pdf.

47 "gobble up all of the air in the room" Transcript of Oral Argument at 16, *Al-Aulaqi v. Panetta*, No. 12-civ.1192 (D.D.C., July 19, 2013),
https://www.aclu.org/sites/default/files/field_document/rt071913-1005
.july_19_argument_transcript.final_.pdf.

47 officials "must be trusted" *Al-Aulaqi v. Panetta*, 35 F.Supp.3d 56, 80
(D.D.C. 2014).

47 legal advice to executive branch agencies "Best Practices for OLC Legal
Advice and Written Opinions," Memorandum from David Barron, Acting
Assistant Attorney General, to attorneys of the Office of Legal Counsel,
July 16, 2010, https://www.justice.gov/sites/default/files/olc/legacy/2010
/08/26/olc-legal-advice-opinions.pdf. See also Reply Brief for Plaintiffs-
Appellants at 7-8, *New York Times v. Department of Justice*, No. 14-4432 (2d
Cir., Apr. 16, 2015), https://www.aclu.org/sites/default/files/field_document
/98._aclu_reply_brief_4.16.2015.pdf.

47 never adjudicated by the courts See, e.g., Frederick A.O. Schwartz and
Aziz Z. Huq, *Unchecked and Unbalanced: Presidential Power in a Time of
Terror* at 190 (New York: The New Press, 2007) ("OLC issues legal rulings
that are the binding final word for agencies within the federal government
on contested issues of federal law.") (emphasis in original); id. ("OLC in
effect often has the 'last word' in terms of what the Constitution or federal

law demands."); Jack Goldsmith, *The Terror Presidency: Law and Judgment Inside the Bush Administration* at 32 (New York: W.W. Norton & Co., 2007).

47 judicial review by secrecy and jurisdictional doctrines See, e.g., *Clapper v. Amnesty Int'l*, 133 S. Ct. 1138, 1147–1155 (2013); *Al-Aulaqi v. Panetta*, 35 F. Supp. 3d 56, 78–80 (D.D.C. 2014); *Al-Aulaqi v. Obama*, 727 F. Supp. 2d 1, 14–35, 53 (D.D.C. 2010).

47 complying with the Fourth Amendment "Authority for Use of Military Force to Combat Terrorist Activities Within the United States," Memorandum from John C. Yoo, Deputy Assistant Attorney General, and Robert J. Delahunty, Special Counsel, to William J. Haynes, II, General Counsel to the Department of Defense, Oct. 23, 2001, http://nsarchive.gwu.edu/ torturingdemocracy/documents/20011023.pdf.

48 OLC opinions said "Application of Treaties and Laws to al Qaeda and Taliban Detainees," Memorandum from Jay S. Bybee, Assistant Attorney General, to Alberto R. Gonzales, Counsel to the President, and William J. Haynes, II, General Counsel to the Department of Defense, Jan. 22, 2002, http://www.justice.gov/sites/default/files/olc/legacy/2009/08/24/memo-laws -taliban-detainees.pdf.

48 challenging the lawfulness of their detention "Possible Habeas Jurisdiction over Aliens Held in Guantanamo Bay, Cuba," Memorandum from Patrick F. Philbin, Deputy Assistant Attorney General, and John Yoo, Deputy Assistant Attorney General, to William J. Haynes, General Counsel to the Department of Defense, Dec. 28, 2001, reproduced in Karen J. Greenberg and Joshua L. Dratel, *The Torture Papers: The Road to Abu Ghraib* at 29–37 (Cambridge: Cambridge University Press 2005).

48 authorizing the methods the CIA had proposed Jack Goldsmith, *The Terror Presidency: Law and Judgment Inside the Bush Administration* at 96–97 (New York: W.W. Norton & Co., 2007).

48 regulate presidential power during wartime David J. Barron and Martin S. Lederman, "The Commander in Chief at the Lowest Ebb—Framing the Problem, Doctrine, and Original Understanding," *Harvard Law Review* 121, no. 3 (2008): 689–804.

48 order the killing of Anwar al-Aulaqi The story may be more complicated than this. On December 24, 2009, a drone strike hit a home in the Yemeni governorate of Shabwah where al-Aulaqi was thought to be meeting with others. The strike killed more than thirty people. It seems likely that al-Aulaqi was the target of the strike, or at least that U.S. officials expected he would be killed by it. Accordingly, when Barron and Lederman approved the targeting of al-Aulaqi, they may well have been ratifying a decision that had already been made. Karen Greenberg, *Rogue Justice: The Making of the Security State* at 219 (New York: Crown Publishers, 2016); Jeremy Scahill, *Dirty Wars: The World Is a Battlefield* at 313 (New York: Nation Books, 2013).

But see Charlie Savage, *Power Wars: Inside Obama's Post-9/11 Presidency* at 230–31 (New York: Little, Brown, 2015) (concluding that Al-Aulaqi was not designated a target until February 2010).

48 memo addressed to Attorney General Holder Charlie Savage, *Power Wars: Inside Obama's Post-9/11 Presidency* at 232 (New York: Little, Brown, 2015).

49 questions they had overlooked Mark Mazzetti, Charlie Savage, and Scott Shane, "How a U.S. Citizen Came to Be in America's Cross Hairs," *New York Times*, Mar. 9, 2013; Kenneth Anderson, "The Lord Works in Mysterious Ways—KJH and OLC Edition?" *Opinio Juris*, Mar. 9, 2013, http://opiniojuris.org/2013/03/09/the-lord-works-in-mysterious-ways-kjh-and-olc-edition.

49 first of his lawsuits against the government The ACLU and CCR had planned to file the suit on behalf of Nasser al-Aulaqi in July, but on July 16, the same day that OLC issued its memo concerning the proposal to kill Anwar al-Aulaqi, the Office of Foreign Asset Control designated Anwar al-Aulaqi a Specially Designated Global Terrorist, the effect of which was to make it unlawful for any attorney to provide "legal services" for Anwar's benefit without first obtaining a license. See U.S. Dep't of Treasury, "Treasury Designates Anwar Al-Aulaqi, Key Leader of Al-Qa'ida in the Arabian Peninsula," July 16, 2010, https://www.treasury.gov/press-center/press-releases/Pages/tg779.aspx. Seeing no other option, we submitted a request for a license. When OFAC failed to respond, we filed a suit challenging what we considered to be an unconstitutional infringement of Anwar al-Aulaqi's right to counsel and of our right to represent him. Complaint, *ACLU v. Geithner*, No. 1-10-cv-01303 (D.D.C., Aug. 3, 2010), https://www.aclu.org/sites/default/files/field_document/2-OFACComplaintFinal_0.pdf. After we filed suit, OFAC issued a license that permitted us to represent Nasser al-Aulaqi and that ultimately allowed us to file suit on his behalf. It also amended its regulations to permit uncompensated attorneys to initiate and conduct legal proceedings on behalf of designated individuals without first seeking a specific license from the government. Notice of Dismissal, *ACLU v. Geithner*, No. 1-10-cv-01303 (D.D.C., Dec. 17, 2010), https://www.aclu.org/sites/default/files/field_document/2010-12-17-ACLUvGeithner-NoticeofDismissal.pdf.

50 "executive branch in times of war" Steve Vladeck, "The Holder Speech and the Mathews Test," *Lawfare*, Mar. 6, 2012, https://www.lawfareblog.com/holder-speech-and-mathews-test; Steve Vladeck, "What's Really Wrong with the Targeted Killing White Paper," *Lawfare*, Feb. 5, 2013. https://www.lawfareblog.com/whats-really-wrong-targeted-killing-white-paper.

51 taken care to avoid this result *Webster v. Doe*, 486 U.S. 592, 611 (1988).

51. to any similar privilege or immunity See, e.g., Jens David Ohlin, "When Does the Combatant's Privilege Apply?" *Opinio Juris*, Aug. 1, 2014, http://opiniojuris.org/2014/08/01/combatants-privilege-apply/; Convention

(III) relative to the Treatment of Prisoners of War. Geneva, 12 August 1949, Art. IV (defining "prisoners of war"); 10 U.S.C. § 948a (defining "privileged belligerent" by reference to Third Geneva Convention's definition of "prisoners of war").

51 thrown a grenade at a passing American convoy Gabor Rona, "When Considering CIA Targeted Killings, Don't Forget International Law!" *Just Security*, Apr. 5, 2016, https://www.justsecurity.org/30426/cia-targeted -killings-dont-forget-international-law/.

52 made the CIA's drone strikes war crimes Charlie Savage, "U.N. Official to Ask U.S. to End C.I.A. Drone Strikes," *New York Times*, May 27, 2010.

52 extend only to war crimes *Al-Bahlul v. United States*, 792 F.3d 1, 10 (D.D.C. 2015).

52 *New York Times* op-ed piece Nasser al-Awlaki, "The Drone That Killed My Grandson," *New York Times*, July 17, 2013.

53 absence of criminal proceeding and conviction *Hamdi v. Rumsfeld*, 542 U.S. 507 (2004).

53 imprisoned as enemy combatants at Guantánamo *Rasul v. Bush*, 542 U.S. 466 (2004); *Boumediene v. Bush*, 553 U.S. 723 (2008).

54 chilling effect on intelligence sources Defendants' Motion to Dismiss at 26–27, *Al-Aulaqi v. Panetta*, No. 12-01192 (Dec. 14, 2012), https://www .aclu.org/sites/default/files/field_document/tk_govt_motion_to_dismiss .pdf.

54 "no substitute for legal or democratic process" David Cole, "Killing Citizens in Secret," *New York Review of Books*, Oct. 9, 2011.

55 "life hangs in the balance" Owen Fiss, *A War Like No Other: The Constitution in a Time of Terror* at 279 (New York: The New Press, 2015).

An index for *The Drone Memos* is available at
www.ACLU.org/TDM/Index.

ABOUT THE EDITOR

Jameel Jaffer, director of the Knight First Amendment Institute at Columbia University and former Deputy Legal Director of the ACLU, oversaw the ACLU's work relating to national security for almost a decade and litigated some of the most significant cases concerning U.S. counterterrorism policy after 9/11. A prominent commentator and speaker on issues relating to civil liberties and human rights, Jaffer has written for the *New York Times*, the *Los Angeles Times, The Guardian, Index on Censorship*, and the *Harvard Law Review Forum,* among other publications, and is the co-author with Amrit Singh of *Administration of Torture: From Washington to Abu Ghraib and Beyond*. Canadian Journalists for Free Expression awarded Jaffer the Vox Libera Award in 2015 and *Foreign Policy* magazine listed him as one of its "Top 100 Global Thinkers" in 2012. He lives in Brooklyn.

PUBLISHING IN THE PUBLIC INTEREST

Thank you for reading this book published by The New Press. The New Press is a nonprofit, public interest publisher. New Press books and authors play a crucial role in sparking conversations about the key political and social issues of our day.

We hope you enjoyed this book and that you will stay in touch with The New Press. Here are a few ways to stay up to date with our books, events, and the issues we cover:

- Sign up at www.thenewpress.com/subscribe to receive updates on New Press authors and issues and to be notified about local events
- Like us on Facebook: www.facebook.com/newpressbooks
- Follow us on Twitter: www.twitter.com/thenewpress

Please consider buying New Press books for yourself; for friends and family; or to donate to schools, libraries, community centers, prison libraries, and other organizations involved with the issues our authors write about.

The New Press is a 501(c)(3) nonprofit organization. You can also support our work with a tax-deductible gift by visiting www .thenewpress.com/donate.